SOCIAL AGENCY POLICY

SOCIAL AGENCY POLICY

Analysis and Presentation for Community Practice

SECOND EDITION

John P. Flynn
WESTERN MICHIGAN UNIVERSITY

Nelson-Hall Publishers
Chicago

Project Editor: Dorothy Anderson
Cover Design: Corasue Nicholas
Cover Painting: *Rural Electric* by William Barron

Library of Congress Cataloging-in-Publication Data

Flynn, John P.
    Social agency policy : analysis and presentation for community
practice / John P. Flynn. — 2nd ed.
        p.   cm.
    Includes bibliographical references and index.
    ISBN 0-8304-1272-7
    1. Public welfare—United States.   2. United States—Social
policy.   I. Title.
HV95.F53   1992   91-12177
361.6'1'0973—dc20   CIP

Copyright © 1992 by Nelson-Hall Inc.

Manufactured in the United States of America

10   9   8   7   6   5   4   3   2   1

TM   The paper used in this book meets the
minimum requirements of American
National Standard for Information
Sciences—Permanence of Paper for
Printed Library Materials, ANSI
Z39.48-1984.

Contents

List of Case Illustrations

Note: the case entitled "Infants with HIV+ Infection" is distributed throughout chapters 4 and 6 as a case example for content and process criteria for analysis. Cases 3 and 5 both deal with "Homelessness and the Mall People."

Preface

This second edition of *Social Agency Policy: Analysis and Presentation for Community Practice* provides theory-based, practical frameworks and models for the analysis and presentation of social policy at the small-scale or local (including state and regional) levels. The book focuses on both the content and process aspects of social welfare policy analysis and provides outlines that will serve as guides for analysis and presentation of policy. Special attention is given to values as criteria for analysis of social welfare policy.

This book is aimed especially at direct service practitioners, those who work with clinicians or who would hope to train them, and anyone who is willing to take up responsibility as a policy practitioner. It is intended as a text for undergraduate and graduate courses in social welfare policy and for courses in public administration, counseling and personnel, community psychology, or other human services areas concerned with social policy practice at the local level. It is also intended as a helpful tool for those social agency professionals who recognize the need to provide policy analysis in their work but who have had no preparation in its practice. Given the relatively recent emphasis on policy practice in a field such as social work and the absence of any attention given social welfare policy analysis in particular, the lack of such preparation affects virtually all social welfare practitioners. This problem is further exacerbated by the lack of tools for small-scale policy analysis at the agency, organizational, or interorganizational levels.

I see an immense need in the area of social welfare policy analysis. Traditionally, social welfare and human service policy have been taught from a descriptive or historical perspective; that is, various important events or structural features of legislative and service agencies have been chronicled. This approach, while important in identifying the social, political, economic, or philosophical foundations of social welfare policy, generally lacks an emphasis on critical analysis as it pertains to policy work at the local level. Consequently, professionals who find themselves with the responsibility for social welfare policy analysis do not have the guides or tools to meet their responsibilities and ethical mandates. The frameworks and models for analysis that have emerged in recent years have been geared to national or grand-scale content and processes; they have limited value to the local-level practitioner. Very few of us have the opportunity to rewrite the Social Security Act or to design a jobs and employment policy and program for the nation. The vast number of social workers and other human service workers must meet their policy responsibilities at the local level—in cities, counties, states, or regions.

This book attempts to provide human services professionals with the ability to analyze and present, and hopefully influence, both the content and process of social policy—in their own organizations and interagency activities and in the legislative contexts (e.g., city ordinances, county resolutions, state legislative proposals) that are meaningful to their professional lives. Local or small-scale issues, such as clinically or direct service-related policy practice problems (e.g., HIV + and AIDS concerns or utilization review policies), personnel policy matters, interagency social action position statements, information security and client confidentiality issues, regulatory legislation or rule-making, and accountability policies are some of the policy analysis issues that we will address.

A number of significant changes have been made in this second edition, which largely reflect the struggles that students experienced with the first edition and the critical feedback generously given by colleagues. The most significant change is the integration of criteria for analysis of values elements into the frameworks for analyzing content and process. Values elements in analysis were considered separately from the analysis of content and process in the first edition, and that artifact left a wrong impression regarding the centrality of values analysis to policy analysis. The format for analyzing values criteria in this edition also helps us to distinguish values in content matters from values considerations in process matters—in itself an instructive opportunity.

Another major change is that this book develops *frameworks* for analysis from which *one can construct one's own models for analysis*. That is, this book includes a number of "laundry lists," as it were, which embody a range of criteria or elements considered important for any analysis. Here are *potential* frameworks—the individual practitioner must apply what fits or what is possible at the moment. In the real world the policy practitioner often does not have sufficient time or information to fill in all the lines; instead, he or she develops temporary constructions for the purpose of facing an immediate analytic task. This book provides extensive *frameworks*; the practitioner builds *models*.

A number of other substantive changes have been made. More emphasis has been placed upon the growing reality of policy-as-practice in considering the rationale for tools for policy analysis. A rather lengthy list of agency-based small-scale policies analyzed by students is provided to stimulate analogues that readers might find particularly relevant to their own practice. Also, the differential nature of formal and informal policy has been confronted more directly. More illustrations and explanations regarding the theoretical foundations of models of policy process have been provided in this edition, and reference to an additional, problem-based framework has been introduced, that is, family impact analysis.

A new case illustration has been provided, dealing with policy issues concerning HIV infection and AIDS. The case of ''Infants and HIV+ Infection'' has been used throughout chapters 4 and 6, the two chapters which develop the frameworks for analysis of content and process, respectively. In addition, the case illustration regarding people on the downtown mall has been revised to reflect the growing need for policy analyses concerning the problem of homelessness and is also subjected to both content and process analysis.

Finally, the last chapter has been completely revised. Chapter 12 provides the reader with issues to consider in the implementation of policy. After all, why bother with analysis if we have no hope to view its implementation or its purposeful defeat or dissolution?

I hope I have responded appropriately and adequately to the criticisms generously offered. I am indebted to the many students who have provided the reality check for the educational process. Many thanks are in order to those who struggled with me in the learning process. Extra thanks go to two special people, however, for giving the kind of honest and sometimes maddening critiques that really help. That kind of collegueship is invaluable, of course. And here I refer to my daughter, social worker Bridget Flynn Timmeney, whose criticism was so gently given, and to my faculty colleague, Edward Pawlak. His honesty is evidence of real personal and professional friendship.

Empowerment and Policy

1

This book is for social workers and other human service practitioners who wish to influence, or are influenced by, the realities of social welfare policies. Its purpose is to empower. If providers and receivers of human services apply and analyze the substantive content of policies affecting them or those whom they represent, they are empowered. If practitioners and beneficiaries, professionals and recipients, workers and clients apply the skills to analyze the processes whereby policy comes into being, they are empowered. Empowerment is knowing that one is able to be a doer. Effective action requires information, and analysis provides enlightened knowledge guiding purposeful social action, whether that social action be at the person-to-person level, in working alone or with others for organizational change, or in group political action at the community level.

Every social welfare professional and every social welfare program is affected by social welfare policy (hereafter referred to simply as social policy). Many practitioners are in a position to effect changes in social programs and social policies, either by themselves, in coalitions, or in other cooperative efforts. While this book is especially written for those who engage in policy-as-practice at the local—interagency and intra-agency—level, it is also intended for practitioners at the regional or state levels of policy analysis.

Social workers and other human service personnel have come to recognize that social welfare policy directly affects their day-to-day practice and that as individuals or members of groups or organizations, they have the opportunity to actively participate in policy analysis and change. A problem, however, is that many practitioners are not accustomed to viewing social policy as a close-to-home phenomenon that can be developed, altered, or shaped (as well as tolerated!) in and through their day-to-day routines.

Social welfare policy has traditionally been perceived as something "up there" or "out there"—a mandate or constraint from on high or from some external system. While this perception is sometimes accurate, policy frequently comes from the environment immediately around us—decisions made by city councils and county commissions, mandates of central administration, decisions of a local or regional policymaking board, rulings of an administrative law judge, or agreements made by local, regional, or state agencies acting together. Furthermore, such policy frequently comes from ourselves and our colleagues as we interpret vaguely stated laws or directives from administrative sources. The impact of such policy is felt largely in the environments of "small-scale systems." At times, the social worker may attempt to influence these policy processes, and then analysis becomes the first major step in empowering the practitioner. By analyzing the impact of policy, for oneself or for one's employer, we take the first step in empowering ourselves or in empowering those whom we represent.

Many practitioners, however, fail to recognize the impact of their participation on small-scale policy systems, probably because policy work has not been viewed as one of their interventive methods, as has management, administration, or the provision of direct services. This alienation or perceived distance from the policy aspects of living systems belies the fact that practitioners are actually very close to social policies at the agency level. For example, many psychiatric inpatient facilities or residential care programs for children or vulnerable adults have (or should have) formal policies for the use of seclusion and restraints. These policies intimately affect social practice and can be effected by human service practitioners. Many have had to develop and/or operationalize policies in their own areas of practice that pertain to the policy principle of "the least restrictive environment" or "the least restrictive alternative," whether in an elementary school setting providing special education services, a juvenile detention facility, a partial day care program for developmentally disabled adults, or an activity program for senior citizens. Or, we find policies requiring team assessments and case planning by a number of disciplines, as in an acute care medical facility. The detail of agency-based policies and the concomitant procedures generated are very much a part of the "policy life" of social agency practice.

Lack of awareness of the role that practitioners play in policy may also be due to the manner in which many social workers and other human service professionals have been socialized regarding the content and process of social welfare policy. That is, the practitioner is more likely to view social welfare policy content and process as the huge mass of information that constitutes the backdrop for learning about social welfare services. Policy might be seen as synonymous with information about the various social services fields, the structure of national service programs, or principles involved in various social issues such as poverty, racism, or sexism. Certainly, this is important information; it helps to give us a full policy perspective. But social agency policy is more than the substantive content handed down by generations of accumulated programs, or the principles articulated in social legislation. Social policy and specific opportunities for policy analysis and policy change manifest themselves in the day-to-day provision of human services. The direct service practitioner has a very real opportunity to "occupy the policy space" when, for example, an agency establishes policy for psychotherapy services in which fee negotiation with the client is required as part of the therapeutic process, or determines agency policy regarding visitation in an inpatient substance-abuse treatment center.

There are other examples. Both agency administrators and direct services staff participate in shaping agency policy concerning negotiations with outside funding sources, such as developing contracts for obtaining global assessment scores on agency clientele and providing the results to a funding source, or drafting interagency agreements about case management responsibilities or case conferencing. These opportunities for policy analysis present themselves through existing policies and through new developments in policymaking.

From another perspective, social welfare policy *process* (as distinguished from *content*) is often seen as "politics." The tendency here is to characterize policy process as happening exclusively in and around the nation's or states' capitols and about broad or inclusive issues such as social security, national health insurance, and public assistance. Little wonder that we tend to look beyond our immediate environments in search of what is happening in social welfare policy and that we feel no sense of empowerment when we look to these large-scale systems in defining our "policy world."

Yet the processes of policy development are often very close to home. For example, social agency coalitions sometimes unite to persuade a city commission to budget a fixed percentage of revenues to fund local human services programs. Both the content and the process of that policy principle and goal require analysis and action at the small-scale level. For example, policy processes are undertaken by local child-care agencies when assisting a state social welfare department to alter its policies and to allow for *purchase* of services, as opposed to only *direct provision* of services by state agencies.

Historical-Descriptive Approaches to Policy

Our understanding of social welfare policy relies, in large part, upon recognition of significant social policy actors who appeared in social welfare history or upon an accumulation of policy events occurring over time. It is a fitting and at times exciting experience to recall the contributions of people who have shaped social policy over the years: Jane Addams, Florence Kelley, Frances Perkins, Bertha Reynolds, Eugene Debs, Clarence Darrow, and Edwin Witte, among others. Remembering these people and their impact on American social welfare policy not only gives recognition to their contributions but also provides a vehicle for identifying the policy issues and programs that have emerged over time. This approach to learning social policy is valuable in that it enables us to maintain our rich policy heritage.

A similar approach is viewing social policy as the accumulation of particularly important documented events—the chronological view of social welfare. For example, the establishment of the state chargeback system in developing mental health policy came about when states levied charges upon localities for the care of indigents and the mentally ill. This policy fostered the dual roles of states and localities. Another example is the fundamental policy principle established by the Social Security Act of 1935 of building in mandatory conditions for grants-in-aid to the states, or the concept of categorical approaches to assistance. Grants to states for assisting special groups were made contingent upon accepting other policy provisions, such as requiring state program administration by civil servants. Much of our policy process understanding is based upon major and visible events and their associated activities, such as the activities of Dorothea Dix and the Pierce Veto, which for decades stopped the entre of the federal government into social welfare. Another example is the intriguing interplay of the Ford Foundation's Grey Areas Project and the President's Commission on Juvenile Delinquency and Youth Crime, each of which had tremendous influence in shaping the parameters of the Economic Opportunity Act. Certainly all of these approaches, taken singly or in combination, provide frameworks for either descriptive or critical analyses of social welfare policies.

Living Policy and Policy Practice

In recent years, there has been a shift in social services arenas from considering policy as history to considering policy as doing. ''Policy practice'' as a term was coined by Jansson (1984) in recognition of the fact that social workers and other human service professionals engage in a kind of direct practice that focuses primarily upon policy concerns. Policy practice ranges from direct work with individuals wherein the emphasis in the helping process is upon policy matters to interventions in larger-scale systems in which the social workers must provide policy expertise, for example. Jansson (1990) suggests that, at all levels of intervention, policy practice requires analytic, political, interactional, and value clarification skills. Given application of these skills, policy practice provides a vehicle for seizing opportunities for intervention into the environmental realm of the client system and goes beyond what Wyers refers to as the ''clinicalization of social work during the 1980s'' (Wyers, 1990, p. 2). In other words, policy practice might be said to emphasize the *situation* in the person-in-situation paradigm so common in social work. Fortunately, there are recent efforts to help social work students who have a primary identification with the direct practice aspects of social work to identify their professional responsibility and opportunities in the policy aspects of their skill development (e.g., Hart, 1989; Meenaghan & Gruber, 1986; Witherspoon & Phillips, 1987; Wintersteen, 1990).

While social welfare policy has generally provided background and context for the methods of social work practice, social policy has more recently been examined as a *method of practice* within the field (e.g., Dear, Briar & Van Ry, 1986; Flynn, 1985; Jansson, 1984, 1990; Pierce, 1984; Tropman, 1984). Cunningham (1990) has articulated a model for preparing social workers for the policy aspects of generalist practice, and an effort to codify policy practice was provided by Wyers (1990) at the 1990 Annual Program Meeting of the Council on Social Work Education as part of the Symposium on Social Welfare Policy and Policy Practice. Wyers identified five models of policy practice which, while not mutually exclusive, facilitate heuristic examination of policy practice.

1. *Social Worker as Policy Expert*

   The social worker, as a specialist in policy analysis and formulation as a central aspect of job responsibilities, scrutinizes legislative or regulatory proposals affecting social issues and client systems. This would be the commonly held view of the ''policy analyst,'' perhaps the easiest for us to conceptualize as the practice of policy. While easily seen as occurring in the context of a state legislature, this policy expertise might also be practiced in county government in the development or management of human service programs or in community welfare councils or United Way planning agencies in which policy is legislated by funding bodies through local governmental decisions or a private body's establishing of funding priorities.

2. *Social Worker as Change Agent in External Work Environments*
   As a part of her/his job and professional responsibilities, the administrator or direct practitioner assists or enables other organizations to confront opportunities for attending to various social issues, for example discrimination on the basis of gender, class, race, age or some other demographic characteristic. Here the policy practitioner engages in community action and is called upon to provide information and/or recommendations on the substantive content of policy or the processes of policy development arising out of disciplined policy analysis.

3. *Social Worker as Change Agent in Internal Work Environments*
   The social worker may also engage in policy change activities aimed at internal policies and procedures. For example, the social worker may engage in program design, that is, policy work which facilitates the design of services that respond to the need for human diversity in agency programs. Policy analysis enables the practitioner to obtain the credibility needed to receive sanction or support for subsequent policy maintenance or change and to impact the design of services to clients.

4. *Social Worker as Policy Conduit*
   As both implementor of policy and the sounding board for its impact on intended and unintended targets or clients, the social worker becomes the representative for diverse individuals and groups that are known to a social agency. In this context, social workers, for example, become the filterers or facilitators of essential communications that can or could impact organizational policy. Their ability to identify the intended and unintended consequences of policy depend upon policy analysis skills.

5. *Social Worker as Policy*
   The social worker, by behavior and professional practice, is also the "embodiment or personification of policy" (Wyers, 1990) and thereby represents the organization and the profession in terms of its actual position on social issues. By their behavior, all human service professionals communicate their own personal values and those of the people or the organization they represent. In many instances, these values may not display respect for human diversity or commitment to social justice. In this sense, the social worker *is* policy and, consequently, *is* policy practice. Policy analysis thereby becomes self-analysis, whether that "self" is one's own behavior or the organizational behavior of the agency with whom one is associated.

Human services practitioners are active participants in their current policy environments. In their day-to-day work they have the opportunity to support existing policies and generate change for new ones. Earlier or external policy events are important to policy practice, but so is individual opportunity, which is potentially within one's understanding and, at times, even within one's control. This is the opportunity aspect of policy practice.

Social welfare policy is made in four arenas: (1) legislative, (2) judicial, (3) administrative, and (4) executive (see Dobelstein, 1990). Policy analysis must take both the opportunities and constraints of these arenas into consideration. Legislated policy embraces not only state or federal laws but also local ordinances or resolutions established by public bodies such as city and county commissions or councils. Furthermore, the policy set forth by legally constituted boards of directors in the private sector may be seen as legislated policy in the sense that board policy governs all other agency policy and either delineates or makes new opportunities for social action in policy processes. These public and private bodies sanction and support programs. Legislation provides the right and responsibility for action and, at times, mandates that analysis and evaluation of the legislated policy occur.

Judicial policy is established both by courts and court agencies: judges decree social welfare policy in deciding contests over statutes and regulations; court agencies, such as juvenile or domestic relations courts, in their decisions, formulate policy which approximates the force of law (at least until it is contested). In the local policy arena this could, for example, entail a clash between individuals who seek a new home as a result of deinstitutionalization and neighbors who contest zoning ordinances in court. Decisions by juvenile courts limiting either the rights of children or their parents provide other examples, as do rules or procedures concerning commitment or guardianship that differ from court to court.

Administrative and executive policy are somewhat blurred in their distinction, yet either of these arenas generate a greater number of policies than do legislative or judicial. For instance, there is a huge body of law known as ''administrative law,'' which is comprised of all the rules and regulations derived from legislated policy. It is common practice to state legislative policy in the broadest of terms and provide that specific administrative rules be established to give direct effect to the enacted legislation. This administrative, or regulatory, area, as it is sometimes referred to, although often overlooked, is far greater in size and scope for the social welfare analyst than the body of legislated policy taken by itself, since laws or statutes often demand and generate a vast body of regulatory policy.

8   Social Agency Policy

Executive policy, whether set by the administrative branch of governments or the executive or program levels within agencies, constitutes perhaps the largest body of policy providing grist for the analysis mill. Executive policy-making may take the form of various word-of-mouth directives, organizational memos, or voluminous policy manuals for an organized set of interrelated organizational policies. Executive policy may be ad hoc and ephemeral, sent by memo as administrative directives, or a highly formalized body of policy as in the case of an agency's personnel policies. Executive policy is generally the level of policy closest to the direct practitioner, since it is only one notch above the "front line" of practice.

Most social workers practice with other people like themselves in small-scale legislative, judicial, administrative or executive policy systems. While these systems are influenced by broad and large-scale social policies, they also generate and respond to their own realities at the local, small-scale level. In fact, opportunities for analysis, development, and articulation or presentation of policy are present virtually all the time in local-level practice. Social workers not only participate in and influence the play of policy at this level, but policy participation is often expected as part of professional responsibility. A major part of human services work is participation in social agency policy, which involves analyzing policy either to understand it or change it.

We can summarize this part of the discussion by citing Jansson's definition of policy practice:

The use of conceptual work, interventions, and value clarification to develop, enact, implement, and assess policies. (1990, p. 24)

This definition implies that policy practice is applicable to the various methods of professional practice, the many fields of service, and the myriad of job titles and organizational positions. In addition, it suggests that policy practice requires the use of various means of research and expositional skills and direct interventions involving policy formulation at virtually any level of human interaction. Policy practice, as emphasized in this definition, especially focuses upon the examination of the values and ethics of serving people in need.

Working at the Policy Level or Policy Space

Policy refers to those principles that give expression to valued ends and provide direction to social welfare action. Policy has to do with principles—what we value most and what we want to happen. "We want quality!"

This expresses a principle, although it is a broad generalization. "We want our clients to participate fully in their treatment plan." This is a more specific expression of a principle that could find its way into policy. In real life, however, policies may be made up of a number of principles. For example, a policy on client confidentiality may consist of principles such as security of records, informed consent provided by clients in releasing information, or informing clients of their rights to confidentiality. Principles become policy when we attach an expected pattern to achievement of the principles. This relationship between principles and policies is evident when we couch a policy statement in terms of "ought to" or "must" or "shall" (often called *mandatory* policy), although most policy principles are pursued as something that we "may" desire or "hope to achieve" (as in the case of *permissive* policy).

What is meant by the "policy level?" "Policy level" on the small scale is comprised of all the resolutions, orders, rules, guidelines, or other statements of principles that derive from such sources as councils and commissions, courts, boards, executives, or interagency compacts that guide and direct professional activities in community social welfare. For the purposes of this book, the small-scale policy system that comprises the social welfare community refers to the local, regional, or state levels of activity. It focuses on those policy actions that center around intra-agency, interagency, and group policy action. "Policy space" refers to situations in which there is an opportunity to effect the nature or shape of policies by altering the relationships of the interacting elements, such as people, programs, or resources. The following are some examples of policy topics or issues that have been subjected to systematic analyses by students in agency internships and by professionals in social agencies using the frameworks and models provided here. Each one illustrates the subject matter of small-scale policy.

A. *Policy Concerning Eligibility*
1. Requiring a physical exam for residents in a juvenile detention facility.
2. Definition of "family" as eligibility criterion in a domestic violence shelter program.
3. Period of eligibility for perinatal care services.
4. Affirmative action policy for Vietnam Veterans in an educational institution.
5. Provision of legal aid services at no cost to clientele.
6. Provision of treatment for nonpaying clients at a private, for-profit mental health agency.

7. Eligibility requirement(s) for special education services.
8. Requirements of primary caregiver in the home as eligibility criterion for hospice services.
9. Financing of housing repairs through deferred and low-interest loans with block grant funds.
10. Mandatory dental screening for children in a Head Start program.
11. Mandatory removal of college students with severe psychiatric disorders from college programs.
12. Restriction on school social workers to provide services solely to special education students.

B. *Policy Concerning Clinical Considerations*
1. The use of electroshock treatment in a psychiatric facility.
2. The primacy of teamwork in a residential treatment facility.
3. Use of volunteers in a sexual assault unit of a mental health center.
4. Room time and confinement policy in a juvenile home.
5. Staff response to suicidal threats in an inpatient facility.
6. Home calls for public assistance recipients.
7. Family notification of periodic review results of patients in a state facility.
8. Mandatory family participation in a substance abuse treatment program.
9. Exclusion of multiple-diagnosed clients in a substance abuse treatment program.

C. *Policy Concerning Administrative Procedures*
1. Mandatory time limits for case closings for child protective services caseloads.
2. Commitment in a labor/management agreement to an employee assistance program.
3. Investigation within twenty-four hours by adult protective services for complaints of abuse or neglect.
4. Full-time enrollment requirement in a professional educational program.
5. Procedures for maintenance of confidentiality (e.g., implications for minors, informed consent, maintenance of materials, etc.).
6. Obtaining apprehension and detention orders in a juvenile court.
7. Insurance risk and liability for volunteers in a social service program.
8. Disposition of leftover food in a congregate meals program.
9. Use of alcohol on a college campus.

D. *Policy Concerning Environmental Relationships*
   1. Brokering in-home services only through prior interagency agreements.
   2. Mandatory reporting of suspected abuse to Protective Services.
   3. Use of service team quarterly meetings for client staffings in a community residential care program.
   4. Movement from a college's mission statement based on a planning model to one based on environmentally responsive strategic planning.
   5. Purchase of service contracting with external providers.
   6. Volunteer recruitment and screening in a big brother/big sister program.
   7. Maintenance of location secrecy for a domestic assault shelter.
   8. Mandatory substance abuse educational programs ordered by the court.
   9. Alternatives to discharge under a diagnostic related groups (DRG) system.

E. *Policy Concerning Client/Staff/Citizen Rights*
   1. Mandatory testing.
   2. Clients' rights to access or review their own records.
   3. Harassment of clients or staff.
   4. Security of clients' files in possession of traveling outreach workers.
   5. Parent participation in a Head Start policy council.
   6. Parental participation in special educational planning for children.
   7. Disability claimants' denial based on lack of cooperation in providing necessary medical evidence.
   8. Claimants' rights to privacy in disability determination.
   9. Voluntary vendoring of AFDC payments.
   10. Conflicting legislated mandates in clients' right to access or review their own records.
   11. Rules for seclusion of psychiatric patients.
   12. Patient's right to be free from physical restraint or seclusion in an inpatient facility.
   13. Posting of inpatients' rights.

Of course, this list is not exhaustive. The policy space here is largely at the program level or at the interface of worker-client contact. A myriad of policy events and significant issues of principle are (or could be) the subject of policy maintenance, change, or control and cry out for analysis.

Our attention is given to policy practice situations at the local level, because that is where the vast majority of human services practitioners spend their professional lives and where the vast majority of social services clientele interact with human services systems. It is also the place where most practitioners meet their ethical and professional commitments. The Code of Ethics of the National Association of Social Workers, for example, provides a number of mandates for its members to take on responsibilities for initiating and shaping social welfare policy. Many practitioners are called upon to analyze the content and/or the process of policies arising from local activities and are sometimes asked to provide reports or presentations based on those analyses. For example, practitioners are often asked to analyze potential policies being considered by their own governing boards, to respond by review and comment within a sixty-day period to a proposed policy published by a state agency, or to give an expert opinion on the potential impact of a proposed piece of legislation or a county budget policy upon client services that their interagency task force wishes to address.

In the area of social policy process, practitioners might be asked to analyze the role or influence of key actors or events in a community issue, such as the merging of a number of human services agencies or the application by a new agency for membership in the local United Way or community welfare council. Practitioners may be required to provide leadership in a social action process aimed at purposively affecting community welfare policy, and their ability to analyze the policy process might be crucial to achieving their goal.

Clearly, if social and other human services workers are to influence policy decision making, they must possess or develop skills in analyzing policy content and process. Mayer and Greenwood (1980) contend that policy research is goal-oriented, requires the analyst to be familiar with a systems perspective, demands the ability to manipulate a large number of variables, is focused on both content and action, and must be conducted in multidisciplinary situations. But do practitioners have the skills to meet those obligations? As Ziter (1983) notes, social workers have developed policy skills only to a limited extent, despite considerable attention to policy content in social work curricula. It would seem, then, that concerted efforts must be made to develop skills in the area that Ziter refers to as "policy analysis and synthesis."

Formal Policy and Informal Policy

The reader may have concluded by now that policy behavior manifested in informal or normative behavior of human service professionals is just as much "policy" as policy that is formally stated or written. Such a conclusion, of course, is a debatable point of view. For instance, Tropman (1984) defines policy as "an idea that has been elaborated and set down in writing, ratified by existing authorities, and designed to guide action" (p. 2). This definition makes good sense when a technical or legalistic approach to questioning or challenging policy principles of a system or an organization is required. For example, how many of us may have asked, very righteously, "Now just what *is* the policy around here?" implying that, if we could find a written policy statement, we would be on the side of the angels in our confrontation.

On the other hand, consider Jansson's characterization of policy. He identifies informal policy as behaviors that develop over time among practitioners who have to "fill in the gaps" for ill-defined formal or written polices. He notes that these practices, sometimes shaped into "collectively defined rules," come to have the same effect as written policy and actually shape the functioning of direct service professionals and administrators (Jansson, 1990, pp. 22–23). Some of these informal policies may respond to deficiencies in formal policy; others may be a result of the unilateral initiatives of practitioners to establish policy for themselves. Agency staff, for example, may informally select certain types of diagnostic conditions for continued services, routinely refer or not refer to particular agencies, or routinely discriminate against some types of persons on the basis of some social criterion such as race or age. In such instances of informal policy, the everyday behavior of agency professionals comes to constitute the principles by which the agency operates. Whether or not these principles have been set down in writing or ratified or legitimated by authority, the reality of their impact upon participants in the system is just as real.

Policy is both formal and informal. Policy, as the principles by which practitioners establish their priorities, guide plans and interventions, and bespeak basic values, is articulated formally and informally.

The Need for Small-Scale Policy Frameworks

Many social workers have the ability needed for such analysis. They have the broad system knowledge, the accumulated experiences necessary for understanding, and the analytical skills. However, it is likely that many do not have the policy analysis frameworks needed at the small-scale level for precisely the reasons stated above: practitioners have been socialized to believe that social policy only happens somewhere beyond their immediate environment. And, if they have been inclined to take an analytical approach to social welfare policy, the literature has been helpful only to the extent that it has provided large-scale or national system frameworks for analysis. Such frameworks are limited as tools for small-scale policy analysis of issues in which most direct practitioners have an opportunity to participate.

This book provides direction for the analysis of policy content and process—the substance and the activity of social welfare in small systems. We will review what the literature has to offer us and extract what is relevant to our needs for small-scale policy analysis. But we will essentially be forging our own tools. We will not only develop that set of tools but also share in the development of that area of social intervention that might be called social policy practice, or social welfare policy practice.

Policy Analysis Work

As suggested above, social policy has heretofore largely been seen as an area of substantive information in support of the various methods of social work practice, such as social treatment, direct service provision, planning, community organization, and administration. One could argue that the analysis of social welfare policy has really existed in other forms or in other methodological orientations, such as social welfare administration or social welfare research and evaluation. Or it might be said that the analysis of the process aspects of such policy has really been the business of the community organization method of practice. In fact, Ziter has said that, "policywork" comprises three practice areas: community organization, administration, and "a technical component, policy analysis and synthesis" (Ziter, 1983, p. 39). Nevertheless, it appears that the essentials of analysis (analysis and synthesis for the purposes of this book) have received the least attention in terms of skill development.

One might also acknowledge the relationship between policy analysis and program evaluation. Policy deals primarily with establishing the principles and goals or objectives or the ends; program deals with how the ends are to be obtained, that is, the means. Programs involve the activities, in the form of social services, undertaken in pursuit of agency policy. Like the rest of the real world, however, virtually everything is interrelated.

The focus of attention and the primary purposes of program evaluation differ, however. For example, in policy analysis we may be interested in determining the efficiency or effectiveness of a particular policy. However, in program evaluation, while we would be interested in efficiency or effectiveness, the focus would be on a collection of services, resource allocation to a set of activities, and (likely) upon a number and variety of concommitant policies enmeshed in those services. So, while policy analysis and program evaluation are interrelated, they differ in their focus.

The intent here is not to stake out any territory or domain. The essential point is that we are in need of frameworks for analysis of small-scale policy, and we will have to develop these frameworks ourselves if we are to be policy practitioners. To see policy, to know policy, to feel policy is not enough: we find ourselves ''doing'' policy and we need the tools, including frameworks for small-scale policy analysis and the presentation of those analyses, to do the job. We need to know how to conduct those analyses and how to convey them to others. As we recognize more and more that there are identifiable and essential sets of knowledge, skills and abilities associated with the ''doing'' of policy we come to realize that, indeed, social policy work is social policy-as-practice. This book is written from the perspective that social policy work is social policy-as-practice; i.e., that social policy is a part of social work practice and an essential element in all human services practice. The business of small-scale policy analysis—of policy content and policy processes—is central to the work of policy practice.

This book takes a general or human systems or ecological perspective throughout, at some points explicitly and at other points only implicitly. The systems approach here is not the typical linear approach of stating goals and objectives, identifying alternatives, and developing feedback mechanisms. Rather, we summarize the underlying principles of systems thinking and weave those principles into the outlines for analysis provided in later chapters. These human system principles will especially be made explicit when we identify value elements for policy analysis.

Chapters 2 and 3 review and summarize approaches to policy analysis in social welfare and an inventory of currently available frameworks for analysis. Chapter 4 sets forth the essential elements of a framework for analysis of policy *content* from which the analyst may choose in constructing his or her own model for analysis. This is integrated with case applications along with an outline for the analysis of content and is followed by more case illustrations. Chapter 5 develops the framework for the analysis of policy *process* at the local level and is followed, in turn, by process-oriented applications of case material. The remaining chapters deal with situations frequently requiring the presentation of policy analyses: legislative analysis, giving testimony, and position statements. Again, the substantive chapters are each followed by case illustrations.

Each chapter that generates an outline for analysis also includes case illustrations. These case examples are either woven into the narrative of the chapter or appear at the end of the chapter. Some cases illustrate both *content* and *values* analysis or *process* and *value* analysis. Cases 3 and 5 focus on the issue of an integrated policy for the downtown mall.

Approaches to
Policy Analysis

2

In chapter 1, we explored a number of approaches to the analysis of social welfare policy; we also briefly considered some of the contexts within which policy analysis in the social welfare area might occur. Now we will examine in more detail what social welfare policy is.

What Is Social Welfare Policy?

We gave a brief definition of policy in chapter 1 by saying that *policy* refers to *those principles which give expression to valued ends and provide direction to social welfare action*. We said that policy has to do with principles, with what we value most and what we want to happen. A conventional way of going about the study of most any subject matter is, of course, to begin with a definition of basic terms. However, David Gil has shown us the tremendous range and number of options available to us if we wish to give definition to the term "social policy." In fact, in addition to citing numerous authors' definitions, Gil notes Freeman and Sherwood's observation that at least four "layers" of an understanding or definition of social policy exist, depending upon whether one emphasizes social policy as a philosophical concept, a product, a process, or a framework for action (Gil, 1976, pp. 3–10). Thus, one's understanding of what constitutes social policy greatly depends upon one's perspective, which could be significantly determined by the task at hand, the job, or one's world view. It could also depend on whether one's focus is the substantive aspects of a policy or policies or the process aspects of policymaking.

The policy definitions found in social welfare literature emphasize the broadest or highest level of human interaction, particularly national policies such as income maintenance, massive provision of social services, and various other questions about distribution of national resources. Very little is available to guide us in policy analysis at the local levels, due in part perhaps to a presumption that local policy analysis phenomena are too idiosyncratic or unique, or perhaps due to the presumed primacy of national policy. However, since our intent is to be of immediate and practical help to practitioners at the local or community level, small-scale definitions are in order.

One-Liner Definitions of Policy

It is perhaps practical to think of social welfare policy in simple terms, keeping in mind, of course, that complex problems cannot really be reduced to simple terms. Our attempt here is not so much to simplify but to demystify and not get lost in large and "bookish" definitions.

Generally speaking, the common ingredients in most definitions of social welfare policy are that policies (1) set forth principles, and (2) deal with human health, safety, or well being. More comprehensive definitions would, of course, include some notions of social interaction, legitimacy, sanctions, availability of resources, and so forth. However, the central concepts have to do with the fact that policies set forth the values that give shape to ends or means, and that social welfare policies relate to the health, safety, and well-being of human beings in social systems.

One uncluttered approach to obtaining a definition of policy is to establish a number of reasonable one-liners. For example, social welfare policy (hereafter occasionally referred to as social policy) is a set of goal statements about desired human conditions. Or, social policy is a set of principles to guide social action. One definition is goal-oriented, the other means-oriented. Looking at a combined ends/means definition, we could say that policy is a statement of desired ends, with selected alternative means. Another approach to definition is to look at policy from a strictly empirical perspective (i.e., what one can see or feel) and simply view it as a position taken by an individual or organization, either implicitly or explicitly. Put another way, a policy is a decision made or not made, as Harvey Cox (1966) would perhaps state it. Another approach is to look at social policy from a technical, administrative, or planning perspective and refer to it as a standing plan (Kahn, 1969) or an organizing principle to shape a system or design a program, for example.

Since social welfare services tend to be inspired by socially sanctioned goals often debated at the community or agency board level, it could be said that policy is the ordering of priorities. The latter would be a simple one-liner, process-oriented definition of social welfare policy. MacRae and Haskins have argued that these economic-decisional orientations to policy analysis currently dominate the field. Frameworks for analysis based upon this approach emphasize criteria of maximization of social welfare measured either by the value of outcomes or the satisfaction of preferences (MacRae and Haskins, 1981, p. 8).

In contrast to these more rationalist orientations to policy, DiNitto and Dye emphasize the political aspects of social welfare policy. They say that public policy is the "outcome of conflicts . . . over who gets what, and when and how they get it" (DiNitto and Dye, 1983, p. 2). This is the conflict approach to social process.

Finally, policy has a special property in virtually any system: the ability to give order and predictability. (This will be discussed in chapter 4 along with the concept of the "stochastic process.") In fact, it can be said that the purpose and desired function of all policy, whether it involves legislation, judicial decrees or mandates, administrative rules, or executive directives, is to give order and predictability to a system. These properties of policy lead to the reduction of disorder. Consequently, a policy provides information to those who are likely to be subject to or influenced by it. Hence, a very practical one-line definition is that policy is (merely!) systematically ordered information. Policy, then, provides a signal, a direction, of what is expected of people—individuals, groups, or organizations.

The following list summarizes these definitions of policy. It may be said, then, that policy is:

1. A formal or informal expression of goals or valued ends.
2. A statement of desired ends with an indication of selected alternative means.
3. The ordering of priorities.
4. An organizing principle.
5. A standing plan.
6. A decision made (or not made).
7. A position—taken implicitly or explicitly.
8. The outcomes of social choice about who gets what, when, and how.
9. Information ordered in a system.

You no doubt can develop a number of other one-liner policy definitions, perhaps more relevant to the context or responsibilities of your practice. For a definition to be useful, it must articulate the fundamental principles or values at stake and must relate to human health, safety, or well-being.

Power and Policy

Since social welfare can either move people to action or delimit their range of potential outcomes, a close relationship exists between policy and power. As Dobelstein (1990) notes, understanding policy requires the understanding of power. A definition of power that is particularly relevant to this aspect of the discussion is provided by Polsby. Simply put, power is the "capacity of one actor to do something affecting another actor, which changes the probable pattern of specified future events" (Polsby, 1963, p. 5). As noted above, policy, by its nature, also introduces a stochastic process in human interaction. That is, policy provides for a certain lawfulness with respect to how people will behave, whether staff can exercise a certain prerogative, and whether a particular agency is free to make a given decision within the promulgated rule or regulation. At times, policy allocates power to individuals or organizations; at other time, power legitimates the ability to make or enforce policy. When power legitimates in this way, individuals or organizations are given authority. Thus, power and policy are inextricably interwoven.

It may also be said that policy is information—it transforms data into information and disorder into order. Policy shapes information in such a way that people can communicate priorities and expectations. When policy is clearly stated and consistently administered, people know what is expected of them or their agencies.

Policy, Power, and Information

The power of policy lies in its ability to give order to and manipulate a system by providing information. This is possible due to the close relationship between policy, power, and information. When a social welfare policy has clarity, consistency, legitimacy, and sanction, that policy may be said to be powerful. The test of a policy's power is first found in the degree of salience or applicability it has for a large number of people or for a sustained period of time. Further, as Meltsner and Bellavita (1983) point out, the policy "message" must be communicated throughout the organization or the system. Consequently, the power of such a policy is evidenced by the degree to which people normatively behave according to the policy's mandates, which explains why policy is so vitally important to social practice professionals pursuing social goals.

The allocation of resources in our society is highly dependent upon the distribution and exercise of power by various interest groups. Policy gives shape, direction, and limits to that exercise of power; policy sets the boundaries and establishes the goals; and the actualities of the policy process frequently determine how or whether those in need will share in our society's resources. Consequently, in the context of power relationships, policy is a key vehicle for achieving social ends. This characterization of the role and function of policy is no less true in small-scale systems than in large-scale or national systems.

It may be said that policymaking is the processing of information wherein the communication obtained and promoted gives order (organization) to the system. Thus, social policy, when processed (as with information), becomes communication that gives order and predictability to a system or its members. It may also be said that the making of social policy is the management of social power, and the power of social policy lies in its ability to order or manipulate a social system. Policy-making is a decision-making process and the making of policy decisions is, in turn, the playing out of *influence*. As McGill and Clark (1975) have indicated, power is the *potential* for having or using resources, while influence is the actual exercising of power through the decision-making process. Therefore, while social policy actually constitutes the substance or content of a particular issue, it also constitutes the processing aspects of power and influence and the ordering of information in a system.

What Does Policy Do for Us?

As Alfred Kahn has indicated, policy enacts practice (Kahn, 1973). Policy shapes and delineates what the practitioner does, how he or she relates to the client group, and the manner in which discretion is allowed or exercised. Policy also provides the priorities within which the practitioner can allocate time and other resources and, consequently, provides a structure for how one's professional role is to be carried out. As policy shapes individual or group functioning, it also shapes functioning at the *program* level, setting the agency's direction, the content of services, and the tone and quality of the milieu within which work is accomplished and services provided. The workers influenced by policy reciprocate and have many opportunities to set, modify, and even negate social policy in both formal and informal ways. Thus, we may infer that social practitioners undertake policy analysis at all times, at least at some level of consciousness, as evidenced by their dutifully or creatively carrying out policy mandates or by their purposefully engaging in social action at various system levels to modify or even resist those mandates. Therefore, it is empowering for professionals to realize their bilateral role in the play of policy, for in awareness there is hope for control. Out of this awareness, one has the empowering potential to subject one's situation to productive analysis.

Dolgoff and Gordon (1976) have suggested that there is actually a continuum of reciprocity between the practitioner and the larger systems from which policy emanates. At one end of the continuum there are only client- and worker-specific policies, such as a mutual decision to depart from an agreed upon treatment-policy principle like the location or frequency of interviews. At the other end of the continuum, there are situations in which an entire service system is altered, as in redefining the authority and responsibility of state and local levels of government with respect to provision of a social service. This is reminiscent of the five models of policy practice identified by Wyers (1990) and listed in chapter 1, that is, the social worker as policy expert, as change agent in external and internal environments, as a policy conduit, or as the embodiment of policy itself.

The direct practitioner is actively involved at all levels in the making of policy decisions. For example, the worker and/or agency makes a policy choice by selecting a particular treatment modality, for example, deciding to provide only behaviorally based treatment, or taking on clients only when the entire family consents to treatment. In such situations the worker or agency acts within the context of having performed a small-scale policy analysis or at least a "quick-and-dirty" rational evaluation (presuming that decisions are made with responsible forethought).

Along the continuum, workers may also make policy decisions that shape and define their own strategic roles, such as becoming advocates, brokers, mediators, therapists, facilitators, or change agents. The individual or the group makes choices regarding who or what the interventive target might appropriately be. The practitioner's choice of strategic role is itself evidence of the agency's and/or the practitioner's own policy position on the appropriateness of a particular intervention modality. For example, a school system's social work unit might arbitrarily or consciously select a child, the parents, a teacher, the school principal, or even the administrative structure as the target for intervention. Some practitioners routinely take on one or a selected number of these targets—as a matter of policy.

Finally, Dolgoff and Gordon suggest that what often really occurs is a blend of the three policy decisions; i.e., choice of treatment modality, worker role, and intervention target. Clearly, however, these three areas of policy decision occur at the smallest scale—that of interpersonal practice. For example, the worker makes a choice (hopefully after thoughtful analysis) about the appropriateness of assuming an advocate, mediator, or therapist role. These role choices are partly determined by agency policy; for example, what services are fundable or otherwise allowable. Treatment methodology is also limited or enhanced by agency policy and/or facilities as is the choice of clients and/ or targets.

Perhaps an analysis of social policy at the program or agency level makes the policy analysis process clearer. Here, program coordinators are called upon to provide the agency director or task force, for example, with a detailed statement of the potential impact of a piece of pending state legislation upon the agency's mission or client population. Or an agency staff member is asked to provide an analysis of the ramifications of taking on a new service or establishing a new outpost at a branch location. In the context of policy process, an agency administrator may have to assess the possible human or social costs and outcomes of entering into a proposed or emerging coalition that results from current social action surrounding a policy issue. These situations clearly suggest that practitioners take implicit or explicit approaches to their analyses of policy.

Policy analysis has a range of functional utilities. Gilbert and Specht (1974) have pointed out that frameworks for policy analysis provide a meaningful set of concepts applicable to a wide range of situations, help to simplify a complex reality, and direct attention to certain elements while filtering out others. An explication of the elements for analysis also helps us to make our own assumptions known and to open our philosophical points of view to examination. Cates and Lohman (1980) have suggested that such analyses can serve to educate personnel to policy changes or consequences, provide a way to determine the local discretion available in new rules or regulations, allow clear position statements to be developed, and help client groups become more informed in order to enhance their ability to lobby more effectively. These practical utilizations of policy analysis provide justification for efforts to build models or frameworks for the analysis of social welfare policy.

Approaches to Social Welfare Policy Analysis

As the reader is probably aware, there are many approaches, models, or frameworks for the analysis of social policy. In the discipline of political science, Thomas Dye (1981, pp. 19–45) has identified eight analytic models that are applicable to social policy. They may be described as follows:

1. *Institutional model.* Policy is seen as the output of institutional events and processes.
2. *Rational model.* Policy is seen as the effect of efficient goal achievement.

3. *Process model.* Policy is seen strictly as political activity.
4. *Incremental model.* Policy is viewed merely as variations and modifications of past positions.
5. *Group model.* Policy is seen as the maintenance or outcomes of group equilibrium.
6. *Elite model.* Policy is seen as the preferences set and/or taken by elite community actors.
7. *Game theory models.* Policy is seen as rational choice-taking in competitive situations.
8. *Systems model.* Policy is seen as system inputs, throughputs, and outputs.

You can see that the analytic approach chosen will likely be dependent upon many factors, particularly the philosophical orientation and the maintenance or change goal of the person or group making the analysis.

Yet another classificatory scheme emphasizes not so much a perspective of what constitutes policy *per se* but, rather, how the policy analysis is perceived. This scheme, described by Dobelstein (1990), contains three models of policy analysis which are said to be on a continuum, at one end of which is complete reliance on empirical data and, on the other, reliance on value choices. These three models are:

1. *The Behavioral (or Rational) Model.* Policy analysis requires a maximum amount of social science information and empirical methods. This approach relies heavily on "systems approaches"—in the context of specification of problems, determination of objectives, identification of alternatives and sets of alternative choices, establishing cost, and choice-taking among alternatives. This approach is based on the work of Simon (1964).
2. *The Criteria-Based Model.* Policy analysis requires dual recognition of possible alternatives as well as extensive recognition of all value ramifications. This approach is an attempt to balance the demands of normative social science methods and, at the same time, to recognize the human-relations aspects of policy formulation and implementation. This approach is located in the middle of the continuum of policy analysis models, according to Dobelstein, and is based on the work of Gallagher and Haskins (1984).
3. *The Incremental Model.* Policy analysis requires primary attention to the interplay of values in choice-taking and emphasizes that policy is the outcome of incremental changes, to tradeoffs with, and approximations of what might actually be desired. This approach is said to focus more on the solution to the problem than on the problem itself, and is based on the work of Lindblom

(1964), whose explanation of policy process is examined in more
detail in chapter 6.

The reader will subsequently see, particularly in chapters 4 and 6,
wherein the criteria for analysis of policy content and policy process
are discussed, that this book gives most recognition to what Dobelstein
calls the criteria-based model where equal emphasis is given to specification of a number of elements that can be empirically established as
well as elements that reflect the values of those who are impacted by
any policy choice.

The foregoing lists make it clear that there is no universal model
for conceptualizing policy or policy analysis. Which approach to take
will depend upon an individual's situation—one's job responsibilities,
level of functioning, and philosophical orientation. In this regard,
Moroney cites Rein's observation that no single academic or professional discipline can adequately develop a universal appropriate tool.
Rather, the analyst must select and apply the approaches used in the
different disciplines and synthesize the analysis into a meaningful
whole (Moroney, 1981, p. 78).

At the large-scale level of social systems, a number of successful
approaches to the understanding of social welfare policy have developed, some of which are found in classic texts, such as Romanyshyn
(1971), Dolgoff and Feldstein (1980), Kammerman and Kahn (1976), or
Frederico (1980). These approaches to policy range from the histori-
cal/descriptive to the critical/analytical. A particularly good example of
historical research on the larger scale is Cates' examination of the development of the Social Security Act (Cates, 1986).

Generally speaking, the approach to analysis has been to explore
the various fields of service (e.g., child welfare, corrections, mental
health, income maintenance), or to identify policy milestones in the
chronology of American welfare history. Some approaches offer practical, descriptive information, such as details regarding the benefits or
eligibility requirements of particular programs, while others provide
critical analyses of the choices taken or the opportunities overlooked in
past policy and program development. It appears that most of the literature has focused on the content, as opposed to the process aspects of
social welfare policy, though this is an impressionistic observation.

The shift has been away from an emphasis upon historical and
descriptive approaches to social welfare policy analysis and toward
analysis of current policy impact or future policy choices. This newer
theme is particularly evident in the emergence of model building in social welfare policy analysis. These efforts are of great value to practitioners in developing their own models for small-scale policy analysis.

Particularly noteworthy are two works by Jansson (1984; 1990) in which frames of reference for policy analysis have been clearly articulated. The latter work emphasizes the practice aspects of social policy. Others, some of whom were noted in the discussion of policy practice in chapter 1, have been provided by Karger and Stoesz (1990), Pierce (1984), and Tropman (1984). The first edition of this book was also a model-building effort (Flynn, 1985).

Frameworks and Models for Analysis

You may have noticed that a number of terms are used interchangeably, particularly *approaches, frameworks,* and *models.* While we do not want to get too technical here, it is important that we point out some important distinctions between *frameworks* and *models.* We are trying to achieve two things. The first is to establish a framework to organize our thinking about policy analysis; the second is to provide a model for the particular application for analysis. And, we are trying to bring this all down to the small-scale system in which most of us spend our professional lives.

It might help to first think of the importance of establishing what might be called a "world view," which we will call here our frame of reference. A frame of reference is what we consider to be most important and what is valued most of all, in common parlance, "where we are coming from." As Lastrucci (1967) noted, the frame of reference suggests *how* or *from what viewpoint* one views the data. It suggests the point of view or perhaps the theoretical perspective taken to a problem or any analytic activity. In real life, if we are reasonable and experienced at all, we tend to select not just one frame of reference but several in order to organize our thinking about reality. This eclectic mix of frames of reference we refer to as our *framework.* You might conceive of an elaborate structure comprised of many elements (representing different frames of reference), such as looking at policy problems and saying, for example, that the role of legitimation is essential in formulating social policy, or that the nature and amount of resources are absolutely critical, or that the nature of communication within and among human systems is a *sine qua non* of social functioning. We build a framework based upon what we think is important in terms of what will describe, explain, or predict reality.

At times we must apply those frameworks to some particular problem or analysis. And the reality may be that we do not have sufficient time or the data is not readily available or its collection is too great an expense. In other words, we may not want to apply the entire framework to the task. So we need a temporary construction of the problem and a smaller tool for the analysis. Here is where the use of a *model* comes into play. As Lastrucci says, a model only provides approximations or tentative interpretations of reality.

> [A model] refers to a parallel form, simpler than the complex subject it represents, but having a similar structure or organization. Models are used to help our minds understand the arrangements of key components and how they function (Lastrucci, 1967, p. 130).

The parallel form referred to is the more elaborate framework, or the more elaborate or complete or complex representation of reality. Models give us something to work with for the task at hand.

Another aspect of a model is its practicality.

> An explicit model, scientific or otherwise . . . introduces structure and terminology to a problem and provides a means for breaking a complicated decision into smaller tasks than can be handled one at a time. (Quade, 1975, p. 48).

This is true whether our model is a flowchart, decision tree, or elaborate theoretical construction without graphics.

A number of references have been made to models that are used in policy analysis. But what Dye or Dobelstein refer to as models may more properly be classified as frameworks, since their classificatory schemes convey the need for more complete or inclusive approaches to constructing reality. Their approaches are at a grander level than that of a model. Models, of course, are temporary constructs developed to help solve problems. Frequently we use models to aid in day-to-day problem solving. For example, if we find our housing inadequate, we might drive around on a Sunday afternoon and look for signs saying ''Model Open.'' We can walk through and touch that temporary construction of reality; in so doing we gather data that narrows or expands our range of choices and find further direction in our decision-making. The model house suggests an awareness of a set of values that identifies a house as a dwelling for human satisfaction and includes some theoretical evidence about the utility, as well as the beauty, of a cantilevered roof. Perhaps the location of the lot is based upon empirical evidence of where and how the sun situates itself upon the house's windows, thereby suggesting that the architect (i.e., analyst) utilized data collection and analysis in development of the model. But, in reality, the model need not be complete in terms of what constitutes a ''good'' house. For demonstration purposes, the model house may not have a basement, whereas one might be necessary. Or the floor covering may be of an inferior quality that needs to last only for a limited time.

Frameworks and models for policy analysis have the same relationship. Practitioners have grand conceptualizations for determining what is important in the overall scheme of things (i.e., frameworks) and have temporary constructions (i.e., models) which draw upon what they have articulated in their frameworks for analysis. This book will develop frameworks for analysis. It will be up to those who apply the elements of the frameworks to determine what is important, what time and other resources they have available for analysis, and then proceed to apply a model, a portion of a chosen framework. Both the frameworks and the models are essentially the same. They are based upon certain values, certain theories about how things ought to work or go together, as well as upon some empirical reality. The main objective of this book is to provide frameworks so that you will be better equipped to apply models. In other words, we will point out what might be important in the bigger picture; you will be asked to figure out what is relevant and available in your particular situation.

In this book we develop and use outlines as expressions of frameworks and models. For example, chapter 4 develops and provides a framework for analysis. By way of illustration, we apply the elements of the framework to particular policy problems. But while we feel obligated to apply every element of the framework to provide illustration for the reader, in real life that complete elaboration may not be relevant or even practical.

Whatever the approach, the process and the product require us to specify what we value, and what our hunches, hypotheses, or theories of cause and effect are, and they must rely upon the collection of empirical data. The frameworks of social welfare policy analysis emerging in the current literature are all based upon these notions. And, while they differ significantly in their complexity, jargon, and emphasis, they all make a contribution and each responds to the expanding recognition of our need for analytic tools and structure in presenting our policy analyses. While we will go into some detail in each of the frameworks or models to which we refer in chapter 3, a limited number will be noted here for purposes of introduction. A more extensive list (and discussion) of authors and models is provided by Lyon (1983) in his report on a survey of required readings in social welfare policy courses in undergraduate and graduate social work programs.

The first framework, selected for discussion here mainly because of its frequent appearance in the literature, was presented early on by David Gil (1976). Gil provides a highly elaborate and detailed framework for policy analysis, based on a perspective that certain social requirements are presumed to be universal. Gil stresses the repeated analysis and comparison of alternative policies in his problem-solving approach. Joseph Heffernan (1979) provides somewhat of an interactionist perspective; his focus is the analysis of the interplay of economic and political choice taking. Gilbert and Specht (1974) emphasize the inputs, processes, and outcomes (though not in those terms) of social welfare policy choices. Prigmore and Atherton (1979) provide an inventory of questions that are essentially basic value choices and practical political and financial parameters in a policy environment. Meenaghan and Washington (1980) provide a framework that derives from a set of basic and universal questions and a set of optional questions or concerns. While these models (as well as those presented in chapter 3) are necessary to understand social welfare policy analysis, they all speak to and are designed for analysis at the grand- or large-scale policy levels. On the other hand, they provide us with direction in constructing another needed tool, a framework for social welfare policy analysis at the small-scale level.

Dilemmas in Understanding

Be forewarned that you will be faced with the same problems with which the authors mentioned above have struggled. As people limited by thought and language, but needing to know and understand, we must make many choices as we proceed with our construction of frameworks and models for analysis. These choices include esoteric labels and tend to be seen as "intellectual concerns," but if we look beyond the jargon and focus on the concepts, we can take more conscious responsibility for what we set out to do. All people make a range of choices in their everyday lives, and they give little notice as they attempt to "make meaning."

We can create our understanding (e.g., our models) based upon the notion that there are certain objective facts and most of what we need to do is identify these facts. At the risk of oversimplifying, this is sometimes called logical positivism. An alternative, called a phenomenological approach, holds that objective understanding is found in the process of events, not the *a priori* conditions that are said to be essential in social systems. This is one duality we face: logical positivism and phenomenology. We do not have to make any forced choices in this regard because our frameworks and models will be eclectic.

Another classical duality is that of inductive versus deductive reasoning. Some perspectives might emphasize beginning with a theoretical point of view and then proceeding to collect the facts appropriate to the theory. This deductive approach gives a good deal of direction to the practitioner and has led to many outstanding discoveries and analyses. The alternative approach, inductive reasoning, begins with the

collection of a large amount of empirical data and then sets out to provide some shape and context to that data via movement toward theoretical explanation. The first approach is taken with a good bit of direction provided by theory; the latter, while less structured, is perhaps
more open to a variety of theoretical perspectives.

Yet another duality is the contest between a task and a process
orientation so clearly treated by Roland Warren (1972), for example.
The first tends to emphasize the goal, the second, the means of goal
achievement. This duality seems to be clearly personified in social
work practitioners. Some staff might be particularly task oriented;
others might be process oriented regarding what they emphasize,
how they perceive their environments, and the importance of things
and events in those environments. Our emphases upon either task or
process are likely to color our analyses, and we should attempt to
achieve intellectual honesty in this area. An excellent discussion of
the conceptual and philosophical problems and pitfalls in explaining
social policy phenomena is provided by Carrier and Kendall (1973),
with particular emphasis on the contest between positivism and phenomenology.

We cannot totally avoid the pitfalls offered by these dualities. If
we are honest, we will simply have to accept the limitations of our conceptual abilities and, as best we can, take what seems appropriate from
the existing approaches available in the field. The frameworks and
models that we choose must have their own integrity and logic. In
chapter 3, a survey of the content and approach of what exists will assist you in making these selections.

Sources of Information

Where do we get our information? In speaking of policy research, Tripodi, Fellin, and Meyer suggest that three sets of information are
available: ''data on the target population, findings from studies of the
use of intervention strategies, and information on costs, staff needs,
and other organizational and administrative factors related to program delivery.'' (1983, p. 163). To this can be added knowledge of the
prior history and individual and collective biases in the group(s) under analysis, and the current political and economic pressures bearing on the issue for which the analysis is undertaken. In short, the
policy analyst needs to have access to and a facility for the use of a
range and variety of information resources in order to conduct an adequate analysis or, more realistically, to at least be aware of the informational deficiencies that exist in the analysis when it is conducted. A
big order!

Summary

This chapter considered definitions of social welfare policy and policy analysis; identified some interdependencies between policy, power, and information as an introduction to seeing what policy actually does for social practitioners; and explored the conceptual and functional differences between frameworks and models. A few approaches to model building in social policy analysis were surveyed. Finally, we considered the conceptual and philosophical dilemmas posed in the dualities of positivism and phenomenology, inductive and deductive reasoning, and in the classical contest between task and process orientations to reality. Next, we will take a more detailed look at some current large-scale frameworks for analyzing policy content and process.

Frameworks and Models for Policy Analysis

3

This chapter will review selected frameworks and models presently available for policy analysis in social welfare. First we will review frameworks that emphasize the analysis of policy content, then those that emphasize policy process. The chapter will help to identify the state of the art and will be helpful in mining the essential features or characteristics of various frameworks that are currently available. Finally, this chapter provides a starting point for constructing the frameworks for small-scale policy analysis and presentation from which you may form your own models.

While we ultimately must develop and construct our own frameworks for small-scale policy analysis, there is a great deal that is of value in social welfare literature to give us direction. The fact that much of this literature has been made available only recently attests to the fact that the focus on policy analysis frameworks in social welfare is a relatively new development. However, although many of these frameworks have much to offer, we still find it necessary to extrapolate from them to the small-scale situation if they are to be of any practical use for policy analysis at that level. Since both the terminology used and its applications are generally large-scale, national, or even global in nature, these frameworks often have limited direct relevance to the kinds of policy problems endemic to local agencies or statewide policy issues or policy action systems.

Before proceeding, however, we must take note of the use of the terms "framework" and "models" in this chapter. Frameworks refer to overall perspectives or viewpoints and encompass the widest possible number of elements or variables. Models are temporary constructions developed to solve a particular problem and are much more limited in their scope or inclusiveness. While models are based upon one or more theories or sets of propositions that make everything a coherent whole for problem-solving purposes, they are limited as compared to frameworks. The term "frameworks" is used in the literature to give recognition and/or conscious visibility to the philosophical or world view as well as the technical and theoretical features embodied in the model. The primary focus here is the development of frameworks rather than models, but the latter term appears to have wider use in the field. As you will see, some of the sources are clearly grand-level frameworks for analysis; others are more modest in their scope and are clearly models within the terms discussed in chapter 2. We will note those distinctions as we move along.

Selected Frameworks and Models

In this chapter, both content and process frameworks for policy analysis will be reviewed and summarized. We will look at frameworks that emphasize either substantive analytic content or the process or activity aspects of policy making. The tasks of policy analysis tend to be either content- or process-specific; our task is to generate both types of frameworks and outlines, which will help the policy practitioner build models for analysis on the job. I do not mean to imply or suggest that content and process are not interactive or interdependent. Indeed, one cannot realistically focus on one to the total exclusion of the other. Content and process are separated here only as a matter of emphasis for the purpose of exploration and focus.

Cates and Lohman (1980) reviewed a number of frameworks and found four different types of analytic categories emphasized by different schemes: (1) the policy values or objectives; (2) the policy target groups; (3) the methods of implementation of policy; and/or (4) the environmental impact of a particular policy or policies. Any framework or application of a framework can emphasize one or any combination of these four categories.

Haskins contends that, whatever approach is taken to policy analysis, all analysts will agree that analysis would include five basic activities: (1) describing the problem situation; (2) specifying criteria; (3) generating alternative strategies; (4) selecting a "best" policy; and (5) assessing feasibility (1981, p. 203).

The simplest framework would include the fewest number of elements or variables. While some frameworks have a number and variety of interconnected elements that facilitate a comprehensive and detailed analysis, other frameworks provide a limited number of elements assumed to be essential. Of course, a simple framework is not necessarily simplistic. Some analysts, however, tend to limit their number of tools in order to eliminate their workbench clutter. Some frameworks are more or less inclusive, depending upon the number and variety of criteria employed for analysis. This does not suggest that the job is any less complicated or complex.

The Centrality of Values in Analysis

Robert Moroney's approach to analysis provides a useful beginning in that, rather than setting forth outcome criteria or feasibility considerations at the outset, he bases his entire analysis on the premise that all "policy formulation is fundamentally concerned with making choices, and those choices are shaped by values" (Moroney, 1981, p. 99). Moroney's position is to keep visible throughout analysis the primacy of values in choice-taking and preference selection. This position is especially appropriate for a practice-oriented profession bound by its code of ethics to deal openly and aggressively with values. In fact, Levy (1979b) contends that values and ethics for professionals tend to converge in that the pursuit of valued ends becomes an ethical mandate for professional practice. That is, what we want (values) and what we must do about it (ethics) converge in professional practice, whereas values and ethics may be quite separate when dealing with these terms in a general sense.

An approach that utilizes a limited number of criteria is the framework provided by Joseph Kelley (1975). Kelley, who offers what is called a change-related (as opposed to a past-oriented) approach, provides a limited number of criteria, each of which is familiar. His three essential criteria are adequacy, effectiveness, and efficiency. Any proposed or actual policy subjected to analysis must be assessed in terms of (1) the extent to which a specified need or goal is met if program objectives are carried out (adequacy); (2) the extent to which the outcomes obtained are a result of policy intent and program activity (effectiveness); and (3) the measure of goal attainment in terms of the expenditure of the least amount of resources (efficiency). One can hardly develop social policy of any kind without considering these basic criteria. Consequently, the three criteria might serve as a foundation for any framework for social welfare policy analysis.

However, Kelley adds what he calls two key "subcriteria" called "identity" and "self-determination." If the substance of the matter is of a social welfare nature, one must also consider the impact of the policy or consequent program upon the self-image of the beneficiary or target (the identity) and the right of consumers to a voice in the determination of those policies that might affect them (self-determination).

Given the nature of the code of ethics of such organizations as the National Association of Social Workers and other human services associations, adequacy, effectiveness, and efficiency are not sufficient criteria. The impact upon client identity and client self-determination are criteria that *must* be included in any framework for social welfare policy analysis. Tropman (1984) gives particular attention to this reality when he notes that social work, for example, is often on the side of what he calls "subdominant," as opposed to "dominant," values. The values of individualism, self-reliance, secularism, equity, struggle, privatism, and work are said to be dominant in American society, whereas the converse values emphasize family, interdependency, religion, adequacy, entitlement, public orientation, and leisure. The task for those who contend with policy (and policy analysis, of course) is to find a judicious balance of those values.

Kelley's framework, on the face of it, appears easy to apply to small-scale policy contexts. Surely, an agency policy may be considered in terms of the current or potential adequacy of its benefits. Effectiveness might be determined by quantitative or soft measures within the local action system. Local measures that determine what constitutes desirable levels of efficiency could perhaps be agreed upon. At small-scale levels, the questions of impact on client or target identity and self-determination are perhaps more realistically pursued. The problem with this first framework, however, is that it posits only a limited number of criteria and is not in itself an adequate representation of reality for an inclusive or a comprehensive analysis. It does help us to recognize, however, the centrality of values in this task. Many in the field have attempted to put forth lists of values thought to be generic to social work practice, perhaps in an effort to develop a consensus definition of the core ethos that glue practitioners together and guide their choices for action. Specific references to two of those values, identity maintenance and self-determination, have already been included. Tropman's list provides many possibilities, too. We will leave it at that for the moment, however, since the primary task in this chapter is to identify perspectives on content analysis and process analysis. We will return to the topic of values and ethics in chapter 4 when we construct our own framework for content analysis and again in chapter 6 regarding process analysis. The digression into the topic of values was necessary in order to remind ourselves of the centrality of values to our work.

Frameworks Emphasizing the Content of Policy

A more elaborate framework is presented by Gilbert and Specht (1974). They suggest two levels for content analysis. The first is referred to as the foundations or major parameters of choice. It includes the identification of the major values at odds in the policy, the explicit or implicit theories giving rise to the policy issues, and the overarching alternatives that are possible. The second is what are called the "dimensions of choice." Those elements, labeled by Gilbert and Specht as (1) bases of social allocations, (2) types of social provisions, (3) strategies for delivery, and (4) modes of finance, essentially analyze the questions of who gets what, through what delivery mechanism, and how the program will be financed. These issues, for example, could be translated into questions of eligibility criteria, forms that benefits might take (e.g., social insurance or public assistance), questions of service system design (e.g., preventative, habilitative, or rehabilitative), and concerns about mode and manner of finance.

Gilbert and Specht suggest that their framework embodies the social, political, and technical process aspects of policy as well as the performance outcomes of actual policies and programs. However, their emphasis seems to center around the substantive content aspects of policy rather than the process of policy development or change. Perhaps the greatest strength of their framework is its emphasis upon the products of any given set of policy choices; however, that feature should be a strength of any framework for analysis.

Meenaghan and Washington (1980) provide a framework that includes a mixture of generally applicable principles (e.g., concerns for ethics regarding work or individualism), basic criteria (e.g., fairness, adequacy, and equality), and generalizable design criteria (e.g., funding and allocation characteristics, types of benefits, or delivery mechanisms). This framework, while perhaps no more comprehensive than some others, does tend to be quite explicit and enumerates a range and variety of considerations in social policy analysis. In their basic framework, which they refer to as "lower levels of choice," Meenaghan and Washington search for the fairness, adequacy, and equality (i.e., more values) in the basic thrust of any policy. They then examine the level of prevention desired, the goal mix, types of benefits (e.g., cash versus in-kind benefits or the redistribution of power), the delivery system design, and financing considerations. Their "higher level" analysis suggests more detailed examination of these elements and examines both the historical and contemporary ramifications of various choices based upon the framework's criteria. Their approach appears to be an attempt to strike a balance between content and process orientations to analysis.

Joseph Heffernan (1979), while giving extensive attention to the political-economic substance of social welfare policy, nevertheless tends to emphasize its process aspects. Heffernan suggests that the main issue in social policy is to link personal problems to public concerns and that this task revolves around two central concepts: political power and economic scarcity. He sees policy as the accommodation of competing and sometimes contradictory demands upon scarce resources, and policy analysis as the articulation of preferences among alternative values and options wherein policy goals, procedures, and consequences are constantly evaluated in terms of what is desirable and what is possible. The primary strength of Heffernan's framework lies in the visibility given to choices among preferences, though relatively little (compared to other analytic frameworks) is offered in terms of substantive criteria for analysis.

Another framework is that of Prigmore and Atherton (1979). Their approach is unique in that they pose a set of questions that serve as an inventory or laundry list. Their framework is comprised of approximately a dozen questions in four major areas: (1) considerations related to cultural values; (2) dimensions of influence and decision-making (political acceptability and legality); (3) knowledge considerations (whether the policy is scientifically sound or rational); and (4) elements related to costs and/or benefits. Prigmore and Atherton's approach provides a range of criteria, which includes a questioning of basic values and premises as well as those items frequently associated with the rational aspects of policy analysis, such as design principles, financing considerations, and delivery mechanisms.

A review of frameworks for policy analysis would not be complete without acknowledging the framework provided by David Gil (1970; 1976). Gil, combining the classical structural-functionalist approach from sociology and a somewhat mechanical (i.e., input-output) view of systems analysis, emphasizes certain basic societal requisites such as resource allocation, rights distribution, status allocations, and the linkage between rights and statuses. Gil's outline for analysis essentially employs a rational and interactive problem-solving approach in which a variety of problem definitions and alternative choices are played out. Gil's framework is the one most frequently cited in the literature, perhaps because of its clarity and comprehensiveness. Yet its detail can be intimidating, if not somewhat impractical in terms of manageability. As with the others, much of its immediate applicability is to large-scale policy systems.

There is one particular aspect of the Gil framework, however, which is unique and receives little mention in the frequent references in the literature. This is Gil's contention that the fundamental purpose of policy analysis is to enable the analyst to become part of a counter-culture through which those interested in maintaining the status quo might be educated to newly found or newly perceived self-interests.

The status quo is assumed to have power and influence and, therefore, the policy analyst is seen as having a mission—to bring new light—and thereby to alter the system's organization of power and influence. Though Gil's approach to policy analysis is fundamentally rationalist in nature, his goals are value-based and pursued in a phenomenological context—a rare mix.

Each of these frameworks (and others in the literature not mentioned here) appears to have been created and developed with broad, large-scale, primarily national policy analysis tasks in mind. While most of the frameworks are inclusive and comprehensive, their language and examples tend to relate to levels well beyond and outside the needs of the policy practitioner at the local or small-scale level. Nevertheless, each offers much to the development of policy analysis tools and we will rely heavily on these works as we develop our own framework in later chapters.

Karger and Stoesz (1990) sketch out a framework for analysis and, in the course of that effort, also identify the properties of a framework for analysis, suggesting a number of key variables for the description of a given policy and giving particular attention to the relationship between policy goals and policy outcomes. They wisely give special attention to issues of feasibility, factors often ignored (at least explicitly) by other authors, through their illustrations to large-scale policy systems.

An exception to the emphasis on the large-scale to the exclusion to the small-scale, however, is provided by Jannson (1990), perhaps brought about because of his emphasis upon codifying "policy practice." Jansson links policy at both macro and micro levels to policy practice, especially by integrating knowledge and skills in both content and process. On the surface, Jansson would appear to offer what has now become a traditional linear-systems approach to policy and planning wherein goals or objectives are specified, alternatives enumerated, and choices taken. However, he has effectively linked content and process and identified particular tasks that are incumbent upon policy practitioners to undertake in both analysis and intervention.

Models Emphasizing the Process of Policy

Explanations of policy process fall more within the category of models rather than frameworks, because they tend to rely on more than one theoretical perspective within a particular explanation while at the same time are more narrow in the number or range of variables or elements included. This would seem to fit within our understanding of models, however, since models are temporary constructions established to solve particular problems. Also, identifying a body of policy literature as policy *process* literature in social welfare is a difficult task. While many books and journal articles related to models and frameworks for the analysis of *policy content* are available, interest in policy process tends to be scattered among a number of fields, including the social problems area within sociology, the political economics area of economics and political science, and the decision-making and communication areas of management, planning, and administration. This may be due to the fact that certain substantive or content concerns of social welfare "belong" to that field while the process aspects of social interaction are endemic to virtually all behavioral fields. That would also explain why explanations of process are so inclusive of a variety of theoretical points of view within any given model. Nevertheless, the task here is to identify a range of process-oriented perspectives that might serve in model building for policy process analysis.

Four process explanations for policy change offer some promise as frameworks for policy process analysis. These conceptualizations will be referred to as models, rather than frameworks, however, due to their limited number of elements or variables that each deals with or includes. This is not an individious distinction, however.

These four conceptualizations of process are (1) the action system model, based on the work of Roland Warren (1963; 1977), (2) the competing problems definition model, based on the writing of Ross and Staines (1972), (3) the sequential/incremental model, from the classical model of politics based on the work of Charles Lindblom (1959; 1968), and (4) the leverage model, the creation of Kenneth Gergen (1968). While we could have looked to the literature on power or community organization, for example, to find our material, we chose instead four disparate explanations of process in the policy context, since this variety promises a range of elements for our own framework construction.

The models to be reviewed are particularly applicable to community action or social change processes and are used here as a context for understanding what might occur in social welfare policy processes. These four models have been selected because they each differ in their emphases on particular variables assumed to be explanatory of social process. Each also gives recognition to both the key events or milestones that are presumed as necessary as well as the importance of the milieu and social structure associated with change processes.

Action System Model

The *action system model* is based upon grounded theory developed some time ago by Sower et al. (1957) in observing social change process in a midwestern rural community. Warren (1963; 1977) has acknowledged those origins and developed much of his work in a grounded and inductive approach to theory development in his work in poverty programs and Model Cities programs.

The action system model is a good model to begin with inasmuch as it is relatively simple and is based upon a common conception of social change, that change occurs in stage-like or phase-like fashion. There is a presumption that certain milestones of process have to be achieved or mastered successfully before actors in a process can move on to another stage. Resolution of each stage is necessary if the goals of a change process are to be realized. However, it should not be concluded that change is also presumed to occur only in linear fashion. Change actually involves circular or iterative processes; nevertheless, successful achievement of certain milestones and stages are prerequisite to others.

In the action system model, the first key event or milestone is referred to as the convergence of interest, the point at which some identifiable actors in a social situation come together and determine a like interest in considering or pursuing a common goal. In our simulation scenario, this may be conceptualized as the point at which people come together over principles that become policy. The presumption here is that there must be a significant number of people with sufficient energy and/or ideas to engage the social system in change. This becomes the rudiment of an idea or an action in which individuals, groups, or organizations check out whether they have significant goals in common and whether they wish to proceed cooperatively in some fashion. This may be the first evidence of perceived self- or group-interest (though the perception of self-interest may also emerge in later stages).

The next step for Warren is what is called the initiation and establishment of the action set, the building of the body of actors who will design and engage in whatever next steps are perceived as necessary for change. The action set is said to have three main tasks: (1) to develop a charter, or template (based upon the common goal), and determine the means for achieving that goal; (2) to determine the availability of means; and (3) to determine who has access to resources or is capable of resource acquisition. The charter, the core condition or substance of an agreement that drives subsequent action, might be said to exist when two or more people commit to a shared goal. The other tasks, having to do with determination of means and their access, are more or less technical functions that go beyond identifying a charter.

The next stage is labeled as the expansion of the action system, the point at which legitimation and sponsorship are seen as necessary and are then pursued. This stage might also entail even the expansion or modification of the original idea or charter as well; the driving values or principles may even be modified at this point. Legitimation might be seen as the right to take action and, at times, the action set may not have the necessary attributes for achieving legitimation, such as title or office. Sponsorship may be seen as the provision of support, and is not necessarily tied to the rights associated with legitimation, such as group membership or prestige. This is the point at which resistance and opposition are likely to emerge.

Once legitimation and sponsorship are obtained, the expanded action system is said to evolve into the establishment of what is called the execution set. This stage may be what most of us visualize when we think of the "policy change process" at the interorganizational or community level. The nitty gritty of social action comes to mind here, such as gathering resources, getting papers of incorporation, obtaining campaign dollars if necessary, recruiting broader support, using persuasion and influence, and in other ways, "pulling it off." It should be noted, too, that different stages may call upon very different sets of actors, with individuals, groups or organizations becoming "specialists" at certain functions.

Last comes the fulfillment of the charter and, in Warren's conceptualization of the model, the transformation of the action system. This "final state" is more or less a practical application of the Hegelian principle that every thesis generates its own antithesis, out of which arises a new synthesis. That synthesis becomes the new thesis, inviting another round of challenges. In other words, change begets change.

There are other variables, of course. For example, the change agents must consider the targets of change, such as whether the objects of change would be ideas, relationships, or the behavior of selected targets. Another possibility is size and nature of the target. There are issues on the means of goal attainment, such as whether cooperation, campaign, contest, or conflict are most appropriate for policy change action.

The essential elements to be gleaned here for a framework of policy process are initiation, support, sponsorship, legitimation, and implementation of group decisions. The model has some utility and has provided the theoretical foundation for studies by Flynn (1973) and Whitaker and Flory-Baker (1982).

Competing Problems Definition Model

The *competing problems definition model* was developed from the perspective of sociologists interested in explaining the process by which a social concern is converted into a "social problem" (Ross and Staines,

1972). This explanation argues that what becomes the agreed-upon principle (i.e., what we shall refer to as the desired "policy") is really arrived at by what goes on in the community's agenda-making or agenda-setting process. This analysis and definition of a social problem occurs in a political (or influence-making) context, and is not a new idea in conceptualizing how a social concern becomes defined as a "social problem." The presumption is that what becomes a "problem" is what gets managed, manipulated, and acknowledged by the greatest (or the most "significant") number of people as being a social concern. Many conditions known to social workers and other human service professionals and/or community activists are often not very popular or well known by the populace until the issues enjoy the favor of the public. Some examples from the recent past are the "popularization" of concern over spouse assault, child abuse, and AIDS, the first two being conditions that existed long before conversion by the popular media into pop sociology issues.

Ross and Staines approach the task in somewhat of a "black box" approach in which their focus is on the inputs and the outputs of social process. Consequently, they especially emphasize the range and variety of input activities. One of the first variables emphasized in the competing problems definition model is private or interest group recognition of a concern and/or group self-interest. Social process does not occur until someone or some group says "I want," "we need," or "we care." Self-interest is perceived here as not the libidinal or selfish motives of individuals but, rather, the collective concerns of people representing a category of interests. Another variable is group ideology, often very clearly present in issues in which the policy principles are not divisible, such as in the pro-life vs. pro-choice contests and conflicts. These group inputs generate debate and dialogue over different definitions of the problem or conditions and what is alleged to be in the community's interest (however "community" is then defined). These self-interests and ideologies compete with one another.

At another level, Ross and Staines argue that there are certain main institutional actors, namely the media, officialdom, and particular members of private interest groups. The first key actor is the media. This refers to obvious possibilities, such as television and radio networks and stations and the press, and other media vehicles. This might be news letters, the grapevine, or even the manner in which churches or associations promote certain messages about a condition or a problem. The media become vehicles for the movement of ideas.

Another important set of actors (i.e., input) is officialdom. This would logically be people in legislative positions or people next to them. The legislative level need not be a state legislature or county or city commission or council; it could appropriately be an agency board or a powerful council of a federated group of agencies, for example.

Yet another important input are private interest groups, those who we would logically and frequently expect to see as well as those who seem to arise on new or single issues. The identity of any particular group could greatly depend upon the issue, the decision to be made, or the structure of power that is in place in the community.

According to the competing problems definition model, the conflict revolves around "what is the issue and how is it to be diagnosed and responded to." People exercise their prerogatives or resources to move an issue along or retard its progress to being defined as a community issue or a social problem demanding social action. The debate evolves from how the problem is to be understood or diagnosed and whose explanation or ideology will prevail. Some possibilities, of course, would include problem definition in terms of individual failures or institutional ineffectiveness, or even serendipity. Next, of course, comes debate over means of resolution.

Overriding all of this is another variable that might be thought of as environmental actors. Some might be seen as "underdog partisans" who have little power, "privileged partisans" not included in the groups mentioned above, or what might be observed as the yet uncommitted "observer system." There are many roles and factions with different ideas to promote, and the reader is free to apply the examples that may pertain to her or his own community change experiences. Nevertheless, what is to be considered a "social problem" or a "community issue" are not givens. The definition of concerns arise out of a social process, and social policy is made in those events. Policy becomes made by those who seize opportunity to offer their diagnoses or remedies for policy change. The competing problems definition model, like the action system model, envisualizes policy change as having a career over time, though the conceptualizations of those career paths might differ somewhat.

Finally, in the competing problems definition model, the possible outcomes might be irreconcilable confrontation, tacit bargaining over tangible matters or reality negotiations over symbolic matters, or some form of legislation or rulemaking. The emphasis in the competing problems definition model is on the dynamic inputs of process, although the outcomes of those processes are certainly of greatest importance in the final analysis.

Ross and Staines' main contribution to the task of constructing an analytic framework comes from their special emphasis upon the role of environmental actors. Tierney (1982) used this model effectively in documenting the preprocess of establishing spouse-abuse shelters in the United States. York (1982) used this model to analyze the politics of defining social problems.

Sequential/Incremental Model

A very elaborate and perhaps the most familiar model is the *sequential/incremental model*, which may be said to be in the spirit of classical political science and is cast in terms of seeing social change primarily in the context of legislative processes (Lindblom, 1968; 1977). Lindblom essentially says that social policy change comes about as a result of a process of successive comparisons in the play of power. Called "sequential/incrementalism," this conceptualization sees gradual change arising out of the exercise of influence and expertise and is perhaps the most conservative view of change presented in the models selected here. New policy is merely a modest evolutionary deviation from positions of the past. Every proposal or new consideration is really only a variation of what used to be. The process consists of a constant comparison of what was, what is, and what might be in the future. This gradualism is said to occur primarily to the play of power that is very "rule-like." Policy change is viewed as never being quite exactly "on target" and is essentially compromise, seldom radical, and, instead, evolutionary.

In spite of the apparent conservatizing conception of change processes presented here, however, sequential/incrementalism would appear to hold promise for those whose business it is to participate in planned social change and policy action. While the action system approach and the competing problems definition approach emphasize the centrality of converting a concern into a "problem," Lindblom holds that policies sometimes spring from new opportunities (or by seizing opportunities) and not from "problems" at all.

A key concept in sequential/incrementalism is the use of political leverage to generate action and response. Lindblom held that "in a quasi-democratic society, the degree of relevance should thus also bear a direct relationship with the amount of actual leverage that people have." Generally speaking, we can easily see that community change agents at the local level have differential amounts of leverage, often depending upon attributes associated with money, prestige, position, or control of resources. Lindblom's view would be that people should have leverage commensurate with their connection with the issue or the problem or the policy and its effect upon them. For human service professionals, this suggests that a major task is to enable those who do not have that leverage to more fully participate in the play of power and the establishment of policy. According to Lindblom, in the absence of agreement on what is to be done, someone has to either seize opportunity or be given the power to decide. Here lies the role of change agents who act on behalf of client interests.

In the sequential/incremental model, policy is seen as a process of cooperation among specialists performing such tasks as initiating, vetoing, coordinating, and planning. Two key actors are: (1) the partisan analysts and (2) the proximate policymakers. For Lindblom, partisan analysts seek ways in which their desires can also serve the values of other policymakers. Partisan analysis is said to clarify the preferences of both the analyst and the target of analysis, to be a valuable aid in discovering the appropriate connection between means and ends in the change process, and to be all-important in achieving "satisficing." Satisficing is the achievement of an acceptable level of goal attainment short of maximization. This and other strategies of "dodges," as they are called, are the means whereby the partisan analyst pursues change objectives. Some of these strategies, besides "satisficing," are referred to as "the next chance," "feedback," "remediality," and "seriality."

The main targets of these efforts are generally not those with nominal power but, rather, those who have the attention and respect of those with nominal power and, therefore, influence them. These actors are referred to as proximate policymakers, persons who might be associate directors, legislative aides, administrative assistants, confidants, or old friends. In the sequential/incremental model, the key actors are proximate policymakers, for it is they who have the greatest influence on the change agenda, its content and its management.

For Lindblom and sequential/incrementalism, the three major propositions explaining the policy process are that: (1) the play of power is a process of cooperation among specialists, (2) policy analysis is incorporated as an instrument or a weapon into the play of power, and (3) the play of power proceeds according to rules that regulate the process. The process, then, may be characterized by the emergence of specialists, the management of cooperation and conflict, and the persuasive and judicious use of authority. For framework-building purposes, however, the key elements are the role of partisan analysts, proximate policymakers, and the notion of rule-like behavior. I regard this conceptualization as inherently conservatizing, given that any policy change is seen only as an incremental change from previous states and/or conditions and because the process fundamentally evolves around compromise. However, perhaps this perspective is also the most realistic in terms of the processes involved in the vast majority of policy formulation.

Leverage Model

The *leverage model*, offered by Kenneth Gergen (1968), has a number of characteristics found in the other three models and, to a great extent, might be seen as incorporating many of the variables of each of the models discussed above. However, Gergen uses the concept of "leverage" as a substitute for the concepts of power and influence. The key variables for this model are three: (1) issue relevance or issue salience throughout the policy system, (2) development and management of change resources available to the action system, and (3) personal efficacy of the individual actors. Consequently, Gergen refers to leverage as a three-dimensional model for assessing the leverage points in the policy formation process.

The relevance or salience of an issue is the degree to which the issue is perceived to affect the greatest number of people in the most meaningful way. Much of the effort of social change entails seizing the power associated with a salient issue or converting an issue into a salient one. This initiative gives rise to energetic change action by significant others. The task, then, for those who wish to engage in social action, is to alter the salience of an issue for those who might be affected by a particular policy position. The task of human service professionals might be to broaden the awareness or salience of those who might be affected by or invested in any particular policy change. A major task is making significant others aware of the importance of the issue. Gergen notes that "in a quasi-democratic society the degree of relevance should . . . also bear a direct relationship with the amount of actual leverage." Hence, the social actionist in pursuit of poilcy change might justify the use of leverage as serving democratic interests and principles.

Gergen sees social issues as having a temporal or time dimension. Consequently, he sees the development, management, and control of resources occurring in overlapping temporal stages. So, for example, there is a process of initiation and education wherein the action system moves to occupy key positions so that it can inform significant others. The process requires considerable staffing, planning and intergroup communication. Gergen also recognizes the power and necessity of legitimation and sponsorship via institutional sanction. The leverage model emphasizes the importance of intra-elite organizing, often called coalition-building, as being of key importance in obtaining adequate financing for the change action. The focus is to gain control of change.

Where Gergen's model departs from the other models, however, is in its emphasis upon the personal efficacy of the individual or institutional change actors. This efficacy consists of certain personal characteristics or capacities that give power to a situation. For Gergen, those characteristics include intelligence, access to information, self-confidence, charisma, reputation, motivation, and a high level of aspiration. While each model of process reviewed gives credence to the importance of systemic factors, the leverage model uniquely stresses the power and influence of personal attributes for bringing about social change. Given this emphasis upon personal efficacy, the leverage model provides an amalgam of many of the variables stressed in the other models of process.

Family Impact Analysis

A different approach to policy analysis has emerged in social welfare wherein the substantive criteria or elements for analysis are not generic across problem areas, as we have so far discussed. Instead, an approach that is problem-specific has come to be called *family impact analysis*, a concept borrowed from or emulating environmental impact analysis, in which potential environmental issues are considered prior to endorsement or adoption of any policy or program proposal. It has been suggested that the concept of family impact analysis was first introduced by Eleanor McGovern during her husbands' 1972 presidential campaign (Zigler, Kagan & Klugman, 1983) though, ironically, the federal requirement of a family impact statement for proposed legislative change was first formally established by the Reagan administration in 1987. Executive Order 12606 required that federal policies and regulations potentially having significant impact upon families shall be assessed in light of the following questions:

(a) Does this action by government strengthen or erode the stability of the family and, particularly, the marital commitment?
(b) Does this action strengthen or erode the authority and rights of parents in the education, nurture, and supervision of their children?
(c) Does this action help the family perform its functions, or does it substitute governmental activity for the function?
(d) Does this action by government increase or decrease family earnings? Do the proposed benefits of this action justify the impact on the family budget?
(e) Can this activity be carried out by a lower level of government or by the family itself?
(f) What message, intended or otherwise, does this program send to the public concerning the status of the family?
(g) What message does it send to young people concerning the relationship between their behavior, their personal responsibility, and the norms of our society? (*Federal Register*, vol. 52, no. 174, Sept. 9, 1987, pp. 34188–89)

This order, with an obvious ideological bias regarding the relationship between government and the family, was given subsequent effect in the specifications for funding applications under the Department of Health and Human Services FY 1988 Coordinated Discretionary Funds Program (*Federal Register*, vol. 52, no. 250, p. 49252) and in the establishment of the White House Working Group on the Family. The White House office did not issue its report and its framework for analysis, as promised, as far as this writer could determine.

Other efforts at family impact analysis have been less political in nature. For example, George Washington University and the University of Minnesota have held Family Impact Seminars in efforts to move analysis to focus on particular implications of policies and programs for American Families (Spakes, 1983). Also, the use of family impact analysis as a framework for teaching social policy has been published by Spakes (1984). Spakes' framework posits a seven-step procedure somewhat like the frameworks for analysis described above. There is one set of criteria, however, that points analysis to issues specific to problems in the area of family policy. Drawing on the George Washington University Seminar, Spakes identifies three criteria in particular. These are a policy's potential impact upon what are called (1) the membership function (i.e., who is considered to be a member of the family in the context of the policy or the policy proposal), (2) the economic function (i.e., the impact on the family's role as both producer and consumer), and (3) the socialization/nurturance function (i.e., the effects upon a family's responsibility for the well-being and care of its members).

The family impact analysis approach suggests that there may be other problem-specific areas within the domain of social welfare policy which might generate their own problem-specific criteria for analysis, such as special analytic criteria for the aged population or for the handicapped. This area of analysis is yet to be developed, however.

The Marxist or Socialist Perspective

Much has been written from a Marxist or socialist perspective on the content and processes of social welfare. Notable examples can be found in the writings of Galper (1975; 1980) and Cloward and Piven (1971). However, the Marxist and socialist oriented literature belong more in the realms of a *perspective*, a world view, and a grand theory for looking at reality. They do not present models. While the socialist perspectives found in the literature provide an excellent overall context for *analysis* or offer the basis for selection of criteria that we value or find compatible with our codes of ethics, as yet no Marxist or socialist *models* for policy process at the small-scale level have been advanced. That is, the Marxist and socialist perspectives have not developed to the point of providing us with *models* with specific decision-making variables that can be broken down for purposes of problem solving.

The socialist literature does, however, offer significant content. Galper (1975) speaks to the value of client self-determination and appropriately emphasizes the social control or regulatory functions of welfare systems and the external environment affecting clients and social service workers. He emphasizes the presence of class antagonisms among and between the sponsors, providers, and receivers of social services and the various degrees of competition and opportunity surrounding control of and access to resources. Of particular note is Galper's critique of the limits of reformism. However, Lyon refers to Galper as providing "the only openly socialist policy monograph" (1983, p. 388). If this is the case, Galper voices many sound criticisms of the bases and priorities of social welfare systems but does not offer a *model* that provides direction at the practice level. Nevertheless, the socialist critique should be kept in mind; it does, in fact, provide us with a useful context for our own pursuit of model building.

Models Emphasizing Quantitative Approaches

A number of models are available that take a quantitative approach to analysis. They are referred to as models because, once again, their scope in terms of elements emphasized is limited. They tend to be used in large-scale policy analysis and, while we will not attempt to incorporate them here, some of these quantitative approaches will be summarized. For those who wish to pursue these models further and who might benefit from illustrations, an excellent primer is available, written by Stokey and Zeckhauser (1978). The quantitative models may be characterized as both deterministic (wherein the outcomes are certain) and probabilistic (wherein the variables, as well as variable values, are unknown). They are often referred to as preference models since their analytic strategy consists of determining the available decision alternatives, followed by selecting a preference from those alternatives. We will summarize a few of these, in particular, input/output models, the difference equation, queuing models, computer simulations, Markov chains and processes, benefit/cost analysis, linear programming, and decision analysis.

The model that appears to be the least quantitative is the *input-throughput-output* approach found in the literature. In fact, these input-output models are often mistaken for "system approaches." In social services, the input might be clients or funding sources; the throughputs the social treatment processes or techniques; and the outputs the solved problems, the satisfaction obtained from service, or other quantifiable measures of the results of the service process. Use of these models requires knowledge of the whole range and dimensions of the various inputs and throughput procedures and, of course, also demands creativity in making outcomes and outputs operational.

Difference equations are used to explore the changes in variable over discrete periods of time. This approach could be applied, for example, to the number of discharges from a hospital on a daily basis or at annual intervals. These equations are generally used only by mathematicians, perhaps due to the reliance upon the use of mathematical notation in the equations and a general lack of comfort with this approach by most policy analysts in the human services.

Queuing models are used to study situations in which the provider of a commodity or a service is faced with a demand that exceeds the supply or availability of what is provided. Key elements in using queuing models in human services, for example, might be the demands or applications (called "arrivals"), the time necessary to provide services (called "service time"), and the "queue discipline" or "queue characteristics," such as special treatment that needs to be made available for crises or priority problem conditions. Queuing models have been used to simulate decisions about the judicious location of satellite offices by a human service agency (Luse, 1982).

Computer simulations tend to be used when a large number of complex and interdependent variables are involved. Simulations are laboratory models in which the analyst attempts to reproduce real-life conditions as represented by an algorithm in the simulation. (An algorithm is a mathematical expression that presumably includes significant variables, with their proper weight and relationship assigned according to some theoretical understanding of the problem.) Simulations and algorithms have been used in decision support systems in making child placement decisions (Jaffee, 1979), in determining service awards for in-home relief (Boyd et al., 1981), in modeling policy processes (Flynn, 1985a), and even in many functions of an entire community mental health agency (Cox, Erickson, Armstrong & Harrison, 1989). A summary review of a few applications to health and welfare problems has been provided by Luse (1980). As with queuing applications, computer simulations allow for an unlimited number of theoretical experiments under virtually an unlimited number of conditions. They are limited by not having relevant data to construct useful algorithms that can be applied to meaningful situations. Their greatest virtue is that they account for the fact that social process often has its own life. Hence, applying theory through simulation helps us to avoid some of the ethical dilemmas and practical problems that may be engendered by intervening in real-life social policy processes.

Fortunately, software clearinghouses have now been established which are repositories of newly developing software, some of which have promise in this area of analysis. Examples are the National Collegiate Software Clearinghouse at Duke University Press, WISC-WARE at the University of Wisconsin-Madison, the Information System for Advanced Academic Computing (ISAAC) at the University of Washington, the Computer Users in Social Services Network (CUSSNET) at the University of Texas at Arlington, CONDUIT at the University of Iowa, and the Clearinghouse at Iowa State University. While the listing of software applicable to policy analysis is sparse, it shows promise of growing.

Markov models provide yet another approach. Markov chains are based on probabilities and are used to follow the flow of people or events through a system. For example, a Markov chain might be used to follow the transition of developmentally disabled adults through a residential training program that provides a continuum of care. While the Markov chain deals with the probabilistic movement of individuals through a system of events, Markov processes allow the analyst to study entire populations. Both approaches require knowledge of the properties of mutually exclusive states or events, the presence of uniform and fixed time intervals, and populations that are constant in size. Therefore, there are limited opportunities for application of these models in social welfare, though they are appropriate and useful in certain circumstances.

Benefit/cost models essentially determine the ratio of benefits to cost, with the favorable outcome being sufficiently higher benefits, presuming a system giving high priority to an economic efficiency principle. Benefit/cost models are perhaps the most frequently used mathematical approach to evaluating expenditures for public services. The difficult tasks in benefit/cost approaches involve specifying all the tangible, intangible, quantifiable, and nonquantifiable variables involved in achieving a net cost. Benefit/cost models have been applied to work training and other direct rehabilitation programs, perhaps because these programs tend to be better defined in terms of inputs and outcomes and, as noted, they are rooted in economic efficiency.

Linear programming is used by policy analysts to distribute a limited amount of resources (e.g., money, time, or staff) to a program or a problem resolution project. It is used to determine the optimum or minimum allowable resource or cost required to complete the range and sequence of tasks necessary for goal achievement. In human services, linear programming (as with PERT, flow charting, or other work plan techniques) can be useful in project planning and demonstration efforts. Another application might involve planning for the carefully scheduled use of facilities by more than one group or agency program. A limitation, of course, is that not all social welfare problems, nor all variables associated with a particular problem, are linear. Some variables are nonlinear or the values associated with some alternatives are not acceptable to the program sponsor or the analyst in the context of a given situation.

The final model to be mentioned is decision analysis. *Decision analysis models* help the analyst sort out the complexity of decisions that are contingent upon one another. Decision analysis is especially useful when decisions must be made sequentially, which is why these models are characterized by decision nodes and decision trees, all of which are contingent upon probabilities and potential payoffs. These models are appropriate in human services when milestones are achieved and subsequent strategic decisions are made along the way. Applications of this approach are finding their way into the human services literature in the form of computerized decision support systems and expert systems. However, much of their use has been applied to administrative design issues or clinical decision making.

Stokey and Zeckhauser (1978) quite properly acknowledge that no magic is involved in the use of quantitatively oriented models for policy analysis. In fact, as with all models for policy analysis, there is no substitute for having the necessary and sufficient information demanded by a thorough, knowledgeable analysis. All models require a conscious valuing of the ends that are sought and the means that are employed.

Summary

In this chapter we have discussed a number of frameworks and models, some emphasizing the content aspects of policy analysis and others the process aspects. Each gives evidence of having its own philosophical perspective and is committed to a set of fundamental principles as well as its own concepts and jargon. A special framework devoted to family policy analysis was given special attention. The Marxist and socialist perspectives in policy analysis were mentioned. A number of quantitatively oriented models were summarized, though we will not draw on these in constructing for our own outlines.

In chapters 4 and 6 you will extract these principles, concepts, and criteria, and add your own in an effort to build a framework for small-scale analysis of policy content and process. You will be empowered to develop your own models for understanding and control of your policy environments.

Content Elements for Small-Scale Policy Analysis

4

The next task is to combine a number of the content elements for small-scale policy analysis, borrowing here and there from what has already been reviewed, and develop analytic tools. To this end, the basic core of content elements that constitute the essentials for a framework for analysis must be identified.

Essential Steps in Content Analysis

A look back at what others have already constructed in grand-scale frameworks currently in use shows that content frameworks require the analyst to engage in five essential activities. Some of these activities are the same as those essential to process analysis, which will be discussed in chapter 6. The five activities are:

1. Identify the policy problem or policy goal(s)—(similar to process analysis)
2. Assess current and anticipated system functioning
3. Determine implications for selected values (same as process analysis)
4. Establish feasibility of the desired outcome
5. Provide recommendations

Obviously, none of these five activities can be seen as discrete events occurring in a rigidly linear sequence; they are interrelated, interactive, and circular in nature. For example, policy goals are intertwined, and values and strategies are often dependent upon feasibility factors. Associated with each of the five activities, however, are particular analytic tasks, which should be identified. The discussion that follows draws on the summaries of grand-scale frameworks surveyed in earlier chapters as well as the brief guide for small-scale policy analysis provided by Flynn (1979; 1985b). You should note that analysis of values is integrated into analysis of the substantive content of the policy. The analysis of values, while more abstract than the substance of a particular policy issue or policy problem, is nevertheless central to the task of analysis.

For illustrative purposes, we introduce a detailed case example in this chapter: a general hospital's policy of providing residential care for infants abandoned in hospitals due to infection with the HIV virus. Therefore, as we move through the discussion and explanation of the elements of the outline for analysis of policy content, applications involving a real policy situation are provided.

One additional comment should be made regarding the application of each element of the outline for analysis. Not every policy analysis needs to apply each criterion in this application. The outline serves as a problem-solving tool that should be applied as it appears appropriate to a given situation. Put another way, this chapter is developing a *framework* for analysis from which you can develop your own working model(s) for your own analysis of a particular policy problem. (Refer to chapter 2 regarding the distinction between frameworks and models.) For purposes of illustration, I have attempted to provide applications for each criterion for this hypothetical situation. No compulsive meta-message is intended; in real life each element or criterion need not be applied. Use the overall framework as a laundry list and pick and choose as you wish.

Case Illustration—Infants with HIV + Infection

The first illustration is a policy that is immediately related to a direct practice issue. Let us explore what is generally considered a knotty problem, both for policy and for direct service practice: infants with a positive diagnosis of HIV infection who are abandoned in hospitals. Assume that you are employed as a social worker in the medical social service department of an urban general hospital, Vistaview Hospital. You and the hospital are confronted with an increasing number of "boarder babies," infants born in the hospital who are ready for discharge and have tested positive for the human immunodeficiency virus. These infants are often referred to as "boarder babies" because they no longer need acute care hospitalization and are ready for discharge but the community will not accept them. Many of these infants are children of parents who have the HIV virus; some parents have

AIDS-related complex (ARC) or full-blown AIDS, and are unable to care for their newborn. A status of pariah has been assigned to these infants by the community. The hospital is now considering the possibility of providing a residential care program outside of the hospital for these infants. You have been called in because of your responsibilities in the Social Service Department and your familiarity with policy analysis to assist a Task Force on Residential Care for Infants with HIV Infection to consider this new policy option.

Vistaview Hospital is a private, nonprofit, acute care, general hospital located in the urban center of a city of 500,000. Like other hospitals of its kind, it is experiencing escalating costs, pressure for cost reduction from third-party payors, and continuing demands for the whole range of acute care medical services. Like many of its cohorts, Vistaview Hospital has recently moved into a number of activities not traditionally associated with moderately-sized, private, urban hospitals through profit ventures under the umbrella of its new holding company, Vistaview Healthcare, Inc. The proposal for developing a residential program for "boarder babies" would be a departure for Vistaview. Neither the hospital nor the parent company has ventured into social service activities outside of the hospital's walls and neither has taken responsibility for long-term care of any kind in the medical community.

1. Identify the Policy Problem or Policy Goal(s)

a. The Problem/Goal and the Policy Statement

The first set of activities for the analysis is to clearly define the policy problem and then develop a policy statement. Decide on a concern, an issue, a felt difficulty, or something thought to be a policy problem. Begin with a clean, clear, and uncluttered statement of the focus of the analysis. At a minimum, the policy statement must answer the following three questions:

(1) What is the problem/issue?
(2) How are people expected to behave as a result of the policy?
(3) Who or what office or agency provides that expectation?

Once answers to these questions are given, the analyst is able to move on to other substantive matters.

a. The Problem/Goal and the Policy Statement—Case Example

Your community problem is that children are left abandoned in acute care facilities, in Vistaview and elsewhere, and the community is unwilling or unable to provide alternative residential care for these children. Consequently, newborns are deprived of the opportunity for care and nurturance in a normal environment, and hospital services are being overtaxed by these care demands. The core of the problem is likely to reside in peoples' fears surrounding the care of anyone with HIV infection. Consequently, the hospital's Board has drafted a proposed policy for further study.

The current draft of the policy now being considered by the Vistaview Hospital Board reads as follows:

> *Vistaview Hospital shall provide community-based residential care and other appropriate assistance for infants abandoned in hospitals due to a positive diagnosis of HIV infection.*

On the face of it, this is not a complicated policy or policy statement. Yet, this short statement indicates the problem condition, suggests that hospital resources will have to be devoted to problem resolution, and it serves as a charge from the Board to the task force. The task force is required to report back to the Board prior to the Board's taking final action on the proposed policy.

b. Bases of Legitimacy and Source or Location

With luck, there may be a policy goal or a policy objective (taken from an annual plan or an administrative manual, for example) that will help in developing policy. Budget proposals, annual program plans, staff manuals, contractual agreements, and executive directives are all potential sources that can give focus to a definition of policy goals and objectives. These statements are often clues to the underlying principles (i.e., the mini-policies) that will hopefully be achieved by the policies or directives. The location (i.e., where the policy may be found) also helps to determine the legitimacy of the policy in the sense that legitimacy may rest with the policy-making authority of the Board or with the influence of experienced or powerful practitioners in the organization. Included in the task of identifying the policy statement is the determination of the policy's foundation or legitimacy (i.e., the right to exist or take action) and source or location. This documentation of legitimacy might be found in articles of incorporation, bylaws, Board minutes, personnel policies, statutes, administrative rules, or memos providing executive directives. Establishing or determining the legitimacy of a policy is a logical early step in any systematic analysis.

It must be stressed, however, that there are also times when it is advantageous to organizations to give low visibility to their policies or preferences, and the analyst may have to use the documents noted above or other sources to confirm what the policy actually is. For example, during periods of tight financial resources, an agency may not publicize the availability of certain services. Agencies sometimes "ration" service this way during periods of financial cutbacks. Or a particular agency may not desire to cooperate with another community agency for some particular reason, but that policy may not be openly stated.

At times the analyst is not blessed with a given policy goal or objective, explicit or implied, but only with a concern, an issue, or a problem. Nevertheless, the first essential task is to "chisel out" a clear and uncluttered conceptualization of what the subject of analysis shall be. For example, in an organizational policy having to do with staff functioning, it would not be helpful to begin the analysis by simply saying that staff are unhappy. It would be much more helpful if it could be appropriately said that staff are dissatisfied with a particular set of events, such as the amount of time spent in group evaluation, assessment, or staffing of agency clients. An even more helpful focus would be, for example, that staff prefer to spend less time in group assessment and treatment planning for individual clients. A greater level of specificity would be that staff prefer to adjust agency procedures so that less time would be allocated to group assessment and treatment planning subsequent to initiation of the original service plan. The statement should be developed to give focus and direction to the kinds of data to be collected for the analysis and to clarify for all that the effort will, in fact, be focused upon the item of shared concern. In other words, the original policy analysis activity—stating the problem or policy clearly—not only gives focus and direction to subsequent analytic activity but is also a way of communicating and checking out shared meanings and understandings with those who might use the product of analysis.

In summary, the analyst should be able to state clearly and succinctly, preferably in one or two sentences, the proposed or existing policy under study. To do this, the analyst needs to identify the policy mandate, the guiding principle, the current operational reality, or the desired policy state. The source and legitimacy must also be made clear, both in terms of the bases of legitimacy and the actual physical location (if any) of any written policy if such a policy is actually formalized. In the case of some activities that constitute informal policy, the "source" can be documented in terms of observable behavior within or around the agency. The policy need not necessarily be in writing. This clarification must come first if the analysis is to proceed on solid ground.

b. Bases of legitimacy and source or location—Case example

This charge, which may eventually become policy of the organization, now emanates from the authority of the Board of Directors of Vistaview Hospital. The Board has the authority to establish policy and allocate resources to programs that support policy decisions. The written documentation of this charge, which might be considered a draft statement of the policy on residential care for abandoned infants with HIV +, will be found in the official minutes of the Vistaview Board. In fact, research by the policy analyst will find that there is extensive background discussion and supporting data appearing in the minutes of the Board's Program and Policy Committee, a standing committee of the Board. Much of the detail in policy development and program evaluation is brought to that standing Board committee prior to bringing any motion to the whole Board. Therefore, a review of those committee minutes and any supportive documents or briefs supplied by staff to that committee, in addition to the Board-level discussion, will reveal a good deal of background data and provide a sense of Board- and committee-level support for the proposed policy.

It is also known that some of the hospital's Social Services Department staff have experience and connections with the child care services system in the community. Staff's speculation is that it will be very difficult to implement this policy, given child care agencies' views in the community that the recruitment of foster care or respite care providers will be exceedingly difficult. Those agencies would also likely insist upon some sort of training and medical backup provided by the hospital. In addition, it is known that the state senate and the federal Congress both have pending legislation that would provide financial incentives for providers of residential care to serve infants abandoned in hospitals due to HIV + diagnoses. These incentives would consist of special training funds for prospective agency staff, direct care providers, and higher per diem support. Hence, the bases of legitimacy are apparently expanding in the political environment.

Nevertheless, this policy would have the full authority of the Board behind it, should the policy move ahead in a programmatic form.

c. Targets and Clients of Concern

Another important task is to specify, early on, who or what the target of concern is. The target of the policy concern or the policy statement should be clear in the mind of the analyst so that all subsequent analytic activities are directed at that target. The target could be multifaceted. In the group staff example, the target might be people (i.e., clients or consumers of services) who are receiving less than the desired amounts of direct services; the work patterns of certain staff who give greatest priority to team interaction and group decision processes; or the alteration of contractual terms with the funding source, such as adjusting expectations regarding the amount of direct services to be provided as opposed to making allowances for collateral activity on behalf of clients. In any event, it is very important to determine early on who or what the target or intended beneficiary of the remedy might be.

Here it is sometimes helpful and instructive to distinguish the *target* system from the *client* system. The target may be seen as that group or individual *in whom* change is being sought. The client system may be seen as that group or individual *on whose behalf* change is being sought (see Pincus and Minahan, 1973). These individuals or groups may or may not be one and the same. In the group staffing example, the client system in one instance might be those receiving agency services, while the target system might be comprised of the staff members stressing group interaction. In another instance, the client system might be the funding source served by the policy change and the target system might be selected staff who provide particular services in a diagnostic or treatment team. These determinations will depend primarily upon the concern or issue and how the analyst casts the analysis, especially the policy statement. And these statements, and how they are cast, are sometimes dependent upon one's view of the world at that particular moment in time.

c. *Targets and Clients of Concern—Case Example*

On the face of it, one might assume that the target of the policy is the newborn infant, with the hospital acting in the capacity of advocate for the child. However, let's think this through.

The group in whom behavioral change is sought, that is, the target system or subsystem in this overall "system" of care for infants with HIV, is not the infants or their families but the residential care service sector. Infants are inappropriately left in the hospital's care because alternative residential care is not readily available to them. Consequently, the target system here is the children's residential care system in the community. This policy, should it come to fruition, may include Vistaview Hospital as a member of that service system.

The client system, the group or subsystem on whose behalf change is being sought, is, therefore, the "boarder babies." It is clear that their interests will likely be served by such a policy. It may not be clear, however, that Vistaview Hospital *may also be* a client system. That is, given Vistaview's moves into new and nontraditional ventures, the provision of residential care for infants with HIV may also serve the interests of Vistaview in diversifying into ancillary enterprises. This speculation remains to be seen and perhaps the analysis will shed more light on it. An important point to make here is that the "client system" of health and human services agencies is not always solely the clients, patients, consumers, students, or residents. Agencies themselves may be affected by policies that serve their own interests. In those instances, the policy initiative may also be on behalf of the organization itself. This condition is neither good nor bad, appropriate nor inappropriate.

d. Eligibility

Eligibility is a criterion that often articulates other explicit and implicit criteria. The criterion of eligibility often applies to the potential clientele's demographic characteristics, such as age or problem condition. Eligibility may also refer to the desired state or condition of the target group, such as those in training or preventive services to assist people at risk of HIV+ infection. It sometimes relates to the client or target group(s)' level of need. And almost always eligibility criteria is applicable in some way to the financial or other resources to be allocated and to a given policy's political feasibility. Nowhere are the eligibility criteria of level of need and political feasibility so visible as in income maintenance policies and programs. However, eligibility also plays a complicated role in small-scale policy systems in such areas as developing service system goals relative to financial and personnel resources and assessing the presence and activity of various interest groups. Living examples can especially be found in the drive toward deinstitutionalization and its relation to the demands upon community mental health systems. Eligibility criteria variously speak to collective treatment goals of a client population, to diminishing resources during a period of increasing demands, and to the contests and conflicts between and among various interest groups competing for the range of residential care, partial day care, outpatient and emergency services, and services for the mentally ill, as opposed to services for the developmentally disabled, and so forth.

d. Eligibility—Case Example

At this point, the criteria for eligibility seems quite clear. Children eligible to be served by this policy are infants born at Vistaview who have been diagnosed as being HIV+ who are in need of out-of-hospital residential care. However, given the policy as presently stated, the possibility exists for "boarder babies" in any hospital in the service area to be placed into residential care under the authority of this policy and within any program developed by this policy. This is an early clue that the policy will require more clarity and specificity in terms of the boundaries to be placed upon the eligible group.

e. Effect upon Maintenance, Change, or Control

Another approach to the target of policy action is to look at the desired outcome of the policy in terms of the effects upon system maintenance, system control, or system change, or any mixture of the three. Some questions to pursue are: Does continued group staffing of cases, for example, essentially provide a holding operation for clients (i.e., system maintenance) and a continued source of required labor for staff (i.e., system control)? Or does it provide for continual evolution of the needs of clients, the needs of staff, and the needs of the agency (i.e., system change)? Put simply, the goal of the policy may be seen as a service system condition as well as a client condition.

e. Effect upon Maintenance, Change, or Control—Case Example

In looking at the overall residential care system for infants, the policy would clearly provide for system change in that the hospital would thereby impact a system to the extent that a group not now served would presumably be provided residential care. From an internal organizational perspective, we may see this as either system maintenance or system change. That is, if the hospital is moved to this alternative primarily to diversify services in an effort to generate revenues, it may be seen as a system maintenance strategy. On the other hand, the policy could enable system change in that the provision of out-of-hospital continuing care of any kind would enable the hospital's metamorphosis into a multi-function, community-based provider of health care, not only in health-related services to children but also in other areas.

f. Explicit or Implicit Theories

It is also helpful to take an early look at how one has cast the problem or the policy goal statement and speculate about what theoretical point of view is expressed by the issue as formulated. As you are no doubt aware, the theory underlying the formulation of the problem is likely to dictate or delimit the subsequent analytic methods selected, the analysis of data, and the resultant solution or recommendation. Theories bring with them a limited set of conceptualizations and values which put boundaries around what is seen and considered. For example, it would serve us well in our group assessment or staffing example to consider how we tend to operationalize the notion of efficiencies. We could see ''efficiency'' as bringing the whole range of professional resources of staff to bear upon the assessment or treatment of the client, on the one hand, or as the minimal allocation of professional time to assessment in the interest of delivering more direct services, given the limited available professional staff time. Or we may tend to operate on some implicit theory that group staffing of assessment and treatment planning also serves other goals of staff orientation and staff development, wherein various staff members share their experience and expertise with newer members of the team.

These theoretical conceptualizations may be explicitly stated at the outset as guiding the problem statement and the policy analysis or they may be stated as conjecture for possible theoretical alternatives. At any rate, it benefits the analyst to bring these theoretical conceptualizations to mind and explicate them as much as possible, if for no other reason than to make a running list of them, to keep the analyst "honest," or to forewarn the person or agency to whom the analysis is communicated that these are the possible considerations.

And finally, as with theories, it is well to think "up front" about what values are being expressed in the problem or goal formulation. However, we have reserved the discussion of value considerations as our third major set of analytic activities and that matter will be discussed in more detail.

f. Explicit or Implicit Theories—Case Example

Some speculation about and/or identification of the theoretical foundations of the policy under analysis can give clues to the incentives for the policy's existence. We have already introduced the notion of the organizational incentives for diversification into nontraditional services by an acute care general hospital.

There may be other theoretical underpinnings to this policy. One possibility is that the hospital is committed to the notion that the earliest days of life in early childhood must be closely associated with a personal care giver. Hospitals cannot provide adequate substitute care for parental nurturing. The policy would hopefully enable that personal care.

Yet another theory might be based upon a redefinition of the proper role of acute-care general hospitals in a community. For those who hold that a hospital has a responsibility to locate itself on a continuum of care, both within and outside of the hospital walls, the policy would support that theoretical perspective. Clearly, a child with HIV infection is not only in need of socialization and interpersonal nurturance but medical monitoring and supportive services as well. This range of needs cannot be separated and the policy would support this concept of the role of the medical care provider.

g. Topography of the Policy System

Systems thinking has taught us the value of mapping the characteristics of living systems or, in other words, to make mental images of the elements comprising a "system." This concept, mapping the topography of a system or determining what is and is not included and their relative positions and interaction, gives us some leads that help to give shape to the policy definition. For example, we can identify implied boundary characteristics, such as what subsystems are included in the definition of the problem, the policy, and/or the system. For purposes of analysis, it is crucial to be aware of the fact that at this point we can both arbitrarily and logically determine which subsystems or elements we might choose to include in the definition of "the system" and, therefore, what elements will be subjected to the analysis. This, then, gets us immediately to the questions of the nature and form of the boundaries that give shape to the "policy system" we have selected. For example, what *does* give shape to the boundaries? Do the origins of agency sponsorship or legitimacy, auspices, legal status (e.g., charter or bylaws), funding, or geographic service area determine what is "in" and "not in?" A review of these characteristics helps us to draw conceptual boundaries around the policy system so we know what we are focusing on. It also leads to an early assessment of the policy system's functioning, such as the openness, closedness, or permeability of the policy system's boundaries—a fundamental measuring stick of system functioning of any kind. More will be said about this later in the discussion of system functioning.

g. Topography of the Policy System—Case Example

This policy obviously expands the typical boundaries beyond the infant care ward or office space of the hospital's Social Services Department. There are many other system elements implicitly involved in this policy of providing residential care for infants abandoned in Vistaview Hospital and other hospitals. There are, of course, the whole range of child care services providers: agencies that provide foster care, adoption services, respite care, home health care, child day care, and the like. In some instances, the child protective services and/or the juvenile court systems would possibly be involved. Certainly, third-party insurance companies would be active participants in many cases, as would the state or county department of public welfare. If child care agencies become more involved, or if the hospital itself decides to provide the residential care, it will be necessary to deal with licensing rules and regulations aimed at protecting children in out-of-home care. These are some of the possible participants in the policy, program, and service system that automatically become implicated, voluntarily or not, in the policy decision to be made by the Board. The Board will need to be adequately advised about the implications of expanding their domain to include these elements. The Board is clearly expanding the conceptual and political boundaries of its own agency as "system" by adopting such a policy.

h. Contemporary Issues or Historical Antecedents

It is also necessary to determine whether there are other related or ancillary issues impinging on the policy under study. For example, in the illustration noted above regarding group staffing of client assessments

and treatment planning, there may be peripheral issues related to certification requirements for third-party insurance reimbursement, or
contractual requirements from one of the funding sources. Some staff
may be included to meet a requirement for insurance reimbursement
or for accreditation by an external agency. These are just some of the
possible factors impinging upon the problem and upon the statement
of the problem.

Another concern should be determining whether any historical
"baggage" is being brought to the problem or the policy. We sometimes
inherit theories or procedures that explain why we do things the way we
do; at other times our behavior reflects a rejection of the past and its procedures. In our illustration of group staffing, it could be that, in the past,
when the agency was functioning entirely at one location and the total
staff was small in size, it was physically easier and therefore logical for
staff to get together. Today, its large staff operates out of a number of
outreach centers. Or group staffing may have necessarily been more frequent prior to the creation and availability of client-service managers
who are now charged with coordinating case services for clients. These
are just some examples of the necessity of considering the relevance of
historical antecedents to the current policy situation.

h. Contemporary Issues or Historical Antecedents—
Case Example

Now we need to explore some of the ancillary issues in our case illustration.

We know that annual estimates by the Surgeon General of the
United States show an increasing number of infants born with HIV.
Much of this growth is attributed to infants being born of parents who
are intravenous drug users and those who engage in bi-sexual activity.
There is no reason to believe that the incidence of the problem will de-
crease to the point of there never being any "boarder babies."

At the same time, there is a tremendous prevalence of misinformation in the environment, regardless of the extensive public education that
has been disseminated, about how individuals actually contract the virus. Ignorance and misinformation about contagion have interfered with
obtaining an adequate supply of caregivers for those with HIV infection.
In addition, there are the prejudices and discrimination toward those
with the disease and the stereotyping of those who are considered to be in
high risk groups. The environment presents a very irrational picture. It is
even possible that the propensity to "blame the victim" even carries over
to the infants themselves and we do have a national history of not treating
"pariahs" very well, given the national story with TB or leprosy, and
even mental illness or developmental disabilities.

On the positive side, however, is the historical baggage that our nation is generally committed to—the ethic that each and every child needs to be nurtured by a family unit and that the family is the basic unit of society. These precedents may exist in support of the proposed policy and its coming to fruition. They are all a part of the historical baggage that accompanies this policy.

The analyst would also need to look to historical events within the agency or the community that might have a bearing on the policy. This case example is a hypothetical one; let's play it out a little. We have already mentioned the issue of whether or not the hospital should properly be involved in longer-term, out-of-hospital, continuity-of-care provisions in the form of residential care. The hospital's recent moves into other ancillary enterprises has also been mentioned. These factors are surely related to the emergence of this policy issue and to decision making concerning the policy. We need to look at previous history related to whether or not health and welfare agencies in the community are protective of service domains or shun hegemony into others' territories.

Summary

To summarize up to this point, it is essential to begin with a clarification of the problem to be studied and/or the goals to be pursued, with particular attention given to determining the bases of legitimacy and the source or location of the policy under study. This is best done by identifying any relevant policy statements and associated issues. The next step in analysis should consider the targets or objects of policy and the likely participants in the policy system, the explicit or implicit objectives of system maintenance, change or control, and any theoretical underpinnings of the policy. After identifying the inclusive topography of "the policy system," one must identify and examine any relevant contemporary or historical issues related to the particular policy.

2. Assess Current and Anticipated System Functioning

Now we have to focus on the organizational, administrative, and/or environmental functioning of the *policy system* and the interaction of the components in that system. Here attention must be given to both current functioning and system functioning anticipated by accepting any proposed policy changes.

When we get to the matter of selecting criteria as guides for what to review for the substantive content in our analysis or what criteria to employ in making our selections, we come to a myriad of possibilities. An important point to keep in mind is that criteria themselves are "little policies." That is, criteria for reviewing or for guiding principles in making choices are themselves policies in the sense that they are human creations that express preferences, theoretical points of view, priorities, or other manifestations of what we value. For our purposes here, however, we need to select a minimum set of criteria for review or choice as suggested by the characteristics that seem germane to policy analysis at the small-scale level. Criteria for analysis are not preordained; the policy analyst operating at the small-scale level can, of course, add any criteria that appear to be particularly germane to the policy under study. We are merely trying to construct a framework for analysis here that can serve as a guide; the analyst can select any criteria for his or her own model. The criteria for analysis are merely part of the tool kit, and practitioners decide what tools they need. Nevertheless, a certain core of criteria have served others well and will be included in our inventory of elements for small-scale policy analysis.

The assessment of system functioning focuses on *how* an existing or actual policy is currently functioning, on speculations about the probable functioning of a proposed policy, or on the current functioning of a policy-action process encountered in pursuing policy development.

Here we might look at the quality of fit between administrative or organizational structure and stated or implied policy goals. Another likely candidate for inspection is the fit between the actual program design (e.g., centralization versus decentralization; or direct service provision versus purchase of service) and policy goals. Other characteristics of system functioning can be assessed, such as the patterns of interaction among essential elements, perhaps among client, target, and action systems or interest groups in the case of policy process analysis, or among various program policies and provisions in the case of policy content analysis.

Case Illustration—Infants with HIV + Infection: Current and Anticipated System Functioning

For our case illustration we will use the criteria provided in our earlier discussion. The criteria selected are not cast in stone but, rather, are to be selected by the analyst. The criteria provide touchstones.

Here we will have to use creative license as we introduce hypothetical factors into our analysis, using the elements of our outline now to be provided. Some clues to our direction will be supplied by looking at whether a program's design would encourage or deter realization of the policy goal of placing abandoned infants in alternative residential care. Another direction is to look at the actual patterns of interaction among those who might participate in bringing this policy to reality.

a. State of System Boundaries

One key criterion to consider is the *extent of openness (or closedness) of system boundaries as a consequence of the policy or the policy process.* This criterion helps evaluate the system's ability to interact and communicate with its environment or the ability of any element within a system to interact with other elements within its subsystem. The policy should enhance the healthy permeability of system boundaries and interaction.

a. State of System Boundaries—Case Example

The first place to look is the state of boundaries that exist between system elements, in this case the boundaries within and among both internal system components and external system components. Internally, the nature, quality and frequency of interaction of all hospital staff that would enable and support the provision of alternative residential care is very important. Do the nursing, medical, and social service staff, for example, work well together and could they work cooperatively and effectively in the new program component established by the proposed policy? How well do they communicate and how effectively do they share responsibility? Externally, the state of system boundaries in regard to the hospital's connections with the community's established child care services system would have to be assessed and improved wherever necessary. Implementation of the proposed policy would surely require the full participation of the child care service system, and positive inter-system interaction will need to be developed and nurtured. The question is how these tasks will be approached and who within the hospital will be given the responsibility to bring these relationships to fruition. Is it likely that the hospital's social service staff would take the lead in this?

Would the patterns of interaction be any more or less permeable as a result of the policy? For example, is there a tendency to exclude certain professions that might be crucial in making this a successful venture, such as nutritionists or health care educators working with child placement foster families?

It is the policy analyst's responsibility to speculate about the effects of this policy on the boundaries around existing and potential social actors and service subsystems that would likely play a part in the policy's implementation.

b. Authority, Influence, and Leadership

It is absolutely essential to consider the location and nature of authority, influence, and leadership in the organization of the policy action system. These factors influence how much power the policy will have—how much scope, salience, clout, or attraction will be present in support of the policy's initiation or implementation. Some questions here have to do with the extent to which such authority, influence, and leadership is formal or informal, centralized or decentralized, and whether the policy has the necessary legitimation (the recognized right to be acted upon), support, or sanction (the attendant and requisite rewards and punishments). In order to gain an adequate perspective, these characteristics must not only be assessed in their current contexts, but retrospectively.

b. Authority, Influence, and Leadership—Case Example

Every policy that is fundamentally meaningful has some aspect of power that keeps it in place. The Board authorized the pursuit of this policy option and is accountable for it. One might also observe the extent to which the agency's administrative leadership, in the persons of the executive director, program heads, coordinators, or other significant actors, provide leadership in pursuing the policy goal. For clues, one might note how often and in what manner policies such as this arise during orientation of new workers or in staff meeting discussions—as indicators of the extent to which the hospital and its staff have taken on the concept to think of patient planning in terms other than the norm of acute care provision. Put another way, one might observe whether the policy, given its legitimacy from the Board, might also be associated with its necessary sanctions (i.e., rewards and/or punishments). Are staff who assist in creating effective techniques for developing community agency relationships or who develop internal procedures that facilitate out-placement valued and rewarded by administrators and staff in discussions? Answers to such questions offer clues.

c. Patterns of Communication

The patterning of communication is often expressed in terms of the presence of "filterers" (spokespersons or interpreters of policy or group positions) or of "gatekeepers" (intake workers, referral and information agencies, planning councils, review boards, and the like). Filterers and gatekeepers play particularly powerful and pivotal roles in human systems.

Systems of human communication often have key persons, positions, or events that serve as important channels or nodes in the conveyance of messages, principles, or values. It is important to the analysis to identify these channels and nodes. Furthermore, it is also necessary to recognize that communication may be either unilateral (i.e., going in one direction), bilateral (i.e., going in two directions, back and forth) or multilateral (i.e., going in many directions). The direction and source of communication are also important consider-ations in the analysis of policy.

c. Patterns of Communication—Case Example

The impact of communication is fairly obvious in the case of planning for alternative residential care for abandoned infants. Unquestionably, for infants with HIV + in particular, there will have to be extensive in-terpersonal communications involved in case planning for discharge, identifying placement opportunities, and orientation and training for the care givers.

The policy will likely expand, to some extent, the gatekeeping power of the social services department staff in the hospital. The nature of the out-placement policy requires detailed information and feedback among all those who plan for the infants' placement. The staff social worker is likely to be a key element in this communication system.

d. Strains and Constraints

The next consideration is the effect of the policy or the policy process upon tension, variety, and entropy. Entropy is the tendency toward disorder or the inability to do work in the policy system. That is, not only should the question be raised of whether such tension, variety, or entropy are present but also whether these characteristics are func-tional *or* dysfunctional. There is a common tendency to see such char-acteristics automatically as being negative, unwanted or dysfunc-tional, but this is not necessarily the case in human policy environments. For example, tension-producing action sometimes brings issues to the fore for examination or resolution; variety some-times generates creative interchange; and entropy may sometimes provide a desirable slowing down of circular degenerative processes that are getting out of hand.

It is helpful to examine the existence of interface constraints in the policy system. Interface constraints are those situations in which two or more elements in a system come into conflict or competition with one another at their boundaries. Those boundaries may be determined by their roles, positions, or needs, for example. Any adjustment in cur-rent arrangements runs the risk of placing components or elements of a system into conflict or competition with one another, because the sys-tem's resources (both tangible and intangible) may be modestly or ex-tensively redistributed. The task of the analyst here is to identify the quality or nature of new interaction generated at the interface of any two or more components in terms of what constraints are now the ''new baggage'' of the substantive policy or policy process. These interface constraints are especially apparent in the clash between competing ideologies or philosophies; limited and fixed resources, such as low-income housing properties and industrial development needs; or in learning new ways of doing things, such as new professional disciplines required by interactive team efforts in service provision.

d. Strains and Constraints—Case Example

Our earlier discussion suggested that policies or procedures that generate tension for a system are generally seen as "bad," whereas the introduction of variety sometimes generates new and creative interchange among or between system components. Surely, variety in perceptions and preferences is at least more likely to occur when a number of new roles and tasks are introduced into the work environment. Our policy illustrated here is likely to introduce new ways for managing patient care. The movement will be away from maintenance in the hospital to preparation for community living. Furthermore, professionals in the hospital will have to interact with a new set of actors, from community agency personnel to foster parents to protective service workers. This change in routine and number and nature of system participants will very likely create some new tensions in the hospital system and should be anticipated.

The introduction of new participants, new individuals, and new organizations as caregivers also adds variety. It might be axiomatically stated that, the more new information introduced into the system, short of overload, the greater the system's ability to do work. The principle of expanding the boundaries and domains of the hospital beyond its walls generates more problem-solving challenges but also more problem-solving resources. Consequently, entropy (the tendency toward disorder and inability to do work) may be reduced by the policy since significant actors with new technologies and new approaches will likely be involved in doing the work of service to newborn infants.

Another presumption is that, as the current policy adds more information to the decision system, each of the parties is offered more criteria with which to plan and make ultimate recommendations and decisions for children and their appropriate care. While more information presumably leads to more enlightened decisions, it also introduces more variables and reduces the *probability* of total agreement in perceptions and judgments. Thus, the policy increases the likelihood of differences or even conflict within the system. This would appear to be one of the costs of enlarging the definition of the task. At this point, at least we can say that the policy (as with the introduction of many other policies) may generate more confusion or disagreement in the care of infants since more people are now participating in the decision processes (assuming that the policy will be implemented to the fullest intention of the Board of Directors).

e. Resistance to Change

A telling criterion of system functioning has to do with the existence and nature of resistance to change. The criterion involves not only an assessment of resistance to change implied by the policy but also of the resources (e.g., money, supportive and ancillary policies, people power, or technology) needed to maximize, optimize, or "satisfice" (see Lindblom, 1968) the policy goals. This also requires an assessment of the opposing issues, forces, or liabilities that might give resistance to or mitigate against change.

e. Resistance to Change—Case Example

The task now is to determine if resistance to the change created by the policy of providing alternative residential care for abandoned infants exists and, if so, what form the resistance takes. The more obvious method is tuning in on staff complaints regarding, for example, the inconvenience of having to take on new responsibilities, having to learn how to interact with new individuals or agencies in the community, and so on. Less obvious indicators of resistance may emerge. For example, a common practice of some medical practitioners is to reduce the number of HIV + diagnoses actually made because they do not want to place an infant in a stigmatized position unless there is absolute and irrefutable evidence that an HIV + diagnosis is in order.

f. Feedback Devices

An important characteristic of living systems is that they include devices and channels that provide information to guide the system toward corrective action based upon its output activities—feedback. Feedback is an important aspect of policy systems. Consequently, it is beneficial to have in one's framework for analysis some assessment capability of the extent to which feedback devices are built into the policy itself. A modern example of a built-in feedback device in social welfare policy is "sunset legislation," through which policies and/or programs are automatically terminated, pending a reading of the monitoring information and the systematic feedback built into the policy review and discussion process. Another example is the setting of objectives and/or policy priorities for time-limited periods, which automatically requires some process of evaluation and/or feedback. Determine the extent to which feedback devices have been built in to perform the functions of monitoring, evaluating, and/or controlling desired policy outcomes. Sometimes agencies or action groups are able to monitor the outcomes of their processes by building in, through policy, routine feedback mechanisms from their consumers (clients, patients, students, customers, etc.). This is achieved by scheduling hearings or review sessions or by implementing client satisfaction surveys or questionnaires. Some action systems create job positions to deal with both positive and negative feedback from the system (community relations specialists, ombudsmen, delegates, recipients rights officers).

The extent to which feedback devices are working can sometimes be determined by effective monitoring and evaluating pegged to specific policy goals. The key question here has to do with the manner in which the policy system manages both positive and negative feedback. For example, is the agency structured such that service outputs can be monitored for the number of dropouts, recidivists, "successes," and returnees? Is the policy process or implementation structured to evaluate the nature of its inputs (e.g., type and frequency of particular problems or referrals) or its outcomes (e.g., success or achievement rates, attainment of contractual goals or treatment plans)?

A key consideration here is what the output (frequency of events) and outcome (actual achievements) *criteria* are, who sets them, and by whose standards. If the analyst is looking at "what is working," then it is imperative to determine by what criteria and standards of measurement that question and answer is evaluated.

f. Feedback Devices—Case Example

On the one hand, the policy would seem to allow for corrective feedback to enter into the system if and when the hospital chooses to implement the policy by working cooperatively with existing child placement agencies. Presumably, such agencies would require and demand extensive supportive services from the hospital beyond what is normally provided to an infant placed in foster care, for example. The commitment to cooperative service provision would, of its nature, require and ensure intra- and inter-system feedback among and within the participating agencies. Those feedback requirements may even be built into interagency contracts or memoranda of understanding.

On the other hand, if the hospital chose to provide the alternative care arrangements itself, evaluative feedback on the needs of the care system would have to be identified in the agency's process of obtaining experience in this new service venture. In other words, the feedback system would not necessarily be self-adjusting but, rather, incremental, and based upon the hospital accumulating experience with this new form and level of patient care.

There does not appear to be any provision built into the policy itself that allows for a monitoring of the effectiveness of the policy, individually or in the aggregate. We might assume that a policy with such good and obvious intentions is automatically effective or appropriate; but nothing in the policy assures us that there is a built-in monitoring of its processes or ultimate effects. Procedures would have to be developed to correct this deficiency.

A key question here is how the system will handle both positive and negative feedback about the functioning of any residential placement. We will need to be assured that the policy comes with necessary monitoring systems in place, such as the nature and frequency of requests for assistance from substitute caregivers, problems in recruitment of or turnover in those caregivers, and issues in reimbursement and payment levels. We will need to develop consumer feedback information, perhaps using surrogates for assessing adequacy of services from the point of view of the infants themselves. These feedback devices should be suggested in the ultimate policy statement itself.

g. Impact on Agency's Dynamic Adaptation

Another important criterion to consider is the extent to which the existing policy, proposed policy, or the policy process enhances the system's ability to allow for dynamic adaptation. The analyst must assess the impact or potential of the policy to enable the system to be more adaptive and self-corrective. Some clues to this characteristic might be found in policy characteristics of automatic review mandates, the range of representativeness in clientele or decision makers involved, or the flexibility of available change mechanisms, whether such changes be available through legislation, ordinance, rules, guideline development, or consensus development. The analyst needs to determine whether the agency uses the feedback information, in either planned or serendipitous ways, to make appropriate adjustments in the policy itself or the procedures or guidelines associated with the policy. This is often the function in "sunset laws," or even the principle behind zero-based budgeting, when installed properly. These techniques, used appropriately, generate ongoing formative evaluations so that the system is ready at the point of renewal to justify continuance or adjustments based upon systematic use of feedback.

g. Impact on Agency's Dynamic Adaptation—Case Example

Evidence of dynamic adaptation might be found in staff attitudes and orientation to taking on new forms of care, roles, and tasks. If not only the social service department staff but staff of the various specialty units and those on the ward have a commitment to new forms of care, then there is evidence of the system's ability to adapt. Another possibility is to examine the extent to which various departments are willing to integrate new procedures into currently routinized procedures for existing forms of care.

h. Environmental Impact

Now we will take a page out of our discussion on family impact analysis in chapter 3. While we will not pursue the detail suggested by family impact analysis, it would be instructive to consider generally, at least, the impact of the policy upon the immediate social or political environment. We can consider what, if any, impact there will be on the general social welfare climate as a result of the policy, what messages or meta-messages might be sent to the environment if this policy were to be embraced by any sponsoring groups, or what the overall implications might be in terms of any setting of precedents, rescinding of prior custom, or tacit approvals being given as a result of the policy.

h. Environmental Impact—Case Example

The impact upon the medical establishment in the community is likely to be very significant in that the implementation of the program would be the first occasion that a hospital facility has taken on responsibility for continuity of care involving actual placement and followup in residential care for any population group. This policy would establish a precedent for the hospital delivering services to individuals beyond the point of discharge from acute care. The precedent more closely resembles the hospitals providing "social services" in the community, although the complexities associated with HIV infection cannot so neatly be divided between "medical" and "social" variables.

3. Determine Implications for Selected Values

Now the task is to focus on the implications for selected values to be used in the analysis of the proposed or desired policy, particularly with regard to the targets and clients/interests affected by the policy. Values provide both the foundation of what we consider to be the important criteria for analysis as well as an essential screen operating in tandem with the criteria for analyzing the substantive content.

Values are particularly central in the practice of social work and other human service professions. Values are different from ethics in that values pertain to desires, wants, or priorities, while ethics pertain more to the behaviors necessary to attain those preferences. However, as Levy (1979b) points out, these distinctly different elements become merged in professional practice. That is, the professional person cannot easily separate values from ethics. Nevertheless, values may be seen as the *principles of ends* and ethics as the *principles of means*. Values indicate our preferences; ethics give directions for how to behave to embrace those preferences. For some, the values and ethics of their professional orientation may provide the driving force for their commitment to social welfare in general and social welfare policy analysis in particular. In this part of this chapter, we focus primarily on values aspects: our purpose here is to examine the substantive content of policy, rather than how we are to behave ethically in our practice.

For the professions as a whole, values are integrating forces that become part of some professions' charters, as evidenced in professional codes of ethics. Consequently, any framework for social welfare policy analysis must give explicit attention to the values elements in order to be consistent with the profession's mandates and meet the professional responsibility owed to the clientele being served.

This section concerning values is organized around three content areas. The first is a consideration of those central values considered generic to social work practice, particularly as they relate to policy analysis. The second refers to a set of values that are consistent with the general systems approach or systems theory of social processes. In the third section, special attention is given to sexism, classism, racism, poverty, and ageism as they pertain to policy analysis. This latter procedure will be referred to as "The SCRAPS Test," since scraps is what one is likely to be left with, so to speak, if there is an issue of Sex, Class, Race, Age, or Poverty in the policy or the policy problem. An analysis of policy for the social work field *must* give conscious and purposeful attention to the implications for the problem and the policy for those who constitute a minority because of gender, class, race, age, or level of income.

A number of possible values could be included in our framework. Reamer suggests that "values considered central to the profession [are] . . . individual worth and dignity, self-determination, adequate living conditions, and acceptance by and respect of others" (Reamer, 1982, p. 10). Lewis includes "justice, security, knowledge, beauty and self-respect [and] . . . liberty and opportunity, income and health, education and aesthetic satisfaction, and self-respect for all persons" (Lewis, 1982, p. 141). Although making particular reference to ethics, Lewis also suggests combating unfair discrimination, providing equal opportunity, and assuring citizen participation in decisions affecting (peoples') lives (Lewis, 1982, pp. 99-100). In a discussion of ethical dilemmas, Reamer (1983) refers to four principles to be applied as criteria for distributing scarce resources: equality, need, contribution, and compensation. Some of these suggestions are good examples of the close relationship between values and ethics perceived by professionals.

Perhaps the most concise but inclusive list of values considerations was offered many years ago by Felix Biestek in *The Casework Relationship* (1957), which is still in wide use. While he spoke ostensibly only to the practice of social casework, Biestek enumerated central principles (i.e., values). In addition to the notions of self-identity and self-determination commonly found in the litany of values central to social work, we can borrow three additional principles from Biestek: confidentiality, individualization, and the nonjudgmental attitude. These principles also exemplify the merging of values and ethics that occurs in professional practice suggested by Levy, noted earlier.

Case Illustration—Infants with HIV + Infection

We will continue to explore the policy of Vistaview Hospital: the organization shall provide community-based residential care and other appropriate assistance for infants abandoned in hospitals in the service area. So far, we have considered a number of elements in our analysis of that policy situation that have value implications. However, we will now give our attention to those elements that explicitly have implications for a *values analysis*. Again, remember that application of each value element in our narrative is meant for illustrative purposes; an exhaustive application of each element may not be necessary or appropriate to all policy situations.

The first three criteria to be considered are adequacy, effectiveness, and efficiency. These three criteria should generally be considered in any analysis inasmuch as they comprise a central place in the value systems of both those who influence social welfare systems and those who are responsible for the delivery of human services. That is, these three criteria frequently bespeak central concerns of many in our society who have opinions about and/or responsibility for social welfare services. These three criteria are often expressed in one breath, as if they were synonymous, yet they are not synonymous. They are treated separately here to make their distinctions clear as analytic criteria.

a. Adequacy

There is hardly a policy that in some way does not demand at least a cursory review of its adequacy (i.e., the extent to which the goal is achieved when the policy is carried out). Adequacy may be thought of as the extent to which all those who were meant to be "covered" were actually impacted (i.e., horizontal adequacy) or the degree to which any particular individual or other target was affected (i.e., vertical adequacy). Adequacy refers to the degree of impact, as opposed to effectiveness (i.e., the determination of the relationship of the goal and any particular selected means employed).

Whether the target of the policy is a service system client group, or individual, it is also instructive early in the analysis to make some estimate of the adequacy of coverage of the target. That is, we need to get some idea of the extent to which the target is "covered by the policy," both in the aggregate (i.e., to what extent is the whole target covered) and individually (i.e., to what extent each target element is serviced by the policy). This gives us an early notion of the power of the policy in terms of its achieving its intended effects and the extent of its remaining problematic.

a. Adequacy—Case Example

It will remain to be seen just how adequate this policy is in terms of the degree to which "boarder babies" are actually assisted to become nurtured in a normal family environment. The present situation is that children in need of normal homes are abandoned; the policy would presumably allow for placement in an appropriate environment. One could first ask, "to what extent does this policy actually accomplish the desired effect of providing more home-like environments to infants abandoned in the hospital? Is there really a responsiveness from the child care community? Is there likely to be? Will conditions really be any different for these children as a result of the policy? What evidence will there be that their situation is any better than if they remained in the hospital? What indicators can be used to answer this last question? If those indicators or that information is not available, the policy analyst needs not only to devise means for obtaining it but to regularly develop such data. The latter may even be one of the resultant recommendations of the policy analysis effort.

b. Effectiveness

A policy's effectiveness refers to the relationship between its goal and the selected means employed to achieve it. This criterion goes beyond the question of adequacy to the relationship of means and ends. Effectiveness speaks to the question of whether there is a logical connection between the means or techniques required by the policy and the policy goal. Means should have a predictive relationship with the ends obtained.

b. Effectiveness—Case Example

This proposed policy would assist the hospital in using its resources for what they are intended to be used for, that is, acute or rehabilitative care. The goal of any care for infants would likely be to provide acute care in the appropriate time frame and return a child to as normal an environment as is possible. The question has to be raised whether or not the provision of residential care provides the most logical or effective means to achieving that goal. While the connection appears obvious, the honest analyst will consider the question carefully and also consider other means to the goal, such as the maintenance of alternative but enriched custodial care in the context of continued hospital placement. Surely, respite care, foster care, or home health care would obtain the same goals for children (i.e., nurturance and adequate care) for much less cost than in-hospital care, though the costs for gearing up a new venture would not be insignificant.

c. Efficiency

The criterion of efficiency refers to the degree to which the means employed can be maximized with the use of the minimum amount of resources. Hence, efficiency is concerned with the particular *relationship* between a policy goal, the means employed, and the *resources* allocated or expended to obtain that goal. Those resources might be time, money, staff effort, space, or whatever.

c. Efficiency—Case Example

We also need to arrive at some estimation of the efficiencies obtained by the policy. In this policy we may want to look at the amount of time and effort needed by staff to appropriately engage the community's child care service system, should the option be to work through existing child placement agencies. Or the comparison should be made to the effort required to obtain the skills and information needed for the hospital to establish its own child care program. This is not to say that there is some pre-established level of "efficient" versus "not efficient" functioning for this policy. Rather, it forces the analysis to make visible the extent to which the means employed in pursuit of a policy goal can be maximized with a minimum use of the resources available. This helps to establish some of the "costs" of the policy, thereby flushing out the more detailed criteria of cost for subsequent policy decision making.

There will be some cost incurred, albeit not likely out-of-pocket costs, for the various disciplines within the hospital to begin thinking in different terms as to the hospital's responsibility for making adequate discharge plans for abandoned infants. This may require reorientation and/or retraining—efforts which would entail significant costs.

Next, we need to examine the problem's or the policy problem's association with values central to those who work within the human services or social welfare services systems.

d. Impact on Rights, Statuses, and Social Justice

According to David Gil (1970; 1976), we should consider the effects of any particular policy in terms of its impact upon individual, group, or organizational rights and statuses. Such considerations not only entail the questions of equity and fairness but also the political feasibility or practicality of a policy's prospects. Policy can impact one's position in a social system (that is, the status associated with a position) or the commensurate rewards, perquisites, prerogatives, and privileges of those statuses. For example, policy on staffing of cases can affect individual or disciplinary perquisites or prerogatives and thereby enhance or hinder the viability of a particular policy.

Next on the list are questions of the overriding value of social justice and whether the policy allows people to be treated with *fairness* (i.e., whether persons or situations are dealt with reasonably and justly as a result of the policy), *equity* (i.e., whether situations in similar circumstances are dealt with *similarly*, and *equality* (i.e., whether persons, groups, or situations are dealt with in the *same* manner). It should be noted that equity and equality are not synonymous. Equity speaks to similar treatment for similar circumstances; equality speaks to sameness. Justice not only invokes consideration of equity and equality but also fairness, the notion that individuals will be allowed due consideration, due process, and due courtesy.

d. Impact on Rights, Statuses, and Social Justice—Case Example

Infants have rights, of course; in this instance, the right not to languish in institutional care and the right to pursue (or have others pursue on their behalf) as normal environment for rearing as is reasonably possible. It might be said that the policy will confer a new status upon those infants, transforming them into passive hospital patients; their advocates will now have newfound authority and impetus to act on their behalf. The policy would change a child's status from hospital patient to a child in the community and asserts that child's right to community care. The policy may also reward the hospital and insurance carriers for reducing the cost per patient for care.

This policy formalizes client rights and statuses. Even if the principles underlying the policy were already embodied in workers' attitudes and practices without aggressively trying to work with community agencies to provide residential placement, the policy formalizes such rights and statuses and says, in effect, that the hospital will now commit resources to that end. The clients' entitlement to expect certain kinds of behaviors is safeguarded by written policy, as are the workers' methods and procedures in bringing the intended policy effects about.

Generally speaking, any policy that opens up the boundaries to more rights and status in participation in the decision process could be considered egalitarian. That is, the client, participant, patient, or recipient of services should be seen as having some identifiable rights and privileges that place him or her in a relatively egalitarian position in relation to the provider of service.

e. Self-Determination

For social welfare analysis, we must consider the impact of the policy upon the right of citizens to a voice in the determination of those policies that vitally affect them. This is not to say that everyone is involved to the fullest in every policy decision affecting their lives. Nonetheless, the *rights* of citizens must be explicitly reviewed and considered, and these rights must be honored in the policy and, of course, in the policy analysis. Whether these same rights of self-determination will be honored equally in the subsequent decisions arising out of the analysis is, of course, another matter. However, the analyst has an ethical obligation in the analysis itself to consider the value element of self-determination of client and target groups.

e. Self-Determination—Case Example

No self-determination is directly supplied by this policy, though it might be argued that the policy allows others to work as proxy for these infants. In that sense, then, others are given the opportunity to take initiative and act on behalf of abandoned infants to determine a type of environment that will be available for the early years of their lives that is different from languishing in a hospital.

The policy directs the agency to move away from the traditional passive reliance upon external child care systems and toward a more assertive position in caring for and planning for children. Fostering aggressive plans to provide alternative care protects the infant's right to self-determination.

f. Identity

You may recall from our earlier discussion of Kelley's (1975) two ''subcriteria'' that the impact of a policy upon individual or group identity and self-determination are important. It would be well to include both of these criteria as part of the ''main frame'' of our framework for analysis in social welfare policy inasmuch as they are so central to codes of ethics for various helping professionals.

If the substance of the analysis is its social welfare nature, we must consider the impact of the policy upon the self-image of the beneficiary (client), the target of the policy. Our first consideration must be to give explicit attention to the impact of social welfare activity on the self-image of people and their need for and right to human dignity. In practical terms, the analysis must take into consideration the policy's impact upon individual, group, or organizational feelings of self-worth and identity. The analysis must assess the actual or probable outcomes of the policy with respect to these "human rights."

f. Identity—Case Example

We have, in effect, already touched upon the criteria of identity to some extent. Since self-determination is of the very essence in this particular policy, the development or protection of a sense of personal identity is fostered in that the client (patient) be accorded rights to continuity of care provided to other hospital patients. Being abandoned does not mean abandoning the right to be treated as a unique individual. The policy would help to dispel the perspective that such children are pariahs.

As already noted, our analysis leads us to conclude that the policy of providing alternative care provides a formalization of rights and status for abandoned infants that legitimizes and supports optimum discharge planning and continuity of care for infants with the HIV virus. In terms of a person's identity, this policy would appear to foster and support, over time, a child's perception of him/herself as a person of worth who not only has a right to care but is important in the eyes of significant others.

g. Individualization

Individualization refers to the need for individuals (or groups or organizations) to be treated in terms of their unique nature, needs and qualities. Individualization may be seen as the opposite of stereotyping and the playing out of discrimination and prejudice. It can be manifested by giving consideration in policy analysis to the value of self-identity, but it relates particularly to the dangers of invidious distinctions and biased policy. In practice, policy analysis should consider the impact of a policy on individualization—the recognition of the unique nature of potentially affected individuals, groups, or organizations.

g. Individualization—Case Example

Individualization, a principle providing that the unique nature of the individual will be respected, is very much assured by the commitment to provide alternatives to abandonment in a general hospital's children's unit. The provision of alternative residential care or, as the policy proposal states, "other appropriate assistance," indicates that individualized planning and service provision will take place. The policy transforms the class of clientele as a dependent category that will remain in one patient status into the role of clients for individualized case planning.

h. Nonjudgmental Attitude

The nonjudgmental attitude is perhaps as much of a quality desired in the policy analyst as a quality sought after in the analysis itself. Surely, all education is a political act, as Freire (1972) has reminded us, and policy analysis unquestionably has a heavy educative function. To be sure, the pursuit of any set of values is a judgmental, political act in itself. This fact notwithstanding, the policy analysis should still give attention to both the judgmental nature of the analysis itself and the extent to which a given policy, in its net effect, makes unfair or improper judgments about the clients or targets of the policy. For example, a policy may make unwarranted assumptions about the competence of individuals or groups (as is often the case in policies affecting handicapped citizens). A notable example in our social welfare history has been the presumption, embodied in some income maintenance policies, that people who are out of money are somehow also lacking in morality or other socially desirable characteristics.

h. Nonjudgmental Attitude—Case Example

The risk of judgmental attitude could be very much at risk in this policy problem. This is due to the problem of misinformation about caring for those who have HIV infection, in spite of the massive public education campaigns that have taken place. Another factor is that children are sometimes seen as having to ''pay for the sins of their parents'' and, to the extent that many people in the community see HIV and AIDS as being punishment for inappropriate behavior on the part of adults, some children will pay the price for those attitudes. The proposed policy will not do away with those attitudes and, in fact, those attitudes may have to be faced more directly in pursuit of the policy goal.

i. Confidentiality

A citizen's right to confidentiality in personal matters is a central and recurrent theme in our society. Numerous federal and state statutes and their attendant regulations address the issue of privacy and confidentiality of information. Surely the analysis of policy should consider this value. In practical terms, this does not refer merely to whether or how personal or organizational records are ''kept secret.'' The issue of confidentiality also plays itself out in more subtle ways, such as the maintenance of security around unique identifier numbers in management information systems, for example, or in how people are required to make personal or organizational "secrets" known, such as family history. A common example is the requirement of financial disclosure, often not even necessary, though sometimes required by agencies as a matter of ritual or routine.

i. Confidentiality—Case Example

The value of confidentiality is very much at risk in this policy issue. Implementation of the policy of providing alternative care would likely mean having to share information about the infant with a number of caregivers. And, given public attitudes and fears regarding HIV and AIDS, the individual's right to privacy will be at risk with the sharing of confidential medical information. At the same time, there are a number of special state provisions regarding confidentiality involving HIV+ diagnoses, and there will likely be a number of situations wherein protection of a child's confidentiality will be compromised or at least at risk.

The Many Faces of Values for Human Systems Realities

Systems thinking offers a set of values that are worth considering in any human systems analysis. However, there are so many views of what systems thinking actually is that these underlying values are often overlooked. For our purposes here, it is extremely important to be aware of which conceptualization we might accept.

Systems thinking from a sociocultural perspective suggests that there are *isomorphisms* (i.e., similarities in structures and processes) among all levels of living things. This view also stresses the notion of the interrelatedness of social structures and processes. At another extreme, systems thinking is sometimes operationalized with mechanistic models of what is and what ought to be, and might be exemplified by simple input-throughput-output models of systems thinking.

The sociocultural perspective taken here places emphasis upon isomorphic qualities of levels of human functioning (i.e., individuals, groups, organizations and communities) that can be seen in the original work of von Bertalanffy (1968), James Miller (1978), David Easton (1965), and Walter Buckley (1967). A prevailing emphasis upon the inter-relatedness of social structure and events enjoys great popularity in the literature and has been exemplified for some time in social work by Pincus and Minahan (1973) and Anderson and Carter (1974). The more mechanistic views have been exploited by state and federal government agencies, particularly the Department of Defense, and have been characterized and critiqued by Ida Hoos (1972). Whatever the emphasis, however, there is a widely held view that systems thinking, being a grand-level framework, tends to be conservatizing. Perhaps because of the emphasis placed upon mapping and description and its strange terminology, systems thinking has not received recognition for the human values that it embodies.

If one examines the basic principles underlying human systems thinking, or its sociocultural perspectives, it is impossible not to recognize its value base. Indeed, systems thinking offers a set of humanistic values that one might even consider "radical" in that they offer a departure from conventional ways of seeing things. "Radical" conceptions of the world generally assert that social problems are caused by inequitable social structures; that social structures are, in turn, determined by economic factors; that social institutions are developed and supported to maintain the existing inequitable structure (or at best to ameliorate such effects—a common criticism of social work); and that social change can only come about through dialectical means (Keefe, 1978).

We would argue here that the basic tenets of systems thinking not only provide an adequate world view but offer an additional set of values for consideration in effective and realistic social welfare policy analysis. Systems thinking provides a point of view for organizing conceptualization of reality. Human systems thinking comes with some important baggage: its own way of expressing what is most important—its own set of values. These values embedded in the systems perspective must also be considered in social welfare policy analysis if we are to honor our commitments to the human consequences of social welfare policies and programs. Four core concepts of system thinking are particularly relevant for our purposes at this point: (1) indeterminateness, (2) multifinality, (3) nonsummativity, and (4) morphogenesis. These may sound like "50-cent" words, but there are solid values and concepts behind them. The ideas, if not the vocabulary, are likely already known to you.

Case Illustration—Infants with HIV + Infection: The Many Faces of Values for Human Systems Realities

In our hospital policy of providing residential care and other appropriate assistance for infants as an alternative to abandonment to hospital care, the practice theory would likely be something to the effect that a child is best reared in a "natural" environment in the community and that an acute care general hospital best serves its goals by addressing its own unique mission, not by providing custodial care for children. These theoretical views are very likely to be compatible with human system values.

In this section we will focus on the particular values underlying the policy that especially pertain to human or socio-cultural systems.

j. Indeterminateness

A classic concept of social thought is a *determinate* view that the end processes of social action are very much determined and preordained by social structure and social processes. For example, much of our Western preoccupation and enchantment with technology leads us to believe that all problems can be solved. Our faith in progress leads us to conclude that those matters that are not now in hand do, in fact, have a solution and much of our social process is merely aimed at discovering the answer. Some of us are quite magical in our thinking in this regard.

The policy analysis could proceed instead from the concept of *in*-determinateness, which recognizes that the end states of social processes are determined and altered *in process*. This, of course, is consistent with a Hegelian view of the evolution of ideas in which each idea (thesis) generates its opposite (antithesis), out of which is formed a new idea (synthesis). Recognizing the dialectical nature of social process helps the policy analyst to see the reality of unintended effects of a given policy and reduces some of the dangers inherent in positivistic approaches to assessment, review, and analysis. The concept of indeterminateness radicalizes the analysis in the sense that end states are not seen as being fixed, linear, and/or simplistic.

j. Indeterminateness—Case Example

This policy in our case example will likely enable the child and the hospital to "swim upstream" in the sense that our society has a tendency to take a determinate view to anyone with a physical or social handicap. That is, people with handicaps are stigmatized and possessing the HIV infection incurs a social limitation on being accepted into the general community. The proposed policy suggests that and allows for a range of other possible outcomes that can be explored under the authority and sponsorship of this policy. This policy seems to imply a faith in the systems principle of indeterminateness, that the end states of social problem solving are actually determined in process, that is, they are not predetermined. By expanding the pool of potential child rearing and living arrangements, the reality of indeterminateness is given the opportunity to operate. The policy allows for the end state to be determined in process.

Given that there are still so many unknowns in the treatment of this disease and in providing care for those infected, there is much yet to be learned in the process of placement planning, resource allocation, types of caregivers to be recruited and trained, and a myriad of other actors yet to be discovered (e.g., period of disease incubation).

k. Multifinality

A corollary to indeterminateness is the notion of multifinality, the concept that original conditions can result in multiple end-state conditions. This is in contrast to common linear Occidental thinking that prior states end in clearly predictable and fixed probabilities. That lineation is seen in the crude stereotypical thinking, for example, that "kids coming from across the tracks all end up the same," or "once a _____, always a _____," or "the policy is this way because that's the way it has to be done," or "we've always done things this way, that's why!" On the other hand, multifinality is evident in many human system realities. The obverse condition is *equifinality*, the notion that different origins can arrive through social process at similar end states. The implication for social welfare policy analysis is that we can avoid the traps of simplistic positivism and recognize the reality of different policies possibly achieving similar results. While these notions seem like common sense, social practice does not give overwhelming evidence of our thinking in such "radical" terms.

k. Multifinality—Case Example

The policy tends to support the notion that a variety of end states can arise out of similar conditions. Contrary to the presumption that the problem is simply to manage and provide custody for a child that nobody wants in our society, the policy allows for the similar initial state (having an HIV + diagnosis) to be seen as an opportunity for a variety of end states. Given the unpredictable course of HIV infection development, there will likely be a range and variety of service requirements and service conditions that emerge as a result of this policy. There will be many changes in the health status of children in care and various needs will require very individualized responses.

l. Nonsummativity

Traditional views of social process and structure are additive or summative, whereas a view of human nature embodied in systems thinking is that social organization is *non*summative. That is, a traditional view of human organization holds that the whole is *nothing other than* the sum of its parts. A human systems view, instead, assumes that human aggregations are nonsummative, or that the whole is *different than* or perhaps *greater than* or *something other than* the sum of its parts. Consequently, any adequate framework for policy analysis recognizes the qualities that emerge when collective policy action occurs; this is the real meaning of "holism." The notion of nonsummativity is manifested in the concept of treating the "whole person," by the recognition of the unique character of some groups "as group," and by the alleged "personality" of some organizations or associations, and by the attribution of "national character" to many nations. Policy analysis must take these emergent holistic qualities into consideration in reviewing feasibility, for example.

l. Nonsummativity—Case Example

The notion that the whole is something different than or more than the sum of its parts is also suggested by this policy approach since the policy fosters the development of a *holistic* approach to placement planning and community care. The inclusion of the broader social service system and the alteration of the role and responsibility of the acute care general hospital opens up the possibility of the reshaping and perhaps even redefinition of the service system. This policy expands the perspective on what constitutes "system" for the child and engenders a more holistic view of the child's world and his or her place in it. Holistic approaches to problem solving may be said to be nonsummative since they view process and outcomes as something greater than the sum of the observable parts.

m. Morphogensis

The notion of morphogenesis (i.e., the recognition that human systems have the capacity to alter forms and processes) has frequently been observed in operation by social work practitioners. This concept, a recognition of the coexistent ability of human systems to maintain stability and also provide system change and/or elaboration, is a radical valuing of systems in that it rejects the more mechanistic notion of system equilibrium. Social workers have long held that individuals or groups are not only affected by their environment but have an effect upon it and that this process continues over time. This humanistic view of the reciprocal interaction of person-in-environment requires the policy analyst to acknowledge and account for the constant dialectic between system components and their environments, which brings about new emergent qualities through human processes. Such qualities are sometimes assumed to be "serendipitous" outcomes of new system purposes, structures, processes, and outcomes, but these outcomes can, at times, be attributable to the play of policy principles.

m. Morphogenesis—Case Example

This policy allows the hospital as an organization to initiate and participate in its own morphogenesis. Vistaview Hospital, through this type of policy change, is able to redefine its boundaries, responsibilities,

and prerogatives, and how it conceptualizes patient need and proper patient care. Morphogenesis is a human systems principle that holds that human systems have the ability to change forms in process. While individual human systems do not manifest any structural or sociopsychological change as a result of the policy (though such change may come about), the change appears to be organizational. The policy allows for a fundamental change in the nature of the interaction of key components in the social agency system by a radical redefinition of the role of the hospital as organization. To that extent, the policy may be said to allow or provide for the morphogenetic nature of human systems—that an organization has within it the resources to fundamentally change in form.

n. The SCRAPS Test

As noted above, special attention must be given to issues of sexism, classism, racism, ageism, and poverty that might be embedded in the problem or the policy. We have given the acronym of SCRAPS to this analytic task as a reminder that scraps are what are likely to be left for those who have a discriminatory "social handicap" due to an issue of Sex, Class, Race, Age or Poverty. We are obligated by our codes of ethics to give conscious and purposeful attention to the implications of the problem and the policy for those who constitute a minority because of their gender, class, race, age, or lack of income.

Another factor necessitating the SCRAPS test is the countervailing phenomenon noted by Karger and Stoesz (1990) wherein we see the tremendous growth in private practice social work in which the clientele are less likely to be poor or members of minority groups. According to Chu and Trotter,

> the commercialization of private practice contributes to the "YAVIS syndrome"—the tendency of clients of private practitioners to be young, attractive, verbal, intelligent, *and* successful. (*Cited in Karger and Stoesz,* 1990, p. 159)

Karger and Stoesz add that "one might add W to the syndrome, since the clients also tend to be disproportionately white" (p. 159). One might say that the SCRAPS test is not only necessitated by the Code of Ethics but also a reasonable countervailing device to compensate for the increasing tendency to overlook those who are excluded, abused, or in various ways disadvantaged by social welfare policy.

As noted in the reference to Lewis, above, some of us value and are in the habit of giving watchful attention to policies and programs that may be discriminatory. Since helping professions have established ethical standards for combating discrimination in our society, they *must* consider issues of discrimination based on gender or sexual orientation; ethnicity or social class, race, economic or handicapping condition; or age in any social welfare policy analysis. Given the insidious and institutionalized nature of the various discriminatory "isms," it is absolutely essential that these factors be routinely and conscientiously considered in our policy analyses. Consequently, the final component of the value element of our framework requires that we review the implications of these potentially discriminatory factors.

n. The SCRAPS Test—Case Example

The vast majority of acute care general hospitals located in the center of moderate to large-sized cities are known to take on a disproportionate share of the responsibility to care for our nation's poorer citizens. To this, add the fact that infants born with HIV infection are most likely, though not in all cases, to be children of parents who are intervenous drug users or children of prostitutes. Consequently, this policy is likely to be of special service to children who are poor and members of minority groups, given the disproportionate number of minorities found among center city groups abusing drugs.

Some of these children will likely be covered by Medicaid, which may alleviate some of the burden. However, because Medicaid or private insurance has never been adequate for virtually any category of need, there is no reason to believe that it will be adequate for this group, either.

The policy surely has racial implications. Give the disproportionate rate of intravenous drug use among the inner city population, agencies are in even more need of minority staff who can assist this client group in making placement decisions and in recruiting alternative caregivers.

4. Establish Feasibility of the Desired Outcomes

We will now focus on the elements that make for achieving resolution of the policy problem or the attainment of the policy goal, having considered the essential variables that make up the substance and values of policy content. The assessment of feasibility has to do with *how* or *whether* a policy goal *might* be achieved. In fact, some of the criteria of feasibility, such as finances or human cost or political power, are directly related to and virtually inseparable from such measures as system functioning or issues of adequacy, effectiveness, or efficiency, for example. Nevertheless, it is helpful in the analysis to give particular visibility to issues of feasibility, even at the expense of some redundancy. Following are some basic considerations:

a. Legality and Foundation

Social welfare policies obviously have to be consistent with legislated and judicial mandates and must coexist with other administrative and executive directives. Such policy is made in legislative, judicial, administrative, and executive arenas and its analysis must take both the opportunities and constraints of those arenas into consideration. Briefly stated, the question is: "How firm is the ground on which this policy is expected to stand?" These four areas of policy generation and support were discussed in detail in chapter 1. In summary, it can be said that the analyst is advised to consider the legislated, judicial, administrative, and executive bases (and/or alternatives) of the proposed policy. Here the analyst might look at the extent to which the policy is founded on any person's or group's right to take action and/or the statutory or customary support behind such actions. Also, the reader is reminded that these bases of support may very well be small-scale and local in origin, such as local ordinances or board or commission resolutions, the rules of court agencies, the rule-making behavior of administrative agencies at any level of government, or the executive position statement given by the director of any public or voluntary agency.

a. Legality and Foundation—Case Example

The proposed policy for providing community-based residential care and other appropriate assistance clearly has legal foundation in the right of the Vistaview Board's right to establish such policy. However, there may be some intervening factors. For example, if implementation of the policy means the hospital itself will be providing alternative care in the community, there may be some licensing or other regulatory requirements that the hospital is presently not prepared to meet. On the other hand, if implementation means capitalizing on existing community resources already established and licensed within the community, then the required legitimation already exists in both the internal and external environments.

At the same time, we should be cautious about jumping to the conclusion that sufficient support will be available from the hospital's professional staff. Given the long history of how the role of an acute care general hospital has been defined, there may be those who would resist this redefinition of role, and the foundation for the policy may or may not be firmly established among the professional staff.

b. Power of the Policy

As Doblestein (1990) notes, an understanding of policy requires an understanding of power. Here is where the human systems concept of *stochastic processes* is very helpful. That is, stochastic processes refers to the phenomenon in which there is an ordering or sequencing of *probabilities* (not certitudes) of events in a human system. We see this so frequently in human interaction that the concept, if not the vocabulary, is commonplace. Good manners, social skills, and protocol or ritualistic behaviors are all examples of stochastic processes. That is, there is an inherent lawfulness in the ordering or sequencing of social events. This lawfulness is the real measure of the power of policy—the ability of policy to relate to the range of human values *while at the same time* giving predictability or order to a human system. After all, isn't that what policy is really all about—the ability to make something happen? The ability to influence what individuals, organizations, groups, or communities actually do, and how they behave? The primary function of any social policy is to give order and predictability and to announce to living systems what is preferred, expected, or desired. A well-developed social policy gives order and predictability (stochasticism) while simultaneously honoring the values desirable in that policy.

Power has been defined by Polsby (1963) as the ability of one actor to do something that specifies the probability of future events for another actor. When power (which is an attribute of social actors) is exercised, it is called influence. Feasibility considerations require assessment of whether the power and influence requirements associated with maintaining or installing a particular policy are adequate and appropriate or whether issues of power and influence must be dealt with *a priori*. There is a common tendency, however, to think of power on the grand scale or in terms of the more obvious play of influence and to overlook the small-scale level, where power and influence may not be explicit or obvious. The future of any given policy is dependent upon the distribution of power in the policy's environment. The subtleties of power and influence are generally not dramatic, as evidenced by the ability of individuals and groups to meet policy with passive-aggressive resistance, for example, or (on the other hand) the ability of policy leaders to lead, at times, with charismatic leadership styles or to capitalize on a trust that has been established over time. That is, only infrequently does the policy process generate headlines and overt struggles. The processes of power and influence are generally subtle.

At this point, the analyst would do well to revisit the section on current and anticipated system functioning having to do with the criteria of authority, influence, and leadership. This exemplifies the fact that policy and analysis is not linear but, rather, a circular or iterative exercise in which there is constant back and fill in the data collection and data analysis. As with systems in the real world, the elements are interrelated. So are the elements of this or any other analytic framework that represents human interaction. For example, the question should immediately be raised as to how enforceable the particular policy is. What sanctions or rewards are associated with the policy? Who makes sure that the policy will be enforced and how do they provide for that insurance? Answers to these questions are essential for an analysis of feasibility.

b.   Power of the Policy—Case Example

Policy has been said to create a stochastic phenomenon in organizations; that is, that policy creates a certain lawfulness or predictability to the sequencing of future events. This is likely to be true of the policy for infants with HIV +. The policy allows for a new level of care to be made available and provides legitimacy to those who would pursue this goal by allocating personal and organizational resources to achieve it. The policy provides positive sanctions to units within the organization that support alternative care.

On the other hand, this analysis could also yield another conclusion: that new program options for infants enabled by this policy makes future events even less predictable. The inclusion of each additional alternative, each with more decision prerogatives than were possible with the child merely remaining in the hospital, may be said to produce a greater number of potential outcomes. In this case, the principle of stochastic processes in human systems helps to generate more light on our analysis and brings to mind even more outcomes that are possible with the inclusion of more key actors in the process.

The proposed policy clearly provides for a fundamental shift in power away from the custodian (i.e., the hospital) to the abandoned infant and to his or her advocates. This is not to say that the child has become a controlling factor but that her/his influence has increased markedly. We also need to look at whether the Board, the agency's administrative structure, and the technology and competence of the staff can assure delivery of the policy goals. Surely the Board has the power (legitimate authority) to mandate such a policy. The adequacy of the administrative structure might be manifested in proper procedures for supervision of staff in regard to the policy. Executive influence might also be observed in the extent to which administrative staff provide leadership in giving visibility to the philosophy inherent in this redefinition of role. The staff, of course, exercise the ultimate power in their influence on the working of the policy. The direct service worker enters at "the point where the shoe hits the pavement." This is where the real power of policy is observed and exercised—or subverted. The staff must have the necessary social treatment skills to ensure skillful mining of the community resources needed to bring the policy goal to fruition.

c. Resource Requirements and Availability

We have already discussed the issue of resource requirements to some extent in considering current functioning of the policy system. Nevertheless, the issue is still fair game when it comes to thinking of demands placed upon finances, space, personnel, time, power, status, prestige, credibility, and so forth. These resource attributes are all of value to social welfare systems and must be considered in the future context when it comes to assessing feasibility.

The notion of cost itself requires a special note in that we often think of cost primarily in economic terms. Yet, many of us are well aware of the fact that cost is also political and social or, more likely, a mix of political, social, psychological, and economic considerations. An important set of questions in the analysis of social welfare policy (and a set of questions that may more likely be answered at the small-scale level) has to do with *who* sets the criteria of cost, the *appropriateness* of the criteria in determining cost for the particular issue under analysis, and *how* or *under what conditions* cost will be determined and/or evaluated.

The fundamental question here has to do with the level of effort and amount of resources to be allocated and spent on the development, installation, and enforcement of the existing or proposed policy, or in managing the policy process. Some obvious "costing" approaches are of value, such as needs assessments, cost/benefit or benefit/cost analyses, and determination of Pareto optima. However, in looking at the small-scale policy analysis environment, our focus is more on the "soft" or sociopolitical costs of the policy under study.

c. Resource Requirements and Availability—Case Example

Cost is always a consideration in health care and social services inasmuch as health and welfare agencies are chartered to serve the public good with social resources. This is true of both publicly and privately supported programs. There is no question that this policy will require additional staff time, though the demands of the policy could be incorporated into existing staff approaches to the provision of service. Additional equipment or space may be required within the hospital for the housing of more discharge planning and child placement staff, whether the hospital itself delivers the new service or not. For the families of these infants, abandoned or not, there presumably would be a cost incurred by the demands upon personal time required for increased family participation because the rights and responsibilities of family participation in placement planning would still be necessary. For the hospital, additional visibility would be given to the agency programs in the community, which would have to be weighed as a cost or a benefit.

In any event, it helps to be reminded that besides the criteria of costs, equally important is the question of who sets those criteria. The policy decision examined here impacts upon staff, clientele, the organization as a whole, and perhaps other components in the community. It is important to consider whether the policymaker (in this case the Board of Vistaview Hospital) has the interests of each of the affected social components in mind and possesses the legitimate authority to unilaterally affect each of those components.

In the short term, this would appear to be a costly policy because it would likely consume more staff time. Presumably, in the long term, it would constitute a wise use of staff resources inasmuch as more appropriate and successful level-of-care decisions would arise and individual children would experience growth at a time of important socio-emotional development. Other cost indices that relate to this particular strategy might include the cost to the hospital's public relations— whether the policy would incur more favor or disfavor with the community in which the hospital is located. In this sense, the policy's approach must be seen as having political costs, and, while these considerations may not necessarily be primary determinants, they should be weighed in the analysis.

d. Rationality

All policies and their analyses must satisfy someone's understanding of rationality. That is, the statement of conclusions and/or recommendations must have some logical link (preferably seen in the connections between a philosophy and a theory) to the original problem statement and the methodology used in gathering the information and arriving at the conclusions or recommendations. To be believable, the analysis must draw on conventional understanding and employ conventional means. This is not to say that policies and their analysis cannot be innovative; rather, the actual *use* of the policy analysis rests heavily on normative conventions. When the analyst goes beyond those conventions, he or she must be aware of that fact. To summarize this point, it is necessary to examine whether both the policy and the policy analysis are based on rational foundations and rational choices.

d. Rationality—Case Example

Earlier we considered the theoretical foundations of the policy under analysis. However, while a policy may be theoretically sound, it may not necessarily be rational in terms of its practicality, logistics, or workability. The policy involving placement of children with HIV infection does not appear unreasonably cumbersome, but bringing the policy goal to fruition will run into community myths and misinformation that will fly in the face of rationality. Community attitudes in general may not welcome this policy, and it will likely be much more difficult to recruit and train an adequate supply of caregivers than might at first be anticipated. The unknowns associated with (1) embarking on a new program initiative of possibly providing direct care in the community and (2) becoming more directly involved in community care concerning HIV infection may introduce some community responses that are irrational. Those who will endorse and implement the policy must be clearly aware of this possibility.

e. Newly Perceived Self-Interests

Finally, in regard to feasibility, we return to the concept introduced in chapter 3 concerning the role of perceived self-interest in the play of policy. It was Gil's contention, you will recall, that a newly perceived self-interest on the part of influential actors holds promise for bringing about policy change. The "self" of self-interest may not only refer to individual self-seeking behavior but the pursuit of interest on behalf of those who one might represent, such as one's parent organization or a client group for whom one advocates. Hence, self-interest is of vital importance as a feasibility consideration in analyzing social welfare policy. These perceptions may generate or free up necessary resources, reduce resistances to either maintenance or change, or become powerful assets in other kinds of social process.

e. Newly Perceived Self-Interests—Case Example

As discussed earlier, an important dynamic for policy change (or policy maintenance for that matter) is the extent to which significant policy actors perceive that their individual or collective self-interests may be served by pursuit of the policy goal. Given that many acute care general hospitals, especially those located in central cities and those who service small, rural constituencies, are being threatened with their economic survival, there may be an incentive in the opportunity to redefine the hospital's role in becoming involved in more active direct patient services in the community. For some, the proposed policy provides for more expansionist opportunities, to put it bluntly. For others, the policy provides for a new means of service delivery. This push-pull of incentives suggests substantial support for pursuit of the policy goal; the pursuit of self-interest may be very much at play.

The policy provides for a more open system. For the hospital staff, the policy provides support legitimated by Board action for pursuit of practice goals that are consistent with professional ethics relating to client self-determination, individualization, and the achievement of personal identity. Consequently, the policy would appear to relate to the self-interest of a number of significant actors and subsystems in the policy field.

5. Provide Recommendations

Having subjected the policy problem to a disciplined analysis by using appropriate criteria such as those found above, the analyst is now in a position to make recommendations. Recommendations on policy made prior to conducting an analysis would be premature, of course, and would likely have little credibility or stature. The task at this point is essentially to review the data already generated, by employing the criteria for analysis of content, particularly by identifying weaknesses, strengths, or factors peculiar to the issue under analysis. In other words, the analyst's recommendations must come from the data and the analysis and not, as is said, "off the wall." In so doing, the resultant recommendations have some empirical bases and stand a better opportunity of being of value to those for whom the analysis is intended to serve.

Summary

These, then, are essential criteria for reviewing social welfare policy and guiding us in making alternative policy choices. You can expand upon the list when certain criteria are particularly germane to your own situation. However, the criteria presented here are viewed as both generic and useful guides. You are not likely in real practice to actually use each and every one of the criteria enumerated here. This list serves as a guide or an inventory of possibilities and a framework from which you, the analyst, can construct a model for analysis suitable to your situation.

An Outline for Analyzing Content of Small-Scale Policy

A. Essential Steps in Policy Content Analysis
   1. Identify the policy problem or policy goal(s) (similar to process analysis)
   2. Assess current and anticipated system functioning
   3. Determine implications for selected values (same as process analysis)
   4. Establish feasibility of the desired outcome
   5. Provide recommendations

B. Content Elements
   1. *Identify the policy problem or policy goal(s)*—A focus on the definition or delineation of the *core principles* at stake in the particular problem, policy goal(s), or specific policy that is to be analyzed. Identification should include:

    a. The policy problem/goal and the policy statement

    b. Base(s) of legitimacy and source or location of the policy (in written form if formal policy or as observed in actual behavior if an informal policy)

    c. Targets and clients of concern

    d. Eligibility

    e. Effect upon maintenance, change, or control

    f. Explicit or implicit theories

    g. Topography of the policy system

    h. Contemporary issues or historical antecedents

2. *Assess current and anticipated system functioning*—A focus on the organizational, administrative, and/or environmental functioning of the *policy system* and the interaction of the components in that system. Attention should be given to both current functioning and system functioning anticipated by embracing any proposed policy changes.

    a. State of system boundaries

    b. Authority, influence, and leadership

    c. Patterns of communication

    d. Strains and constraints

    e. Resistance to change

    f. Feedback devices

    g. Impact on agency's dynamic adaptation

    h. Environmental impact

3. *Determine implications for selected values*—A focus on the implications for selected values to be used in the analysis or desired in the proposed or desired policy, particularly with regard to the targets and clients/interests affected by the policy.

    a. Adequacy

    b. Effectiveness

    c. Efficiency

    d. Impact on rights, statuses, and social justice

    e. Self-determination

    f. Identity

    g. Individualization

    h. Nonjudgmental attitude

    i. Confidentiality

    j. Indeterminateness

    k. Multifinality

    l. Nonsummativity

    m. Morphogenesis

    n. The SCRAPS test

4. *Establish feasibility of the desired outcomes*—A focus on the elements that make for achieving resolution of the policy problem or the attainment of the policy goal.
   a. Legality and foundation
   b. Power of the policy
   c. Resource requirements and availability
   d. Rationality
   e. Newly-perceived self-interests
5. *Provide recommendations*—A focus on the strengths and weaknesses or factors peculiar to the issue and suggested by the data generated by the analysis.

Case Illustrations of Content Analysis

5

In the pages that follow, four case illustrations are provided to illustrate "An Outline for Analyzing Content of Small-Scale Policy." The first case example, entitled, "Multiple Mandates of Confidentiality," concerns a policy that affects all human service agencies. The particular focus on confidentiality is given to the many forces impinging upon an agency and its staff in carrying out confidentiality policy. The second case example, entitled "Utilization Monitoring and Purchase of Service," relates to a variety of policy situations involving contracting and purchase of services. The third case, entitled "The Homeless and the Mall People," focuses more on factors external to an agency that relate to content analysis. The fourth case, entitled "Participation of Birthparents," refers to a policy change which would provide for more direct and active participation of birthparents in the decision and placement process of children being placed into adoption.

Case 1: Multiple Mandates of Confidentiality

In this case illustration, we will examine a policy that no doubt cuts across all agencies providing social services—confidentiality of client information. Our perspective in the analysis will be to examine the policy in a multiprogram agency and particularly to focus on the diverse or multiple sources and mandates for a policy on confidentiality.

While it appears that all codes of ethics in the helping professions include a commitment to confidentiality, the operationalization of this principle is less than automatic when one is confronted by diverse pieces of federal and state legislation legitimizing a policy of confidentiality. There are significant differences in the many pieces of legislation governing confidentiality. Furthermore, confidentiality as a principle frequently runs head-on into accountability to funding agencies or support sources. Consequently, maintaining confidentiality in the social services setting is hardly a *pro forma* assurance, regardless of individual professional commitments to ethical behavior. In our analysis, we will focus on the multiple sources and mandates of confidentiality and give special attention to the interface constraints between confidentiality and accountability.

Our fictitious agency, Community Services Organization, Inc. (CSO), is a typical multiprogram private child and family service agency located in a large city. CSO is a member of a statewide federation of such agencies and offers programs in family counseling, child welfare services, case management and training services for the developmentally disabled, and community consultation. Its sources of funding are varied, with support from the United Way, third party payment from various insurance carriers and Medicaid, contracts with the county community mental health board as a contractual provider, fees directly paid by clients, and a few other sources. The agency is organized around three main program units; client records are not shared from unit to unit. Only in the case of adoptions would a state agency see the client record. While the county's community mental health director is technically the holder of the record for clients for whom services are provided under mental health funding, client files are held at CSO. The agency is very much integrated into its community by virtue of its variety of programs and their associated funding sources.

1. Identify the Policy Problem or Policy Goal(s)

Focus on the definition or delineation of the *core principles* at stake in the particular problem, policy goal(s), or the specific policy that is to be analyzed. Identification should include the following items.

a. *The Policy Problem/Goal and the Policy Statement*

Generally speaking, the universal policy goal of confidentiality is to assure recipients of services that their associations with the provider of services will be maintained in secrecy insofar as the law allows (i.e., excluding information concerning felonious behavior or potential harm to others). Confidentiality is also viewed as one of many vehicles for sound social treatment. A variety of policy problems occur when confidentiality is violated: for the individual, loss of security and privacy; for the agency, loss of integrity; and for the community, a loss of trust. To a great extent, loss of confidentiality by the providers of service removes that agency as a viable option for services by those who value the provision of services with a safeguarded right to privacy.

b. Base(s) of Legitimacy and Source or Location

The confidentiality policy at CSO is simply stated: "Community Services, Inc. shall respect and attempt to safeguard the rights of clients to confidential treatment of information exchanged, to privacy in their relationship with the agency, and to rights of redress" (*CSO Manual*, p. 2). While the confidentiality policy is a strong statement of values, it should be noted that the statement does equivocate to some extent in the sense that only the "attempt" to safeguard is assured. This wording would appear realistic, given the variety of legal and judicial sources that bear on the matter of confidentiality. Each piece of legislation has its own administrative rules and, in some cases, exceptions. It would be improper for the agency to generalize in a cavalier or falsely reassuring manner regarding this policy.

The primary foundation of confidentiality in policy is provided in the U.S. Constitution, Article IV, which provides for "the right of people to be secure in their persons, houses, papers, and effects" and that this right "shall not be violated." In the state in which CSO is located, its various programs also have a variety of legitimating sources in state law for the confidentiality policy. The child protective services program has its source in the Child Protection Law. Both the foster care program and the adoption program have separate provisions in the Child Care Act. The programs for the developmentally disabled relate especially to provisions in the Social Welfare Code, the Mental Health Code, and the state law for mandatory special education. Each program is bound by the provisions of the state's Freedom of Information Act. At the federal level, the agency policy and practice are bound by the Education for All Handicapped Children Act, the Freedom of Information Act, and the Family Rights to Privacy Act. No doubt this sounds familiar to many readers. On the one hand, we are assured in our hypothetical policy analysis that the policy under study guarantees legitimatization; on the other hand, we are reminded that there are likely to be many confusing and/or competing provisions. Added to the mandate for maintenance of confidentiality is the heavy demand for accountability—the requirement that each agency provide adequate and timely information to its source of support, attesting to the fact that funds are used appropriately.

c. Targets and Clients of Concern

The targets of concern in confidentiality policies are generally limited to the providers of services—the caseworkers, clerical staff, and administrators who represent the agency in community situations are the targets of this policy. It is their behavior that is delimited by the policy's intent. Our policy analysis, then, should ensure that each of the provider groups has been adequately oriented and supervised with respect to the policy. Do new staff receive adequate orientation, not only to the letter of the policy but to the spirit and function of the principle of confidentiality? Do administrative staff have proper procedures in place, such as security and availability of files and proper and effective client release of information procedures? Does the board of directors have a workable hearing procedure when grievances or alleged violations of the policy take place?

There is no uniform provision in each of the relevant statutes regarding the question of privileged communication of social service personnel. The child abuse legislation, for example, mandates reporting by social workers of suspected child abuse but not of adult abuse under the adult protective service legislation. The law in our hypothetical situation grants immunity for breach of confidentiality in reporting suspected child abuse. Other pieces of legislation do not provide for privileged communication by social workers, but some protection is afforded some categories of licensed psychologists and psychiatrists.

While the identity of the targets of the policy might be clear, the identity of the client systems (i.e., those systems *on whose behalf* change or services are sought) is not quite so clear. This is perhaps due to the variety of legislation that legitimates confidentiality practices in the various programs. We see the rights of parents, children, and of the public to know how, and even, in some instances, to whom, some services are provided. Our analysis here, then, would necessarily have to focus on the manner and extent to which the legal and ethical provisions for confidentiality are satisfied by internal policy and procedure. For example, in order to meet the expectations of the mental health code and mental health funding sources, we could examine the materials and procedures of informing clientele at first contact with the agency exactly what their rights are in the area of confidentiality, and what clients might do in situations where they have concerns about confidentiality practices. Here we would need to examine procedures and determine how the policy is communicated and/or explained, how "informed consent" for the release of information is determined and by whom, what forms were developed and how adequate they are, and, thereby, undertake some "policy audit" of these practices and materials. These types of procedures and materials would likely need to be reviewed for each of the agency's programs in regard to each relevant piece of legislation and for each funding source.

The most obvious benefit accrued to the client group as a result of the policy is the freedom to share relevant information in the interest of problem solving. Clients are reasonably assured that sensitive personal information can be shared with agency staff for the purpose of obtaining help or some service without their being embarrassed or having disclosed such information to unauthorized persons. For the staff-member-as-target, the policy gives a guide for action, and gives legitimization—provided by law, the courts, and the CSO board of directors—to a central value held by the workers' professional association. Here we have a mixture of mutually supportive self-interests.

d. Eligibility

Generally speaking, eligibility is not a question for this policy, because it is universally applied to all of the agency's clientele and staff. However, it should be noted that clients do, in a sense, disqualify some information for protection, depending upon the particular legislation and the particular information. For example, the agency does not technically need to formally obtain release of information on each incident of information-sharing with other mental health funded agencies in a mental health funded client situation. (This technicality exists because of the state attorney general's ruling that the county's mental health director is the "holder of the record.") However, the worker is not precluded from explaining to the client the reasons for sharing information, the conditions and time limitations placed upon sharing that information, and so forth. Furthermore, the worker cannot unilaterally declare *all* information to be eligible for confidential treatment inasmuch as information regarding commitment of a felony, for example, is exempt from coverage. In some states, minors cannot expect complete confidentiality in all situations requesting services (e.g., seeking information regarding family planning or contraceptives) though, at this writing, the status of this legal principle is now being debated in many quarters.

e. Effect upon Maintenance, Change, or Control

Hence, the policy may be said to perform system control, as opposed to system maintenance or system change functions. The policy provides a mandate primarily for the providers of services.

f. Explicit or Implicit Theories

The explicit theoretical basis of the policy arises out of the constitutional provision that citizens have a right to privacy in their persons and their papers, by essentially providing that this fundamental right shall be protected in the policies and practices of all forms of social interaction. The theory behind the problem would appear to be three-pronged: (1) confidentiality is a cornerstone of professional ethics and must be honored unequivocally; (2) clients cannot be assisted when secrecy is not assured; and (3) the integrity and reputation of the agency cannot be maintained when staff do not protect confidentiality of client information. The appropriateness of the policy to the problem, then, can be seen in both ethical and pragmatic terms. The strategy for implementation of these policy goals supports the constitutional and statutory rights of individual citizens, the legal bases of the social system, and the fundamental rights of individuals as persons.

The implicit social treatment theories underlying this policy are related more to the presumed beneficial effects of the trust relationship between the provider and receiver of social services necessary for effective help to be given. Inherent in the confidentiality principle is the idea that the rights of the individual or group are protected while, at the same time, the helping relationship is built upon the assumption that the recipient of services is free to disclose any and all information thought to be pertinent to problem resolution. The provider may give assurances that disclosure of that information will not occur. As noted above, however, these complete assurances cannot always be guaranteed, as, for example, in the case of suspected child abuse or of information regarding impending harm to another citizen. Consequently, a theory of sound social practice is frequently in conflict with socio-legal expectations.

The analyst will need to determine, then, the extent to which staff are well informed about the reality and the management of this dilemma. The policy analysis can be helpful in identifying any existing disparities and can be beneficial in developing remedial materials or procedures for staff and clientele.

As an overall approach to helping clients feel a sense of trust and confidence in the agency and its staff, the policy puts the matter to a stiff test. In choosing the vehicle of confidentiality, the agency asks the client to take a high risk: to share meaningful secrets about his or her personal life with people he or she likely has never before known. On the other side, the agency stakes its own reputation on the presumption that it can deliver on its promises (which, by the way, is reason enough for the agency and its staff not to make false and unlimited promises about its ability to maintain secrecy at all costs and in all circumstances).

In terms of organizational strategy, the agency has taken the most conservative of approaches by formalizing the movement of information about clients from one program to another, even within the agency. As the CSO policy statement indicates, the agency has even noted in its policy manual that persons thought to be aggrieved have a right to redress. Consequently, the agency has made not only a commitment to deliver on the promise of the policy but has provided assurances that, lacking such delivery, the client will be assured the right to redress. The analyst would do well to examine those complaint and grievance procedures to see that they function adequately and have been used properly.

g. Topography of the Policy System

The conceptual map of system components and system interaction is rather crowded and complex in the case of confidentiality. Given the variety and nature of the legislation that legitimizes the policy, as well as the various funding sources involved, many organizational actors can be seen in the field.

Some examples are the local and state departments of social services pertaining to child protection, adoptive care and Medicaid reporting, and financing requirements; and the local and state mental health requirements regarding recipients' rights and information system reporting. Since much case activity involves the participation of more than one agency or provider of services, there are a myriad of individual and organizational actors, not to mention the clients and the agency staff themselves.

In terms of policy analysis, it would be helpful to determine whether interagency agreements or understandings are in place with each of the above funding components or other contractual partners regarding procedures and expectations in the management of client information. This determination would require review of contract provisions, for example, regarding the right to data, or review of forms providing release of client information, with appropriate safeguards for all parties with whom the agency interacts. These are just some of the possibilities.

h. Contemporary Issues or Historical Antecedents

While confidentiality of client communications has long been a cornerstone of social work practice, confidentiality and privacy, strangely enough, are relatively recent preoccupations of modern America, arising perhaps out of its emphasis in the civil rights area. Invasion of privacy has loomed larger in recent years, in part due to the explosion in information technology and in part to the erosion of commitments to confidentiality by providers of services in a variety of fields.

In our hypothetical case illustration, recent events in the community involving child abuse situations that, on the surface, appear to have been unreported by professionals to the state protective services agency, have renewed local debate on confidentiality practices in the social services. Also, the recent death of an elderly woman who lived alone and refused social services has engendered heated debate over whether agency workers have a responsibility to inform "proper authorities" when someone presumably in need refuses services.

As noted above, we have the two-pronged historical background behind confidentiality: the long-established commitment to confidentiality held by social workers and other human service workers, and the more recent emphasis arising out of the civil rights movement. Contemporary events in the judicial system across the country add another thread wherein the competing interests of recipients of public services (e.g., parties to a contested divorce, or natural and adoptive parents) each have claims to information provided or obtained in the course of the provision of social services.

2. Assess Current and Anticipated System Functioning

Focus on the organizational, administrative, and/or environmental functioning of the *policy system* and the interaction of the components in that system. Attention should be given to both current functioning and system functioning anticipated by embracing any proposed policy changes.

a. State of System Boundaries

Here we need to look at the permeability of system boundaries pertaining to the policy. From one perspective, the boundaries must be impermeable: the strictest of privacy must be maintained and no information should pass over the agency system's boundaries without explicit client permission. From another perspective, client information, for purposive uses to which the client agrees, must be free to move about: the confidentiality system's boundaries must be semipermeable in this regard. Furthermore, the procedures for implementing the confidentiality policy must not be so inflexible that a client's refusal to share information does not necessarily preclude the provision of appropriate services. The policy analyst would do well, then, to concentrate upon the extent to which the policy and its implementation actually shape or condition the boundaries that exist between clients and staff or between agencies. Subsequently, the analyst must make some judgments about the appropriateness of those boundary conditions.

b. Authority, Influence, and Leadership

The recipient rights officer, for example, has the authority to hear complaints and make recommendations directly to the executive director of CSO. The executive director, in turn, exercises leadership by being a good listener and by developing consensus in a model of shared decision making with administrative staff. Consequently, once policy is made, it is generally widely supported. The task of the analyst here is to be assured that the consensus model of leadership does not adversely affect, or somehow benignly squelch, negative feedback from clientele. Given that assurance, the policy would appear to have broad support, with appropriate leadership given by the influence elements within the agency.

c. Patterns of Communication

The nature of confidentiality policy and the maintenance of privacy gets to the very heart of communications and communication patterning. In the administration of this policy, however, appear two types of communication patterns. One could be characterized as the flow of information pertaining directly to individual clients for the purposes of case management or client services management. The other relates more to reporting and providing information about clients in the aggregate to funding or sponsoring groups. One could almost say that for every dollar that comes in, a report element goes back out.

Communication, then, could be said to be bilateral in either instance. Ironically, confidentiality generates a bilateral flow of communication, as opposed to the stereotyped image of the secret unilateral flow of information. Thus, in a real sense, confidentiality (ironically) tends to open the flow of communication. The task for the policy analyst is to determine whether the information patterns indicate that the information is provided along proper channels, from the right sources, to the right destinations, and in a timely manner—all with the client's proper consent. Where that consent requires implicit or explicit permissions, it is the job of the analyst to determine the means whereby the essential principles of the policy are honored.

d. Strains and Constraints

We said in chapter 4 that information gives order and predictability to a system. The confidentiality policy, with its attendant rules and guidelines, also gives order and predictability to a system. Hence, while a surface view may suggest that more paperwork and rules contribute to disorder, the policy would appear to promise more order, less entropy, and the ability for the system to work more effectively. While the overload of paperwork (e.g., written and explicit releases of information) would appear to produce tension in the workplace, especially when action needs to take place, tension is actually reduced for the client who, presumably, is informed of what is happening by the mandates of sharing information. The task for the policy analyst is to determine the realities of actual and perceived tension and to establish whether, in fact, the policy fosters the reduction of disorder in the service system.

In CSO, each program requires its own release of information prior to such a release to other program units in the same agency. Though not unusual, this is not a common practice in agencies of this size. While the requirement places agency components into competition, so to speak, it nonetheless ensures a greater emphasis upon the agency's commitment to the policy. Our analysis should confirm or challenge the necessity of this practice because, generally speaking, a client may reasonably be presumed to provide information to an *agency* and not to a program or a person. The agency may be said to have ownership over the operation of the service, not its professional or clerical personnel.

e. Resistance to Change

There is no question that the codification and specification now required in confidentiality procedure places the professional worker in a situation of less discretion. Considering that social workers (and others) have held commitments to confidentiality predating the surge of emphasis in this area, they are apt to show some resistance to policy implementation. The analyst should not be alarmed if such resistance is evident but, rather, should consider the extent to which it mitigates against achievement of the policy goal.

f. Feedback Devices

As noted earlier, it is helpful to have built-in monitoring provisions in the policy or in its rules or guidelines. Requiring written and signed releases of information provides an automatic monitoring device because releases are available through a review of agency records. The analyst needs to establish the existence and location of those releases. Another task is to determine the expressed satisfaction or dissatisfaction of clientele with the functioning of the policy, perhaps through such means as client feedback instruments implemented during and subsequent to receiving services.

This particular policy enjoys some aspects of an automatic, built-in feedback device inasmuch as clients can refuse to grant permission to share certain types of information. The policy analyst could, then, have some clues to the extent to which confidentiality is felt by clients to be assured. Presumably, a high rate of refusals, generally speaking, could be indicative of the clientele's lack of faith in the agency's or worker's implementation of the policy. In some situations, signed releases are required to be completed by clients prior to release of information. An auditing of those materials in case records would be useful in the policy analysis.

g. Impact on Agency's Dynamic Adaptation

Here the analyst needs to determine whether the agency has in place a designee person, office, group, or committee with the authority to make adjustments as a result of feedback concerning the policy. In the case of CSO, the recipient rights officer is the conduit for such information and has a direct line of communication to the executive director.

h. Environmental Impact

The agency policy concerning confidentiality would likely not have a significant or outstanding impact on wider community practices because the policy's underlying principles are so much in concert with those of the rest of society at this time. Also, strict adherence to the principles of the policy could lessen the potential for abuse in the area of automated data retrieval systems, data banks, management information systems, and the like. In that sense, the confidentiality policy could help to sustain countervailing values opposing the rise in the management of information for its own sake rather than for support for those who provide and use social services.

The impact on the agency itself should also be considered when analyzing the policy. Communications could surely be said to be more formal and routine as a result of the policy. The effects of this phenomenon should not automatically be assumed to be negative; rather, they should be identified descriptively by the analyst prior to making evaluative judgments.

3. Determine Implications for Selected Values

Focus on the implications for selected values to be used in the analysis or desired in the proposed or desired policy, particularly with regard to the targets and clients/interests affected by the policy.

a. Adequacy

We want to determine adequacy in terms of the extent to which the policy assures confidentiality for individual clients and provides guidance to those individuals who administer it. We also want to determine adequacy from the point of view of the policy's aggregate effects on clientele and providers of services. Some indicators for the analysis are individual client feedback, for example, via systematic feedback from both clients and staff upon termination of services at the agency regarding how well they felt the practice of confidentiality was sustained. Another approach would be to observe or otherwise study the attitudes and behavior of clients at the point of intake to determine their reactions to front-end procedures and information regarding confidentiality. Concerning the aggregate effects upon adequacy, the policy analyst might observe the number and nature of recipient complaints pertaining to confidentiality matters and/or obtain staff comments regarding problems in administering the policy as it might affect, for example, the timely flow of information or the quality of helping relationships.

b. Effectiveness

The assessment of the policy's effectiveness should be based upon the extent to which the policy achieves the desired effects of client trust, privacy, and confidence in the context of the agency's information management procedures. Again, this would have to be done by gathering the views of clients and staff alike.

c. Efficiency

The question of efficiency might be addressed in the analysis by the extent or degree to which both client and staff efforts are allocated in pursuit of the policy goal and in the policy's administration. Some indicators might be the extent to which both client and staff efforts are allocated in pursuit of the policy goal and in the policy's administration. Some indicators might be the extent to which services were or were not provided in a timely manner as a result of the policy's implementation. In this case, CSO has had some complaints from clients, agency staff, or other agencies regarding cooperative services not being provided in a timely manner as a result of the policy. While some agencies have tried to deal with this problem by asking clientele to sign blanket *a priori* release of information approvals, this is not legal under some statutes and rules and, furthermore, the approach is not consistent with the principles underlying confidentiality. The analyst may need to determine very specifically whether the problem exists only in certain programs of the agency or under certain emergency conditions, or whether it is a manifestation of differential administration of the policy by different staff members.

d. Impact on Rights, Statuses, and Social Justice

The large number of statutes, administrative rules, and guidelines surrounding the issue of confidentiality give ample evidence that client rights and agency responsibilities have been codified to a great degree. This growth in legislation and regulations has led to new statuses ascribed to the client population and has given agencies the responsibility of specifically ensuring the protection of privacy—the policy cannot be taken for granted. The analyst needs to confirm this formalization of rights and responsibilities through observation of the management of client records, conveyance of management data, and listening to verbal manifestations of commitments to the policy.

The uniformity and consistency of policy implementation would, in the main, be more assured by having standardized procedures for client release of information in place. The analyst should see whether such procedures, as well as forms and staff training, are in place. Equality of application might be observed by examination of the different staff's practices surrounding the policy. The issue of fairness could be pursued by determining how the agency's own information regarding particular clients is handled in the other agencies with which CSO cooperates. Some indices of equity, equality, and fairness could be obtained, or at least clues given, by examination of any standards review for certification or accreditation undertaken by the agency, because most guidelines or requirements for standards reviews by certifying or accrediting agencies would likely include confidentiality provisions.

e. Self-Determination

The policy does not generally speak to the value of client self-determination, per se. Self-determination, the principle wherein the client has and retains the right to make those choices and decisions that vitally affect his or her destiny, is not generally promoted by the principle of confidentiality. However, the principle of confidentiality in an agency's policy could very well encourage a client to articulate thoughts and preferences that otherwise might not be presumed safe to utter. To the extent that the confidentiality policy enables frank and honest expression, self-determination is also enhanced.

The confidentiality policy also relates obliquely to the question of self-determination when one looks at the other side of the demand for information—the public's right to know where its social service resources are going. The public does have a right to hold the agency accountable, but the agency may in part achieve that accountability by a reporting of services activity. However, the policy does not preclude the individual's right to withhold personal information that is not central to the service provided in order for the agency to satisfy the public's competing right to know.

f. Identity

The confidentiality policy provides to some extent for the maintenance and development of the client's sense of identity in his or her dealings with the agency. This occurs through the policy's underscoring of the rights and prerogatives held by the client as a person in his or her own right and runs counter to the propensity of both public and private agencies to require that forms be filled out and information collected for information's sake alone. Some organizations providing services to the public do not routinely provide appropriate safeguards (or at least assurances that they will provide safeguards) to protect the confidentiality of the personal information provided and obtained.

The policy of confidentiality in information provided about clients and services is bound to impact favorably upon the self-image of clients since their individual prerogatives are not subsumed under unilateral procedures by agency staff or faceless organizational procedures. However, some of this positive impact upon self-concept and identity fostered by the confidentiality policy may be reduced by the manner in which the agency administers the policy, how individual staff workers apply the policy, or how the agency transmits information to other agencies. The client has a right to know, and needs reassurance, that the policy is strictly carried out at all levels. Otherwise, its beneficial effects are undermined.

An additional right, which contributes to a sense of identity, is the client's right to redress, that is, grievance, complaint, or appeal. This right not only informs client groups that confidentiality is valued but assures them that there are certain sanctions to guarantee this right. Furthermore, the client is given notice of the right to exercise those sanctions.

g. Individualization

Individualization is not apparently a consideration in terms of this agency's confidentiality policy. That is, there is nothing in the policy or its implementation procedures that suggests that individualization is either fostered or impeded. As in the case of self-determination, it could be suggested that the confidentiality policy is not inconsistent with the principle of individualization. While assurances of confidentiality do offer some promise that the agency will not treat clients "like a number," the relationship between the two principles is tangential.

h. Nonjudgmental Attitude

The confidentiality policy does not completely embrace the concept of judgments not being made by agency staff about a client's behavior. This is true due to the requirements of most rights-to-privacy and confidentiality legislation or rules, which require that law enforcement officials be notified of information obtained regarding felonious behavior. However, it should be stressed that the confidentiality policy does not actually place the professional helper in a compromising or conflicting position. First, as stated above, procedures for providing informed consent should be routinely implemented. Existence of such procedures would forewarn the client regarding limitations on information that can be shared with an expectation of the maintenance of secrecy. Second, the professional helper is able to maintain a nonjudgmental attitude regarding the alleged felonious behavior. That is, the worker need not attach personal value to any behavior reported by the client.

It may be said, then, that the principle of a nonjudgmental attitude is neither unsupported nor hindered by the confidentiality policy. However, the degree to which the principle and the policy are separate may be somewhat subtle and, while the separateness may appear clear to the policy analyst, that clarity should be confirmed with staff in the policy's implementation.

i. Confidentiality

This is the topic central to this particular case illustration. Confidentiality, the principle wherein the client is assured privacy in the communication and maintenance of personal information, is one of the cornerstones of professional service ethics. However, as noted in our discussion of content elements, this assurance does not cover information regarding violations of law or situations wherein harm may be done to oneself or others. Therefore, confidentiality itself has its limitations and constraints. It is very important that each client is *explicitly* informed of the limitations on confidentiality—that client awareness in this area should not be presumed.

Guidelines and procedures for the policy should give special attention to each detail of requirements for "informed consent." Staff should be oriented in such a way that informed consent is uniformly and consistently addressed with each of the agency's clients.

j. Indeterminateness

The confidentiality policy (and its various sources of legitimation) support the notion that the end states of social systems are determined during the life of social interaction. The policy essentially communicates the meta-message that the client is free to provide information concerning the problem or need, and subsequent decisions will be jointly made regarding the distribution or sharing of that information. This broad characterization has its qualifications, of course, as with allegedly felonious behavior: a client is not guaranteed confidentiality when disclosing information regarding felonious acts. At the very least, the confidentiality policy provides that end states will not be predetermined because of a sharing of private and personal information. Indeed, the question of the use of that information is independent of the sharing of that information.

k. Multifinality

The confidentiality policy would appear to have little to do with the principle of multifinality—that similar initial states may produce different end states. However, one could argue that the confidentiality policy does suggest an environment in which all of the information is encouraged to be put "on the table" prior to making any analysis (i.e., diagnosis or assessment) or before deciding what problem resolution steps (e.g., social treatment plan) might be taken. To this extent, there is a relationship between the principle of multifinality and confidentiality.

l. Nonsummativity

The principle of nonsummativity—that the whole is something different than or greater than the sum of its parts—is consistent with the confidentiality policy in the sense that individual bits of information are actually meaningless until considered in a holistic context. This leads us to conclude that the policy is not in conflict with this particular principle.

m. Morphogenesis

Inherent in the principle of confidentiality is the notion that, given necessary and sufficient information for problem resolution, the client not only can be helped but the policy can provide the genesis of that helping process. This notion is entirely consistent with the human systems principle of morphogenesis— that human systems have within themselves the ability to change their forms and structures. We sometimes give life or shape to this phenomenon by noting that someone is a "new person" after having shared significant information. While this expression is frequently associated with an individual's confession of guilt or sharing of uncomfortable secrets, its application is far more generic. The confidentiality policy offers that opportunity for growth in human structure.

n. The SCRAPS Test

The confidentiality policy does not appear to have any particular implications for issues of sex, class, race, or poverty, inasmuch as its meaning to client groups and application to service agencies is universal. However, it is very important that we make a conscientious review of potential discriminatory factors to help us guard against our own unwitting participation in institutional "isms."

For example, if there is a differential between the socioeconomic class of the recipients and providers of services, we could logically infer that the development of trust is much more difficult than when similar socioeconomic groups share information. In addition, symbols, jargon, and slang that are communicated may not have shared meaning. Therefore, confidentiality is an important element in the development of the necessary trust required in shaping this new and/or infrequent relationship. In the same vein, people who are poor or oppressed may feel they are in an untenable position precisely because of the policies or programs of the institutions represented by the agency and/or professional service provider. Recall the saying that "there is no such thing as a free lunch." Again, the maintenance of confidentiality is all the more important in the development of a trusting and otherwise positive helping relationship.

4. Establish Feasability of the Desired Outcomes

Focus on the elements that make for achieving resolution of the policy problem or the attainment of the policy goal.

a. Legality

As noted earlier, with this particular policy we have legitimacy in constitutional, legislative, and judicial law as well as roots in the ethics of the professional association. Perhaps very few policies enjoy such legitimacy and sanction. In some respects, the administrative rules arising out of much of confidentiality legislation give more specificity for direction (e.g., the mental health code and its recipient rights requirements) than any other new policy governing agency relationships with its clientele.

b. Power of the Policy

Clearly, the power is with the client in this policy because the Constitution, state and federal legislatures, the courts, and administrative agencies are there to ensure the client's rights. Thinking in terms of feasibility, we can look to the administrative structure to implement and maintain the policy, and we can conclude whether or not the structural arrangements are adequate to carry out the various mandates. The mandates are not in question; the organizational and procedural arrangements for carrying them out are.

An avenue for our analysis might be to identify the locations of influence in the policy system and determine whether those individuals or those loci are, in fact, supportive of the various expectations for confidentiality. Some possibilities are the executive director, program heads, the recipient rights officer, those who audit for certification standards, licensing authorities and, of course, key staff workers.

The principle of stochastic processes in human systems—that there is a lawfulness inherent in the sequencing of events—is clearly in evidence with the confidentiality policy. In fact, it may be said that the principle and assurances of confidentiality, as with much of policy, themselves create the potential for a probable sequence of events. This probable sequencing is based upon the trust fostered in the client by the professional person and the agency as a result of observable commitment to the policy. As noted previously, policy itself provides for the sequencing of future events—policy makes life more predictable and probabilistic. The policy of confidentiality sets the tone and increases the likelihood of successful treatment by the trust created in the client-worker relationship.

c. Resource Requirements and Availability

Except for computing the prorated amount of time spent by the recipient rights officer and by agency staff in completing client release forms, informing clients regarding the agency policy, and managing the grievance procedure, it would be difficult to determine the cost of implementation of this policy. However, one may conclude that a very large amount of staff resources have been committed, both formally and informally, to its implementation. One obvious and proper cost is found in orientating and training staff to implement the policy. The analyst has to establish some kind of "soft" criteria of cost, such as anecdotes or estimates of time that could be required to comply with policy expectations. In one sense, the analyst could compute an estimate of the opportunity costs (the costs foregone by not taking action) in *not* complying with the legislative and funding requirements associated with maintaining confidentiality. However, this would appear to be a purely academic exercise since the policy is mandatory.

The accountability side of information management is likely to require more resources than the actual provision of confidentiality assurances. That is, the record-keeping and auditing of confidentiality procedures and the reporting of the information obtained on aggregate client activity are likely to be more costly in terms of personnel and equipment than the implementation of confidentiality itself. To be sure, the maintenance of confidentiality is not trivial. However, the development and maintenance of confidentiality itself is an integral part of the helping relationship, such that it would be impractical to factor out the confidentiality element.

One aspect of determining resource availability is to examine the extent to which staff have been properly oriented and trained in carrying out the technical aspects of maintenance of confidentiality. The analyst would do well to prorate the training cost over the appropriate caseload of the agency to get an estimate of confidentiality's share in the costs per units of service in the agency.

d. Rationality

The policy is rational in the sense that it comes with the support and sanction of a variety of powerful legitimating sources and is consistent with basic American values. Furthermore, the policy is consistent with social treatment theories and, therefore, represents both sound administrative practice as well as a proper principle in social practice.

e. Newly Perceived Self-Interests

As noted before, policies are partly accepted and/or sustained by the perceptions held by key actors that self-interests (of individuals or the groups they represent) can be served—there appears to be something in this policy for everyone. For clientele, increased assurances are provided that their constitutional and statutory rights are to be protected in the process of receiving services. The professional providers are reassured that their code of ethics has the support of law and the board under which they serve. Administrative officers of the agency can be assured that they administer a policy that has the support of the board, the staff, and the clientele—they are not placed in a compromising position. In fact, the policy analyst would do well to frequently ask whether deviations from guidelines and procedure compromise the interests of any of these groups or components in the policy system. That question would provide a useful foil for breaking into the analysis at various points.

5. Provide Recommendations

Focus on the strengths and weaknesses or factors peculiar to the issue and suggested by the data generated by the analysis. At this point the analyst is now in a position to make any recommendations that are suggested by the information obtained in the analysis.

Summary

In Case 1 we examined the multiple mandates of a confidentiality policy in a private, multiprogram, child and family service agency. Here and there we noted the policy's contingent ramifications with the expectations of accountability. Many suggestions for exploration were provided. In real life, the analyst must rely on his or her own creativity and intimate knowledge of the inner workings of the actual policy system. The framework given here merely serves as a tickler and a guide. The analyst must use this guide in constructing his or her own model for analysis and, in the real world of work, that analysis must be augmented by professional experience, knowledge, and sensitivity. Each element of the outline was considered, not in an attempt to force application of each part, but to provide illustrations for use of the outline in policy analysis.

Case 2: Utilization Monitoring and Purchase of Service

Our next case illustration involves a policy piloted by the state which mandates utilization reviews for Medicaid to be conducted by the local county offices. This policy illustration could analogously be played out in a number of similar situations. Given the expanding use of purchase of services by state and private funding sources through contracting, and given the push to install more responsibility and accountability at the local level, this policy allows us to explore a number of issues simultaneously. The issues embodied in this illustration go beyond Medicaid or federal/state/local relationships and are likely found in many intergovernmental and interagency (either private or public) contractual relationships.

Our case illustration is driven by a broader policy—the federal mandate that each state administering the Medicaid program must maintain statewide surveillance and have a utilization control program for Medicaid usage. In our case illustration, the State Department of Social Services (SDSS) has decided, through a pilot program, to employ a policy strategy requiring that the county offices of the SDSS shall monitor and provide safeguards for the appropriateness and quality of all reimbursed services by means of a postpayment review process. This strategy, which we will call the Service Monitoring Policy, has been inserted in agreements between one half of the local county offices and the state funding agency. For purposes of illustration, we will focus only on those aspects of the Service Monitoring Policy (SMP) that pertain to prescription drug purchases. Given the extensive relationship between pharmacotherapy and deinstitutionalization, this policy exploration has other obvious associations with many current policy concerns of human services workers.

This policy has a mixture and variety of client and target groups. It has tiers of superordinate-subordinate relationships and associated and controlling administrative rules. Nevertheless, the policy illustration is not unlike many contractual and/or purchase of service situations in which the policy analyst must consider the obligations of each party to the other and, through the analysis, play out the implications of contract provision.

The utilization monitoring of Medicaid provisions policy is one in which the State Department of Social Services (SDSS) exercised its discretionary authority in meeting federal regulations by assigning the responsibility for monitoring to the local county offices. The state established this strategy as a pilot policy in one-half of the state's counties and, for purposes of our analysis, we focused only on those aspects of the Service Monitoring Policy (SMP) that pertain to prescription drug purchases. The policy requires that the county offices of the SDSS monitor and provide safeguards for the appropriateness and quality of all reimbursed services by means of a post-payment review process. This provision exists in the program and funding contracts between SDSS and the one-half of its county offices involved in the pilot.

1. Identify the Policy Problem or Policy Goal(s)

Focus on the definition or delineation of the *core principles* at stake in the particular problem, policy goal(s), or the specific policy that is to be analyzed. Identification should include the following items.

a. The Policy Problem/Goal and the Policy Statement

On the face of it, this policy addresses the two-pronged problem of inappropriate service being provided to citizens and the inefficient use of financial and medical resources. Put another way, policy goals have to do with getting appropriate services to those who are eligible and in need at an expenditure level commensurate with the level of service needed and provided.

A corollary problem and goal would be the concern over the massive levels of government involvement in service provision, and the interest in shifting more responsibility and accountability for the delivery of services to local levels of government.

b. Base(s) of Legitimacy and Source or Location

The policy statement, legitimated by federal Medicaid regulations under the Social Security Act, Title XIX, is taken from the SDSS Service Monitoring Manual, as follows:

> The purpose of the Service Monitoring Program and Policy is to safeguard against unnecessary or inappropriate use of Medicaid services and against excess payments . . . and to assess the quality of these services. . . . The local agency shall establish a post-payment review process whose purpose is, among other things, to allow for correction of misutilization practices of recipients and providers.

A reading of the section of the manual pertaining to prescription drug purchases would lead us to conclude that the policy essentially has a negative thrust, pertaining primarily to cost containment and misutilization. However, a review of the entire document gives a balanced emphasis to the dangers of the problem for the state's citizens, inasmuch as there are obvious implications for individuals overutilizing drugs without appropriate supervision, as well as other community issues in improper management of drug prescriptions and purchases.

c. Targets and Clients of Concern

In the policy system under study, it is difficult to separate the client system from the target system. In theory, the clients (i.e., the component on whose behalf action is taken) are those eligible citizens who are current or potential beneficiaries of the prescription drug provisions of the program. The targets (i.e., those in whom behavior change is being sought) would presumably be the providers of service, in this case dispensers of prescription drugs. On the one hand, we find the reality of over one-half of the dollar outlays for Medicaid actually going to health care providers, not to the client group, which suggests some confusion in the identity of the client group. On the other hand, the client/recipient group (not the target group) would appear to be the group in which change is being sought. (Perhaps this lack of role identity gives rise to some of the confusion that exists in the program.) We might conclude that the client system in this policy is either the aggregate citizen group called "Medicaid recipients" or even the law-abiding provider groups, while the target system is really a subsystem of abusers within each client and target system.

For the client group, the policy goal is presumably to conserve the financial resources in such a way that benefits will be delivered to those who have proper entitlement. Also, an additional major client benefit is intervention in any process wherein any one person in the client group has become involved in the illegal or medically inappropriate use of prescription drugs. For the provider group (i.e., pharmacists and physicians) the benefits would presumably center around assurances that, given adherence to the monitoring policy requirements, reimbursement will be forthcoming with minimal delays on the part of the monitoring agency.

d. Eligibility

All Supplemental Security Income (SSI) recipients, Aid to Families of Dependent Children (AFDC) recipients, and those on General Assistance are eligible for benefits and are, therefore, encompassed under the policy in the pilot area. All counties and all recipients so covered in the state will be covered by the policy; therefore, the policy may be said to have universal applicability in that regard. This has tremendous implications for criteria of feasibility, which will be discussed later.

e. Effect upon Maintenance, Change, or Control

From an overall perspective, the policy is one of system control in the sense that it attempts to reduce the overuse and misuse of drugs under the medical assistance program and to reduce overall or, at least, unnecessary costs. From a systems change perspective, the policy is aimed at altering the behavior patterns of clients and providers that pertain to a particular client's health status.

f. Explicit or Implicit Theories

The key policy option has been taken by the State Department of Social Services in its decision to transfer the task of monitoring to the local county level. Except for whatever monitoring devices that the state decides to employ, the implementation strategies are found at the local level. The policy analyst would be well-advised to review the features of the state-local contract for the program (or the guidelines published in lieu of such a contract) to determine the local implementation options. Some possibilities might be deviations allowed in error rates or ranges allowed in maximum allowable reimbursements.

A prevailing implicit theory in this policy approach might be that clients need an external control mechanism to help force them to reduce their drug use and change their behavior. However, another view implied by the policy is that professional judgments and intentions of providers may not always be taken at face value.

Another theoretical explanation is that the policy supports a more basic premise—that all public welfare programs exist only as residual programs whose fundamental goal is to help the client achieve independence as soon as possible while using the fewest resources. This premise is contrary to the reality that a certain number of Medicaid recipients will require ongoing care. For some citizens, no amount of control will provide support at a level or in a manner that will effect independent client functioning.

Yet another theory might be that, given the positive political value attached to public opinion that there is sound cost containment in any public welfare program, the policy would, on the whole, be beneficial to the entire SDSS, its county programs and, ultimately, to all recipients of public welfare benefits. The strategy would presumably foster public confidence and wider acceptance in this and other public welfare programs. Furthermore, some professional providers themselves suggest that some clients/patients tend to overuse the system and, as providers, they feel impotent in attempting to create their own unilateral restrictions when, technically, "official" provisions are available. Ironically, these groups support any policy that provides legitimacy outside of their own professional discretion.

Many regulatory provisions have their foundations in the theory that equity is obtained for the citizen entitled to benefits when provisions are uniformly and consistently applied. This assures both the potential recipient and the general public supporting the program that equity is being achieved. A corollary is that programs enjoy continued support when the public is assured that services are provided in an efficient and effective manner and, in the case of monitoring, the agency's efforts at assuring appropriateness and quality of services should develop and maintain public support. Indeed, the client/recipient of services also desires reassurances that services are appropriate and of a sufficient quality.

An overriding theory is that government intrusion in the area of medical care is best only after the professional client-provider experience has occurred. This is manifested in the provision that the reviews shall be conducted *after* the point of payment, which suggests respect for the inviolateness of the client-provider relationship.

g. Topography of the Policy System

The conceptual map of the policy system is, of course, heavily populated and complex. There are the various levels of government agencies with obligations and interests, from the federal down to the local levels. In addition, there are a large number and variety of professional associations and provider groups, contracting agencies, client advocate groups, citizen tax abatement movements and their associated groups, welfare watchdogs, and so forth. Given the formal and complex nature of intergovernmental obligations and expectations, the auditing apparatus itself is demanding, especially since the policy involves extensive amounts of funding, encompasses one-half of the entire state and its counties, and revolves around the very salient issues of accountability and appropriate medical care.

h. Contemporary Issues or Historical Antecedents

There are many issues embedded in the question of control of distributing and paying for prescription drugs (and many other health care procedures, for that matter) through public programs. Health professionals in the service system (in this case, the state) have expressed concern regarding misuse of the Medicaid provisions concerning prescription drugs. Some clients may be harming their health by overuse of certain drugs (even to the end result of fostering addiction or complicating health problems). Authorities have some suspicion of criminal behavior, with reports that drug purchases by Medicaid clients have been made for profit. Certain drugs have been singled out as being especially subject to misuse or abuse.

Another issue, as one might expect, is that any attempt to control the management of a medical procedure, including the prescription and/or administration of drugs, runs the risk of the provider agency coming into conflict with the client's personal physician or clinic. Thus, we hear the cry of "governmental interference in medicine." (This, of course, could as well apply to the "intrusion" of any social agency into the professional relationship, not only in health care but in other areas as well, e.g., client-attorney, tenant-landlord).

Then, of course, there is the issue of cost control. Public welfare programs of an income maintenance nature, whether by cash or in-kind devices, tend to be under constant scrutiny for cost control.

Finally, there is the baggage associated with any suggestion of "drug abuse" and all its attendant fears. While misuse of a prescription drug provision may have nothing at all to do with drug abuse *per se*, the two issues become intertwined and provide a political backdrop for the policy analyst to take into consideration.

Medicare and Medicaid provisions of the Social Security Act have been in existence for over twenty-five years and, as is well known, the expenditure levels have increased geometrically, as have charges of abuse of the system. These realities tend to belie the fact that the program has tremendous value to a great many citizens in need.

The program has seen, along with other "quality assurance" and surveillance thrusts in public welfare, a shift in accountability from the federal government down to the states to the local levels of government. This is the point at which we are now engaged with this policy. In this situation, the state is obligated to control the utilization of services with post-payment reviews—a task that has been delegated to the local levels.

2. Assess Current and Anticipated System Functioning

Focus on the organizational, administrative, and/or environmental functioning of the *policy system* and the interaction of the components in that system. Attention should be given to both current functioning and system functioning anticipated by embracing any proposed policy changes.

a. State of System Boundaries

The policy results in much tighter or relatively impermeable boundaries in providing access to prescription drugs and physician visits. The boundaries allowing for interaction have been tightened by reduced discretion of the client group and by a more active "filtering" role by the local monitoring agency. The mechanism of requiring prior authorization through a voucher has served as the primary vehicle to tighten these boundaries, and the local monitoring requirement has, at least until proven otherwise by the pilot, sealed the gatekeeping function. Given that many of the eligible clientele also have, on the whole, limited transportation options available to them, access to the system is further limited by the voucher requirement. Given that few staff workers in the counties "cross the boundaries" by making home visits, access to the system is more constrained. This fact may run contrary to the overarching policy goal of providing appropriate service to those citizens who are in need. The policy, then, could possibly achieve an unintended effect; thus, systematic monitoring of this aspect of the policy should be developed via the analytic process.

b. Authority, Influence, and Leadership

The policy maintains a hierarchical patterning of authority (i.e., the right to take action) in that each level is accountable to the next *higher* government level. However, while the power of authority over the next *lower* level tends to be the same for each level, the power of influence differs. Defining influence as the actual exercise of power, influence behavior is necessarily constantly exercised by the local county agency in order to meet its responsibilities. The higher the level, the less is demanded of affirmative influence action, which is entirely the point of passing on responsibility to the lower levels of government.

This allocation of influence also affords an opportunity for the local monitoring agency to provide leadership in its own county by the way it sets the tone for exercising its responsibility. The policy analyst would do well to examine the procedures used to implement the policy, since clues to the nature of those procedures will be found here. For example, the analysis could determine whether the procedures or guidelines encourage proper and appropriate distribution of services to those entitled to them. The leadership of the monitoring agency may instead be characterized by negative or exclusionary gatekeeping behavior that discourages service utilization. In either event, the monitoring agency's style of leadership sets the tone for the overall system's orientation to providing services, and the analysis should bring this to light.

c. Patterns of Communication

On the one hand, it could be said that communication between recipients and their physicians would be reduced since, presumably, the requirements of a voucher for a physician's visit would constrain contact between patient and physician. On the other hand, if clients actually do obtain prescription drugs without their physician's assistance, then adequate communication would not be occurring. In fact, it could even be argued that those clients who actually experience a medical condition needing pharmacotherapy would have a propensity to contact and communicate more fully with their physicians. Again, however, this requires an aggressive and articulate client/patient and also presumes the availability of a physician with a propensity to listen.

The increased caseload activity required by prior voucher authorization is likely to create tension in the client-caseworker relationship as the caseworker's ability to handle an increased caseload is strained. This, of course, also has implications for the analyst in terms of the feasibility of the program.

d. Strains and Constraints

Tension in the overall system is likely to be created by increased demands upon the client to pursue necessary services for the casework providers, the monitoring group, and the pharmacists and physicians who will need to keep a paper trail of their transactions for the pilot project. Some clients may choose (or be forced) to start paying some of their physician and prescription bills themselves because of their inability to come to the local office to obtain a voucher or communicate their needs adequately. This could result in a reduction in their spendable incomes in other necessary areas of their budgets and create additional unwanted and unintended tensions.

Due to lack of information and/or preparation about project billings under the pilot policy, some providers may provide services to clients without having the necessary vouchers and, therefore, not receive authorization or Medicaid reimbursement. This could create tension not only between the provider and the service and monitoring agency but also between the client and all elements of the system.

Presumably, however, an important outcome criterion in the policy evaluation would be less variety and more uniformity within the counties participating in the pilot. Also, if one could argue for more efficiency in the overall system as a result of the policy, one could also demonstrate that the policy enables the system to perform more work and provide more overall benefits, and prove that the policy did not foster entropy in the system.

The point of greatest constraint between the various components of the system would likely fall upon the client and any component with which the client interacts. In other words, the client would feel the more negative effects of the policy in terms of relations with providers (caseworkers, pharmacists, or physicians). While caseworkers, pharmacists, and physicians would also be likely to feel the negative effects of this policy in their client relations (assuming that the resource pool will *not* increase while the client pool *will*), there will be other clients with whom these providers will have the opportunity to interact. Thus, providers may remain active participants in the system while the client group may not.

e. Resistance to Change

The key element of change is primarily in the shift in locus of responsibility to another governmental level. While there might be some resentment regarding the new responsibility, there is little likelihood that significant resistance will be manifested, because the sanctions for the local level would be too severe. Both the client population and the monitoring agency would suffer due to reduced funding. This is characteristic of "quality assurance" programs that focus on cost controls.

f. Feedback Devices

Thinking in organizational terms, we would have to look at the timeliness, accuracy, and utility of the data reported to the central state office *and* its flow back to the local agency responsible for monitoring. The monitoring data needs to be obtained and exchanged between each level, and plans are needed for corrective action in ways that both appropriately meet client needs and properly distribute agency resources. We should also look at the effectiveness of the communications between the monitoring agency, the clients, and the providers potentially affected by any adjustment in service provision.

Feedback is built into the policy in the sense that, as a monitoring device itself, the policy assumes that deviations from the desired policy goal of reducing misuse will be identified and corrected by the local regulatory activities. The very nature of the policy is permeated with the feedback and corrective-information features of the regulator intent—from the federal level, to the states, and (in the case of the state in our example), down to the local county level. Printouts showing clients' physician visits, drug usage, and emergency room use will be maintained in the state central office and shared with the local offices. A requirement of client authorization by means of a voucher form obtained before going to a physician or getting a prescription filled or refilled provides for immediate engagement with the information system and for automatic corrective feedback.

g. Impact on Agency's Dynamic Adaptation

The utilization monitoring policy could effect dynamic adaptation of the system to the extent that the feedback about client need, client utilization, and inappropriate provider distribution of services is used to adjust agency practices. Dynamic adaptation, the organization's ability to appropriately adjust forms of organization, could be a beneficial outcome of the policy. The analysis should search for ways in which the corrective feedback could lead to automatic organizational adjustments, such as incentive systems for providers who provide timely reports to the monitoring agency.

h. Environmental Impact

Since public opinion generally favors restrictions on virtually any public welfare program, successful implementation of the pilot policy would curry public favor; conversely, failure in its implementation could further erode public confidence. The policy poses certain risks in this regard because, given the reduced levels of public funding and the danger of not having enough staff resources for implementation, the policy leaves much to chance.

The policy could also erode the client group's confidence in the local SDSS offices. Local control in this policy instance means carrying out the regulatory function without preempting the state's prerogative of setting the goals and the guidelines. Except for the actual review of the particulars through staff investigations, local control essentially consists of making recommendations and giving advice to the applicant or client. The applicant/client must provide proof that his or her health needs warrant a drug prescription and that physician visits are not excessive. Consequently, the client may begin to see the county staff as less of a provider of services and more of a gatekeeper for state resources.

3. Determine Implications for Selected Values

Focus on the implications for selected values to be used in the analysis or in the proposed or desired policy, particularly with regard to the targets and clients/interests affected by the policy.

a. Adequacy

Aggregate adequacy is not lacking in this policy, because the entire state population of service recipients and their providers are presumably covered. However, the ability of the policy to provide for adequate coverage is very difficult to determine in our analysis. The adequacy of appropriate and sufficient coverage is a highly individualized matter for the recipient and, of course, adequacy is a subjective matter when left to the individual discretion of those who prescribe drugs. In our analysis, it would be necessary to review any studies available on the relationship between different medical conditions and average quantities or dosages. Again, because only normative conditions would become apparent, only aggregate adequacy in coverage would be estimated, and only approximations would be suggested for individual adequacy.

b. Effectiveness

The effectiveness of the policy might be determined by samplings of error rates in inappropriately filled prescriptions, the number or nature of alleged or proven fraudulent charges, self-reports from the client population about whether the policy achieves its desired effects, or other means. The analyst should consider field studies involving clients and providers as well as reviews of secondary data in the analysis since the policy's implementation leaves so much to judgment and the partly political application of the criteria.

c. Efficiency

The question of efficiency might be approached by making benefit/cost comparisons of the alleged rate of inappropriate use of particular drugs compared to the frequency of client complaints or appeals, or to the costs incurred in follow-up investigations. The latter approach could also be based on some sampling approach to gather data. The client feedback approach is fraught with considerable danger, however, because of the reliance on a clientele that is vocal, articulate, mobile, and willing and able to register their own concerns. However, this could be overcome in part by an outreach program not only to clients but to others of significance in their lives.

d. Impact on Rights, Statuses, and Social Justice

It is difficult to determine equity (i.e., that persons in similar circumstances are treated similarly) in the absence of a thorough familiarity with standards and guidelines used to implement the policy. Standards delineate the policy objectives in the course of implementation; guidelines provide some clues as to whether those standards are being properly adhered to by the means selected. The analyst would have to become familiar with the guidelines and obtain some evidence that they were systematically applied in the field in order to make any inferences regarding equity. Furthermore, the question of equity runs straight into the matters of individualization of treatment and the prescription of drugs. Therefore, the question is not easily resolved.

Equality is more likely to be assured, but only if the policy is administered uniformly and consistently throughout the state. The analyst could make some inference regarding equality in application if the guidelines are clear and widely published. Another technique might be to determine whether adequate in-service training has been provided to the staff who administer the service and/or conduct postpayment reviews. Yet another approach of value for the analyst might be to determine whether reports of alleged misuse or abuse occur disproportionately throughout the state.

Fairness, wherein persons are thought to be dealt with equitably as a result of the policy, could be determined by such measures as studying the nature of grievances and complaints or, perhaps, determining the extent to which persons had been allowed particular benefits only to have those benefits removed without apparent cause. (Again, this determination would depend on a vocal and articulate group.) In the latter instance, criteria for "just cause" would have to be established and applied case by case in at least an adequate sample.

From the perspective of the client group, they are given no choice whether they wish to participate in the policy pilot. Consequently, their rights appear to be constrained, if not violated. While the responsibility for accountability continues to be left with the state, according to federal regulations, the state's utilization review policy shifts more of the implementation responsibility onto the local providers of Medicaid provisions (in this case, dispensers of drugs). Yet there are no commensurate rights allocated to the localities as a result of the shift in these responsibilities. In fact, the localities actually take on more of the role of a regulatory agency. For the purposes of policy analysis, the analyst could simultaneously focus on two levels. The first level could be a search and identification of what new rights or entitlements the locality and the local agency might have due to a shift in responsibility. The second level would be a determination of the extent to which the local provider agency and its staff are able to undertake the new regulatory function. This may entail plans for staff development, for example.

e. Self-Determination

The policy suggests far less opportunity for self-determination, since the recipient of prescription drugs would undoubtedly enjoy less autonomy in utilization as a result of closer scrutiny by the provider agency. Prescription drug purchases under Medicaid (as well as visits to physicians and other treatments) would be monitored at the county office level. Furthermore, there would likely be a reduced incidence of clients taking the initiative to seek voluntary or preventative medical care because the monitoring agency would tend to discourage such use of the medical care system. Consequently, the criteria for "success" would differ for the client components and the provider components in the use of the medical care system.

As with most regulatory policies or rules, the self-determination of the subjects is reduced or constrained. Individual clients *do* retain the right to share in decisions about their receiving services. However, their ability to take unilateral action on a matter such as getting transportation to the office to obtain a voucher could preclude their ability to exercise self-determination. Our analysis could conclude that the clients are not actually restricted from receiving any benefits to which they are not entitled, but our content analysis has shown that, given other limitations placed upon people who are poor, the constraints on choice are likely to be compounded.

The professional providers of prescriptions and prescription drugs will of course, be constrained in the exercise of discretionary judgment. Such constraint will be especially true of the prescribing physician; the local agency will not have the authority to overrule medical decisions, but the physician's decision will be subject to scrutiny, perhaps engendering a caution not previously present. On the more positive side, however, the policy provides for a *post-payment* review. This is important to note in that the regulatory arm of the agency will not intrude at the time of the original professional decision nor at the point of the provision of services.

The state's allocation of the monitoring responsibility to the local agency has left little choice for local self-determination regarding this particular provision. (Not included in this narrow focus in our analysis are constraints on client self-determination caused by the limited number of service providers who are willing to take Medicaid patients.)

f. Identity

We can consider the impact of the policy on the self-image or identity of the client group, the target group, and the county agency itself. The reader would likely agree that the primary purpose of a review of values should be to determine if the policy or the organizational behavior has implications for ethical commitments to the client group. However, this particular policy, given its triad of components, provides opportunity for a more extended analysis.

The client group—on whose behalf the action is taken (in this case, the recipients of services)—would not be affected, because federal regulations require utilization monitoring, regardless of the level of government performing the task. However, the practical reality is that monitoring, given adequate funding and staffing, is likely to be more frequent and perhaps more thorough when carried out at the local level. In terms of client identity, then, the client is cast more in the role of a subject of investigation. He or she is not so much a citizen entitled to a service as a claimant to entitlements subject to scrutiny. Aside from the fact that the policy satisfies the public's need for accountability, its net impact on the client group is likely to be adverse in terms of their feelings of worth and dignity. Much depends, however, on the manner in which the policy is implemented and the nature of the monitoring relationships directly impacting upon the client group.

From another perspective, the analyst could argue that the policy enhances the self-identity of the client group. Because the policy goal is to provide safeguards for the appropriateness and quality of all reimbursed services, it could be argued that the policy supports the client and implicitly views him or her as a citizen who is entitled to quality medical care. In this sense, the policy has a positive effect upon client identity.

The target group—those who are the targets of the action to be taken—consist of the providers of services, such as pharmacists who dispense prescription drugs, and the physicians who see the client group and write the prescriptions. By implication, the professional discretionary judgments and ethical or administrative practices of that group will be called into question. Consequently, aside from the benefit of maintaining public faith in the functioning of the services system, the policy would likely have a negative effect by challenging the integrity of the provider target group.

For the local agency, the new role of regulator has definitely been established—in addition to the extant role of services facilitator. The proper conduct of this new role by staff and the local agency as a whole would require commensurate orientation and training of both field and administrative staff.

g. Individualization

The principle of individualization should not be challenged or threatened as a result of the policy. The client will likely be individually assessed in terms of medical needs by the attending physician and the prescription would be filled appropriately by a pharmacist of choice. Some limits would likely be placed upon the client due to standardization of services available or the constraints engendered by limited fee schedules. However, these features are limitations put in place by the Medicaid program in general and not by the particular provisions of the utilization monitoring policy.

h. Nonjudgmental Attitude

The policy does not appear to threaten the ethical principle of the maintenance of a nonjudgmental attitude toward the client. The policy mandates a review of the appropriateness and quality of all reimbursed services. It does not suggest that any judgments be made regarding the appropriateness of the motives or behavior of the client as an individual or group.

i. Confidentiality

On the face of it, the policy of utilization monitoring should not impact on the principle of client confidentiality. However, the analysis should caution us that, given more involved staff actors and more intrusion into the services relationship, the risks to the maintenance of confidentiality are greater. As a result of the policy, there will be forays, investigations, and people participating in events surrounding the provision of public services to citizens. More information will be collected, stored, recalled, analyzed, and reported, and the agencies involved will need to take additional security precautions.

However, from a technical perspective, the client's rights to confidentiality are not breached by the policy. The funding agency is entitled to this use of information as a condition of providing public social services to its citizens.

j. Indeterminateness

The policy seems uncertain regarding the principle of indeterminateness—that the end states of social-problem solving are actually determined in process. On the one hand, the indeterminateness principle seems to be reflected in the procedural aspect requiring that monitoring be effected by means of a post-payment review. This would suggest that individual situations and needs are played out in the client-provider relationships and that monitoring and reviewing take place only after the point of service provision. On the other hand, the policy seems to say, in effect, that the decision about the appropriateness and quality of services would be made after the fact. By implication, there appears to be only one possible end state (though perhaps a variety of relationships in process). The end state is determined by rules, payment schedules, and the like. The provision of services is not viewed as an indeterminate phenomenon; rather, the implication is that there is only one "right" way for proper provision of services.

For the policy analyst, this means that the human systems principle of indeterminateness (if it is to be valued by the agency) will itself have to be monitored in the implementation of the utilization monitoring policy. The manner in which this is done will fundamentally affect the nature of the relationships between the agency, the client group, and the provider groups. In a sense, the tone of the policy's implementation may be set by the commitment to the value of indeterminateness. This tone would be reflected in the agency's reasonable flexibility on the one hand, or rigidity and officiousness on the other. Given the earlier observations about uniformity, consistency, and equity, the policy sets a difficult task for the agency.

k. Multifinality

Multifinality is the human systems principle that a variety of end states can arise out of similar conditions; the obverse is that of equifinality, that similar beginning states can produce a variety of end states. The utilization monitoring policy, being based upon statute and associated administrative regulations, is likely to be incompatible with this principle. Statutes, rules, and regulations tend to demand specificity and standardization. The definition of beginning states, in this illustration, revolves around determination of eligibility. While there are a variety of conditions relating to need for drug prescriptions under Medicaid, the actual identification of eligibility status is specified and does not suggest a commitment to the principle of equifinality. Consistent with this is the fact that the determination of appropriateness of benefits is not a multifinal phenomenon—the range of appropriate benefits is virtually fixed. The principle of multifinality might be more appropriate to the determination of "quality," because of its subjective nature, although no doubt the policy analyst will play a role in developing standards and guidelines for what constitutes "quality."

l. Nonsummativity

The principle of nonsummativity, that the whole is something other than or greater than the sum of its parts, appears to be recognized in the policy. This is evident in that the major elements of the service system in this instance must be included—the client/patient/recipient, the provider(s), and the county agency itself. The clients' needs, the providers' judgments, and the agency's regulatory task must be taken into consideration *in toto* for utilization monitoring to effectively take place, since monitoring is not only of the recipient or the provider. Assessment in the review must be based upon a mixture of criteria involving eligibility, appropriateness of services, quality of services, and, no doubt, the appropriateness of the fee level.

m. Morphogenesis

The principle of morphogenesis holds that human systems have the ability to change forms in process. Nothing appears in the utilization monitoring policy that enhances the county office's ability to adapt its structures or processes as a result of the policy's implementation. Neither is there any suggestion that the condition or behavior of the client or provider groups would change as a result of the policy. Morphogenesis, therefore, is neither fostered or hindered by the policy. It could be that the coercive effects of the policy might alter the behavior patterns of the few who abuse the availability of the services, but there is no evidence to suggest that this is true.

n. The SCRAPS Test

Persons of low income are eligible for Medicaid provisions of any kind, not just prescription drugs. Experience shows us that not all providers of services in various communities have been willing to participate in the Medicaid program. Some have refused because of the level of the payment schedules; others because of the inconvenience encountered in working with large government agencies, and others because of ideology. The utilization monitoring policy, regardless of its positive rationale and effects, would likely place even greater limitations on the pool of willing providers who would make their services available to citizens in economic need. Concurrently, the client group would likely experience more stress.

   The policy analyst would do well to study existing demographic profiles of the recipients of services and determine whether there are any differential characteristics based upon sex, age, or race. For example, there may be a disproportionate number of citizens in certain age or racial groups receiving certain types of services. While such disproportionate representation, in and of themselves, may not be undesirable, the implications should be studied. The analyst may find a propensity to limit certain kinds of drugs to women, for example (as has been noted in some studies in the area of pharmacotherapy), or that certain patterns tend to appear among client groups living in particular neighborhoods. The policy analyst has an opportunity here to identify institutional, albeit unintentional, sexist or racist effects of either the service system or the policy implementation itself.

4. Establish Feasibility of the Desired Outcomes

Focus on the elements that make for achieving resolution of the policy problem or the attainment of the policy goal.

a. Legality

It is clear that the policy has sufficient legitimacy. The benefits available, assuming the client and provider have met all requirements, are provided by federal law; the requirement of monitoring is established by federal rules and published in the *Federal Register*. There is nothing in the federal rules or the statute itself that precludes the states from passing the monitoring tasks down to the local level; the states are still left with ultimate accountability. There do not appear to be any implications for the judicial aspects of legality concerning this particular policy.

b. Power of the Policy

Clearly, in this particular policy, power, in the form of legitimate authority through statute and rule, emanates from the federal level and moves down to the local level. The state has been able to exercise influence in shaping the implementation of the policy by making the discretionary decision to place the task of implementation at the local level. It has been feasible to mandate the policy of service monitoring from the highest level, given the leverage of the grant-in-aid device. So, it appears quite feasible to implement the policy of monitoring utilization at the local level, given appropriate and sufficient resources in staff and logistical supports.

This policy is a prime example of the stochastic nature of social policy—endowing order and predictability to the ordering or sequencing of events. In practice, the utilization monitoring policy provides for more predictability for the recipient of physicians' examinations, prescriptions, and the prescription drugs themselves, because notice is given, *a priori*, that subsequent review will be forthcoming, based upon certain standards. The same holds for the providers of services under the program. The behavior and decisions of the provider become more probabilistic as they become more limited by assurance that decisions will be audited in a post-payment review. Thus, positive or negative post-payment reviews probabilistically affect subsequent behavior and decisions of providers. Consequently, the policy may be presumed to achieve the power desired in most policy— the giving of order and predictability to subsequent events. The policy would also appear to have considerable power due to its ability to cover the entire state and the entire range of both recipients and providers.

c. Resource Requirements and Availability

We need to look at the hard-cost criteria, such as the dollar value of benefits appropriately and inappropriately provided, and the full-time staff equivalents necessary for policy implementation. Softer criteria should also be examined in terms of resources to be allocated, such as any potential alteration in the quality of the relationships between clients/patients and their medical-care providers or the potential impact upon the relationships between the monitoring agency and the medical-care providers. These changes will affect the functioning of the entire delivery system and, consequently, can be expressed as a cost. Will the system relationships become any more or less cooperative or contentious? The tighter the monitoring, the more contentiousness is likely in system interrelationships—this is a cost in policy implementation that analysis should make visible.

Implementation of the policy requires massive amounts of increased staff time, both clerical and professional, as well as extensive expansion of the computerized management information system. Voucher authorizations and authorizations for payment would require systematic review. Each of these elements would have to be integrated with monitoring procedures in the expanded management information system. The analyst would have to integrate whatever has been done to cost-out these increased resource requirements.

Also, we should not overlook the increase in resource expenditures necessitated by the client group. Inasmuch as the policy would presumably require more frequent trips to the provider of prescriptions, and more costs for medical reviews, we would have to explore these and other costs to the client effected by the mandatory utilization review policy.

d. Rationality

The most forceful argument for the rationality of the policy resides in the local level of government implementing what is, ultimately, a federal goal. This is reasonable—given the history of success in placing responsibility for broad social goals in the hands of those who are nearest to the place where these goals will ultimately be achieved. Alternately, it would be unreasonable and irrational to expect a federal workforce to carry out the monitoring tasks.

From the perspective of the state, the policy is rational in that the state's legitimate power over its county offices is being properly used. However, there is some risk that, given insufficient clarity in implementation guidelines or insufficient financial resources, the policy might not be rational. Were these insufficiencies to occur, implementation from county to county might be inconsistent and the state's obligation to provide services equitably would be undermined.

e. Newly Perceived Self-Interests

There are no self-interests for the client or the local office in this pilot policy. It is primarily the self-interest of the SDSS that is served. The mandates of the federal statute and the federal guidelines would be served in either event, that is, monitoring by the state or local agency.

5. Provide Recommendations

Focus on the strengths and weaknesses or factors peculiar to the issue and suggested by the data generated by the analysis.

At this point, the analyst is now in a position to make any recommendations that are suggested by the analysis.

Summary

In Case 2 we have used our framework as a guide to analyze the pilot policy initiated by the State Department of Social Services requiring that mandatory reviews of all Medicaid provisions be conducted by local offices of the department. This illustration is not unlike many situations involving interagency relationships, public or private, in which contractual relationships with another agency require analysis of the obligations incurred in each provision.

While our application in this illustration has dutifully marched through each part of our "Outline for Analyzing Content of Small-Scale Policy," we again remind the reader that an actual application need not include such compulsive recognition of each detail. The outline serves as an inventory, so to speak, of elements in the warehouse. At the risk of stretching the reader's imagination here and there, we have attempted to apply each element of the outline for purposes of illustration and to stimulate thinking. In doing so, we hope to "tease the mind" of the analyst to assure a consideration of some essential value elements in policy analysis.

Case 3: The Homeless and the Mall People

This illustration of the analysis of policy content involves a policy issue touching upon a situation of concern to many individual citizens, communities, and service agencies. It is the social problem of homelessness, which is compounded by the "problem" of what goes on in gathering places in many central cities. In the case at hand, we will look at what is to be done about the homeless, in particular those who congregate in the central city. The analysis is complicated by the fact that there are others who congregate in the central city besides those who are homeless. In some communities, people who congregate downtown are often referred to as the "mall people," "drifters," or "bag ladies." We will also continue with a discussion of this problem in chapter 7 when we apply the outline for policy *process* analysis after introducing the process elements for analysis in chapter 6.

In our case illustration, the community of Rapid River is attempting to deal with the issue of constant complaints from business people, the police, and the general citizenry about the number of "vagrants" congregating around the downtown mall and frequenting the mall's shops. Complaints are also received from citizens who frequent the mall and from many social agency personnel who work with them. Many homeless individuals and families feel that they are often victimized or portrayed as second class citizens and undesirables in the community. They claim that what is considered by some business people as "loafing" or "loitering" is nothing more than harmless recreational window shopping, and what some shoppers call "harassment" is often a gesture of friendliness. While the police have attributed instances of assault and theft, including shoplifting, in the mall area to the "mall people," many such reports are unfounded.

This policy analysis example is seen from the perspective of Frances LaRose, city commissioner of Rapid River. She has received the whole range of complaints and inquiries concerning the issue and is perceived as a commissioner who is understanding of human resource issues in the community.

In addition to the policy proposal provided by Commissioner LaRose, our analysis in Case 3 also considers the complementary approach of providing certain social service supports to some homeless citizens and developing a public education program concerning this policy issue.

1. Identify the Policy Problem or Policy Goal(s)

Focus on the definition or delineation of the *core principles* at stake in the particular problem, policy goal(s), or the specific policy that is to be analyzed. Identification should include:

a. The Policy Problem/Goal and the Policy Statement

A general view of the problem is that there is a dispute over the ownership of and entitlement to the resources of the community; in this case, the downtown mall. The mall is comprised of pedestrian walkways on a closed thoroughfare, enclosed arcades on various levels, a variety of shops, a hotel, and meeting rooms. Like many reconstructed central city centers, it was built and is jointly funded by a combination of private enterprise and city revenue and is perceived as a community treasure.

The problem may be cast in terms of "who has access to those facilities and under what conditions?" This approach to the problem takes into consideration conflicts between perceived rights of some individual citizens—downtown business people and "mall people"—and the rights of the community as a whole. Another view of the problem might be that the city has not adequately provided support services for all elements of the community who use the downtown mall facility. Inherent in the latter view is the question of whether the city, other units of government, or even the private sector is responsible for resolving the problem.

b. Base(s) of Legitimacy and Source or Location

In this situation, we do not have the luxury of beginning with a policy statement. At this point, we can only speculate about what our policy might be inferred to be, or what policy might be desirable. Lacking our analysis, it would be difficult to issue a final policy position. However, given what we all might know about such social situations, we could suggest a few policy *principles* that might be suitable or reasonable. We will use the following policy statement, proposed by Commissioner LaRose, as a heuristic approach just to get the analysis process going.

> It is the policy of the City of Rapid River that all citizens of the community shall have equal access to all public facilities associated with the Downtown Mall; that the civil rights of no citizen of the community will be violated by any policy or procedure related to any activity of any public or private group while associated with the Downtown Mall; and that all ordinances of the city and laws of the State and Federal governments shall be observed insofar as those ordinances and laws pertain to conduct of citizens on the Mall.

Commissioner LaRose begins, then, with principles that would appear to advance the rights and responsibilities of city government, honoring the rights of all parties involved, and simultaneously acknowledging the responsibilities of all of the community's citizenry.

c. Targets and Clients of Concern

On the face of it, the targets of concern expressed in the problem statement appear to be the homeless in general, and the "mall people," in particular. In this instance, these groups are cast in the role of pariahs. However, the policy proposed by Commissioner LaRose suggests that all elements of the community should be the targets of the concern. That is, we see in the policy a concern for the rights and responsibilities of all citizens involved. This perspective, were it to be viable in its political context, should allow for a democratic or generally impartial approach to problem resolution. Nevertheless, the arbitrary assignment of who the targets actually are is a crucial element in giving direction and a philosophy to the policy analysis.

In this instance, the "client" (i.e., that element on whose behalf action is taken) and the "target" (that element who is the object of action) may be considered one and the same. Policy change and interventive efforts would be aimed at all of the citizen elements noted above and benefits would presumably accrue to each of these elements. The desired result of the policy would be for all citizens to be free to frequent the mall area and all merchants to be assured that their community development and commercial success efforts are supported. The various strategies would be targeted to each of the population elements.

d. Eligibility

There is no eligibility criteria, *per se*, associated with this issue, although one could reasonably suggest that there is actually some sort of "admissions" requirement to the mall and its facilities (and, in effect, any location in the city). Issues associated with eligibility are more likely to emerge when and if the agencies having responsibility for various individuals or groups within the mall population develop supportive programs, such as day treatment, an activity center, social skills training, and crisis intervention services. Particularly important would be adequate housing arrangements. At that point, turf and domain issues will likely develop regarding agencies and programs, along with the associated competition for resources. These matters will be examined in detail in Chapters 6 and 7 in our analysis of the process elements of policy analysis. At this point, we are considering the analysis of policy content.

e. Effect upon Maintenance, Change, or Control

The overall approach of the proposed policy is one of strict control of rights-violating behavior, and enforcement of the city ordinances and other pertinent laws. Hence, the approach is essentially legalistic and regulatory. This approach, as noted above, is likely to succeed only if complementary supportive services are provided. Such supports would likely be educational (e.g., public education of merchants and the general citizenry) and interventive (e.g., day treatment services, a downtown activity alternative program, crisis services for acting-out persons, and housing for those in need).

f. Explicit or Implicit Theories

The general stance of the business community—that government should intervene—supports the theory that government is the proper regulatory instrument to manage interrelationships of the city's citizens, at least in the area of central-city commerce. This posture rests on the assumption that the rights of all parties are easily definable and distributable. An opposite view is that publicly supported facilities should routinely be made available for broad public use. This view would not necessarily include indiscriminate use of these facilities, however. Implicit in Commissioner LaRose's policy is a classical democratic theory of government—that all people should have equal rights until and/ or unless laws are violated. In essence, part of the policy task is to come to some clear statement of the policy principles for the situation. The opinion of a city attorney or other arbiter could help in giving direction to subsequent action and policy analysis.

The two approaches to the problem—regulation and enforcement on the one hand and supportive services on the other—suggest very different values in problem resolution. The regulatory and enforcement strategy gives the highest value to social control. Social control is not necessarily a negative or unwarranted strategy. Nevertheless, the approach assumes that the policy goal can best be achieved through legal management and relational restrictions.

The services strategy values the provision of supports through development of individuals' social skills in such matters as taking the bus, engaging in appropriate behaviors in shops and restaurants, and learning how to properly greet others on the mall. This strategy is also aimed at public education— education of all members of the community. The fundamental assumption is that individuals are in need of remediation and that community resources should be made available to meet those deficits.

The two approaches have compatible values, however, thereby suggesting the potential for their combined success. While each is rooted in a different perspective about social behavior, they are complementary policy thrusts.

g. Topography of the Policy System

In drawing our conceptual "map" of the components of this living policy system, we have already located a number of people actively engaged in the issue, ranging from merchants to various groups among the homeless. A number of state agencies and their local counterparts also suggest themselves, such as public welfare, mental health, corrections, senior services, and the schools. The city transportation system and the location of its bus stops are also involved, as are the police, operators of residential care facilities providing homes to many of the mall people and other homeless individuals and families, and, no doubt, the local Chamber of Commerce as well as various professional associations with an interest in the issue.

It might be said that in a physical context, our mapping of the issue involves only the central city, and the mall in particular. However, the fact that the central city is the only logical place for so many people to congregate is evidence of the absence of appropriate programs or other alternatives elsewhere in the city or in nearby communities. It also suggests that adequate resources are not being devoted to helping many citizens who find themselves in the role of "the homeless." Such resources might appropriately be directed to assisting citizens in obtaining the skills, resources, or supports necessary to function in a personally satisfying way in the community.

h. Contemporary Issues or Historical Antecedents

One basic issue involves the control of a valuable resource (i.e., the city center) in the community and the distribution of that resource. No doubt, there are differences of opinion within the community about the various purposes to be served by the mall—commerce, recreation, aesthetics, housing, entertainment, and so forth. A related matter is the extent to which the public is responsible for supporting and encouraging the success of free enterprise, and the public good to be served by that support. Another is the role of city government in regulating how individuals use leisure time and/or choose to relate to other citizens in the community.

From a social welfare services perspective, there are other issues related to the identity and needs of the mall people. First is the question of who the mall people actually are. Commissioner LaRose finds that a large number of the controversial citizens are persons who have been treated for mental illness in the state hospital located in the city and who are not functioning at an optimal level within the limits of their handicap. In other words, these are the "deinstitutionalized" found in so many communities. However, there are many other groups involved. Some of the mall people are adolescents, many of whom are enrolled in school programs but who regularly skip school; others are

school youth conducting legitimate business after school. Another group is comprised of men residing in a large "half-way
house" recently located in the city by the state Department of
Prisons, all of whom participate to varying degrees in job-
training programs in the community. Another group is comprised of developmentally disabled adults who work at a sheltered workshop in the downtown area, shop at the mall, use
mall restaurants, and congregate at the many bus stops in the
mall area. Yet another group is comprised of senior citizens who
use the mall as a place to meet friends. *In other words, some are
not at all homeless.* For many of these groups, the central issue
evolves around the question of whether an adequate system of
supports is in place. A related question is the extent to which
various agencies are responsible for the provision of those supports and the level of resources to be made available for such a
system.

One obvious bit of relevant historical information is the shift
in emphasis from institutionalization to community care for the
mentally ill and the developmentally disabled. To some extent,
this shift is also true of correctional programs for criminal offend-
ers. Coupled with this are years of neglect of programming outside of schools for young people and, except for a few "senior
centers," nothing for independent and mobile senior citizens.

Adding to the mall problem is a recent rash of hostilities
around the state concerning the development of group homes
for former patients of state institutional programs. Recent cutbacks in state services in all areas of government finance have
led to reductions in institutional programming. As a result, dollars have not followed these citizens into the local communities
to provide the financial support needed for community programming. Program planners and government decision makers
have found, on the one hand, that the general citizenry is not
willing to finance services at the levels of recent years. On the
other hand, demands are being made on government agencies to
"do something."

2. Assess Current and Anticipated System Functioning

Focus on the organizational, administrative, and/or environmental functioning of the *policy system* and the interaction of
the components in that system. Attention should be given to
both current functioning and system functioning anticipated by
embracing any proposed policy changes.

a. State of System Boundaries

The boundaries of actual and symbolic access to the mall are effectively restricted for all elements of the system at the current time. Merchants, "mall people", homeless individuals who just happen to pass through, and other citizens do not feel free to use the mall's resources and exercise their basic rights. The proposed or potential policy would at least give shape to these boundaries by opening up opportunities for participation and collaboration.

b. Authority, Influence, and Leadership

Leadership is lacking in present problem resolution and would likely have to come from representatives of key interest groups. The proposed policy would provide legitimacy if leadership efforts are centered on certification and protection of rights. Authority to take other actions would likely have to be the result of joint community agreements. However, the sanction and legitimacy afforded this process by the proposed rights-oriented policy would give impetus to such cooperative efforts. Agencies and individuals having access to such legitimacy and leadership would have to play active roles in exerting their influence on the policy process.

c. Patterns of Communication

Patterns of communication in one sense are unilateral, with some elements of the community telling others that they are "undesirables." There is an absence of dialogue. Social service agencies could play a key role in bringing about bilateral communication and in opening up the closed intrasystem boundaries now existing between and among elements. Public education would perform a particularly significant function in this regard, as would any agency efforts at enhancing individual mall people's functioning.

An important activity, then, would be to identify key modes and channels of communication. Individual "mall people" who play leadership roles in the various groups could be very helpful, as could certain active and influential individuals associated with planning and funding agencies. The city manager's office could play a key role as communication coordinator or convener, particularly with a city commissioner playing an active role.

d. Strains and Constraints

The present situation is not able to tolerate the variety of inputs (i.e., behaviors or attitudes) contributing to the mall environment. This has resulted in tension and increased entropy, or a decrease in the community's ability to function effectively. The proposed policy would provide for more order and predictability and, consequently, less entropy as well as the inclusion of more variety in the mall area. However, the systemic tension will likely continue in the absence of supportive measures and services. While variety may be increased and disorder decreased by a firm enforcement and protection of a citizens' rights approach to policy, without these service supports, tension may in fact be increased by such an approach.

Interface constraints exist to the extent that various elements are placed into competition with one another. In this situation, the clash appears to be over both resources and ideology. From a resource perspective, the mall is a resource and its elements are in competition beyond its control. From an ideological perspective, the clash is over the uses of the mall; e.g., a commerce center, recreational area, meeting place, or bus terminal. Both the resource and ideological issues will have to be negotiated more fully and openly by various elements in the community if resolution is to be obtained. Current policy does not provide that channel. The proposed policy, while it would support and be compatible with efforts to resolve these clashes, will not in itself provide the resolution.

e. Resistance to Change

In the absence of viable alternatives that address all elements, there will be great resistance to change. Lacking any change in supports provided to the homeless—the "mall people" in particular—or in any behaviors that are seen as undesirable, merchants will likely continue to press for restrictive solutions. Without supportive programs and services, the mall people will have no other choices in their search for a "community space."

Other users of the mall are also resistant to change. Continued dissatisfaction could result in shoppers moving their business and entertainment activities to the suburbs or other outlying areas. Continued participation in mall activities will probably be determined in large part by the ability of the mall people and the merchants to come to successful resolution of the problem. In effect, the continued participation of the general public in mall affairs will also be greatly determined by the success of the human service agencies in providing the kinds of supportive services that will resolve this conflict.

f. Feedback Devices

As noted above, automatic or built-in feedback devices are useful to provide monitoring of policy effectiveness. These feedback devices are manifested in complaints to the police, referrals to mental health crisis services, searches for emergency housing, or occasional referrals to adult protective services—all on an ad hoc basis for specific problem intervention. The proposed policy would suggest more police enforcement but not other, more service-oriented monitoring and corrective adjustment efforts.

The feedback device built into the current approach is obviously in place, as evidenced by the outcries from the community, though the self-corrective nature of the feedback is unquestionably ineffective. However, a self-corrective feedback measure is built into Commissioner LaRose's proposed policy statement, in that the principles of citizens' rights to equal access and the protection of civil rights (i.e., of "mall people" and merchants alike) are monitored and corrected through the enforcement included in the statement. Consequently, the proposed policy has promise of including its own mechanism for monitoring and control, a desirable feature of social policy. However, it is important that supportive community social service be made available to all elements associated with the mall if self-corrective feedback is to be realized.

g. Impact on Agency's Dynamic Adaptation

There is currently no office, agency, person, or group with the authority or responsibility to adjust arrangements in the system to make the proposed policy workable. Possible solutions could be the appointment of an ombudsman on site at the mall or increased Police Department foot patrols schooled in human relations. However, these efforts would most likely provide only individual problem resolution, not system-wide adaptation. And the community-wide needs of the homeless would be thereby ignored. Given the diverse nature of elements having controlling and vested interests in mall activities, adaptive efforts would likely have to be made by a variety of agencies and offices, perhaps all coordinated by a central office, such as that of the city manager or a social agency under contract.

h. Environmental Impact

The quality of the downtown mall environment at the present time is one of tension and, at various points, hostility and fear. The proposed policy could lessen some realistic fears and suggest that individuals and businesses receive adequate protections. However, tensions or hostilities would not likely be eased by the proposed policy alone.

3. Determine Implications for Selected Values

Focus on the implications for selected values to be used in the analysis of the proposed or desired policy, particularly with regard to the targets and clients/interests affected by the policy.

This policy problem clearly represents a clash of values concerning the uses of community resources and the determination of what should constitute "appropriate" or "acceptable" behavior in public places. As the reader will recall, there are two policy strategies under consideration in this analysis. The first is Commissioner LaRose's strategy of regulation and enforcement, aimed at protecting the rights of all elements of the system. The second strategy complements the first and includes providing supportive social services for the mall people and public education efforts for merchants and other downtown visitors. Our analysis will proceed with these two approaches in mind.

a. Adequacy

From a perspective of aggregate adequacy, the current approach to the problem is not adequate. That is, right and responsibilities are not clear to a sufficient number of elements in the policy system. From the perspective of individual adequacy, the current approach does not provide sufficient protection for any particular individual. Merchants and individual shoppers alike do not feel adequately served or protected. On the other hand, should each individual's and group's rights and responsibility (implied in Commissioner LaRose's proposed policy) be made clear, the remaining question of adequacy would lie only in the area of regulation and enforcement. The commissioner's proposal implies uniform enforcement.

b. Effectiveness

The policy implied in current community behavior is obviously not effective, as there is an insufficient connection between the goal of open and unrestricted participation or cooperation and the means of regulating behavior. Presumably, the proposed policy makes a direct connection between the means and the end, achieved by integrating principles of citizens' rights to public facilities with the enforcement of ordinances. The efficiency of the proposed policy remains to be seen in the level of effort and resources needed to achieve the goal; the current approach is obviously neither effective nor efficient.

c. Efficiency

If the mall people are to be treated equitably by all citizens of the community, however, some will have to be provided with the skills to function within normative expectations. Service agencies in the community will need to target the development of such skills as appropriate routines when waiting for and riding the bus, methods of properly greeting others in public places, and appropriate behavior in the various shops. Providing people with specific social skills will increase their opportunities for equitable treatment; the social agencies have an opportunity and a responsibility to provide supports to help people obtain those skills. It would also be beneficial if efforts were made to provide some public education for merchants and other people who use the mall, in helping them to understand the nature of the problem and the purpose of efforts to deal with the problem.

d. Impact on Rights, Statuses, and Social Justice

We do not have adequate information at this point in our analysis about particular mall people groups not being treated similarly in similar circumstances (the question of equity). We do know, however, that the mall people and the homeless in general are treated differently compared to other citizens. All citizens on the mall are treated equitably in the sense that there are no flagrant restrictions imposed upon any group wishing access to the mall. However, the principle of fairness is certainly lacking at the present time and would likely be remedied in the commissioner's proposed policy. However, the policy would need to be backed up by other community supportive services, such as crisis intervention or a downtown day treatment or day activity center.

The commissioner's proposal appears, if enforced, to assure the realization of rights of all elements in the community and would likely accord a higher and appropriate status to the mall people. Properly enforced, the policy would protect the rights of the merchants and shoppers on the mall, while not imposing any unfair or improper status on the mall people.

e. Self-Determination

The opportunities for self-determination by all elements on the mall are constrained under the current circumstances. Some merchants feel their freedom to conduct business is restricted by the behavior of mall people. Some shoppers do not feel comfortable in freely moving about. Many of the mall people feel constrained in their movements in the community at large, the mall situation only being symptomatic of the broader community problem of homelessness and inadequate support services for various citizens in need—homeless and otherwise.

The proposed policy provides restrictions on all elements. However, the policy strategy is based upon legitimate authority (i.e., statutes and regulations) and not upon the capricious use of authority or power.

f. Identity

The self-image and feelings of self-worth of the mall people are certainly under assault at present, with some merchants asking for their removal from the mall area and some citizens claiming sole ownership of the downtown mall. Some merchants are losing faith in the city's leadership, feeling that personal investments of time and resources in the central city have neither been properly acknowledged nor adequately protected. Collectively speaking, the identity of the downtown mall as an attractive place for business and recreation has suffered. Community pride has suffered as many suburban citizens refuse to bring their business to this area.

The commissioner's proposed policy relates to the maintenance of individual dignity and identity in that its legislated rights approach treats all elements of the community equally. Development of mall people's social skills would enhance their self-concepts and identity in that more appropriate behavior will likely elicit more rewarding community responses.

The proposed policy hopefully would enhance the self-image of mall people without reflecting negatively on the character of others in the community. The focus on the principle of citizens' rights in the proposed policy obviously has a direct connection to the principle of self-determination.

g. Individualization

The current situation has led to the labeling of a certain category of city residents as "mall people"; this, in itself, constitutes a loss of individualization. As individual behavior and needs are arbitrarily placed into categories, individualization is threatened. Prejudicial attitudes toward stereotyping of some of the mall merchants also exist. Some merchants have been labeled as greedy or uncaring when, in fact, they have made positive efforts to make the mall a favorable environment for all citizens of the community, including the mall people.

The proposed policy would allow for individualization only insofar as individuals have entitlements to legitimate access. The complementary social services strategy, designed to provide housing and other support services as well as skill development commensurate with some individual's needs, would certainly foster individualization.

h. Nonjudgmental Attitude

The present environment provides extensive evidence of judgments being made about the behavior of many people and the motivations of others. The proposed policy would permit no prejudgment of individual behavior unless and/or until such time as an ordinance or law had been violated.

i. Confidentiality

Generally speaking, confidentiality is not at issue here. However, if agency services are not provided discreetly, some clients could be singled out as "agency people." Such a practice would not only be dysfunctional from a programmatic perspective, but would violate clients' rights to confidentiality.

j. Indeterminateness

Both Commissioner LaRose's and the supportive services approach express an indeterminate view of social process. The regulatory and enforcement approach does not suggest a precon-

ceived notion of social relationships and social ends. Rather, the
end states of social relationships would be determined in process and, in keeping with the policy, handled accordingly
should anyone's rights be violated. The services strategy also
depends upon the actualities of social process, through such
means as assessments of individual needs for supportive services, helping individuals to gain control over life events, and
public education.

k. Multifinality

Neither policy approach suggests that uniformity or sameness is
expected in any element of the downtown mall social system.
The multifinality principle—that a variety of end states can arise
out of original conditions—is supported. As long as neither merchants nor mall people are stereotyped and unilaterally cast into
role expectations, the principle of multifinality will be fostered
by the direction of policy.

l. Nonsummativity

The principle of nonsummativity—that the whole is something
other or more than the sum of its parts—could be realized in this
situation if the various elements were brought together. If the
situation is dealt with holistically (as a community problem),
the principle of nonsummativity is more likely to be realized.
That is, each of the key elements will have to make their own
contributions to problem resolution. Both the regulatory strategy and the supportive services strategy foster achievement of
that goal, which means that the ability of *each* element to cope or
deal with the problem will be enhanced.

m. Morphogenesis

The principle of morphogenesis—that human systems have the
ability to change their own forms in process—is not necessarily
enhanced by the two policy strategies. Labeling and demands
by some elements for exclusion or restraint of others would require considerable change in community attitudes. The regulatory and service strategy is aimed primarily at changes in behaviors. However, the community propensity for name calling
and/or demands for exclusion and withdrawal could be altered
if, over time, these same community elements were to witness

the positive effects of behavior change. This view, of course, is predicated on the assumption that changes in behavior breed changes in attitude; the efficacy of this assumption remains to be seen.

n. The SCRAPS Test

This policy problem and its resolution have particular implications for young people, the city's senior citizens, and especially for those who rely upon public welfare, mental health, and correctional services. As was noted earlier, the mall people population includes school youth, men residing in a correctional "halfway house," developmentally disabled adults working downtown in a sheltered workshop, senior citizens, and individuals on aftercare following release from state institutions. While many individuals have client relationships with various human services agencies, many are citizens who are not formally associated with any community organizations. Nevertheless, it is clear that the problem is more of a burden for certain age groups in the community, for those in difficult economic conditions, and for many who possess multiple handicaps in coping with society.

The commissioner's proposed policy appears to treat all of these elements equitably. The regulatory and enforcement strategy is a leveling device. The supportive services strategy is, on the other hand, predicated on the primacy of the majority's way of conducting affairs on the mall. Ironically, the services approach places a greater burden for change on the victims, currently perceived by many as those with the problem.

4. Establish Feasibility of the Desired Outcomes

Focus on the elements that make for achieving resolution of the policy problem and the attainment of the policy goal.

a. Legality

The current situation tends toward exclusion of mall people from the mall area and therefore has no legitimacy in legislative, judicial, or administrative policy. It discriminates against the homeless and other groups with social handicaps. The proposed policy would have legitimacy in constitutional law, state and federal statutes, and local ordinance. In addition, courts have clarified some requirements of access to public facilities and have prohibited discriminatory service to citizens in public places. The rights of citizens on public properties adjoining the mall are less clear and depend on very particular circumstances. At any rate, the legal foundations of relationships are not essentially at odds in this issue. The issue revolves more around exercise of rights and role expectations of various citizens.

b. Power of the Policy

The authority of the law gives a great deal of sanction to the proposed policy, but its power is essentially in its impetus for other efforts to be undertaken. The reality of legal sanction would give more power to the mall people than at present but leadership, rather than raw power, is needed to achieve the policy goal. Influence will have to be exercised by the Merchant's Association, the executives and boards of the major funding sources (e.g., corrections, mental health, and public welfare) and by the city commission and/or the city manager's office.

Both policy strategies suggest a probable alteration in the sequence of subsequent events, to the extent that attempts at behavioral change are successful. Both the commissioner's regulatory policy approach and the supportive services strategy are intended to narrow the range of probabilities of citizens' behavior with respect to the mall. Each strategy aims at channeling or shaping the types of behavior on the mall, one through control and the other through education and/or training. Each generates more predictability and lawfulness in the sequence of social processes to follow, and each supports the policy goal of making the mall attractive and readily available to all citizens of the community.

c. Resource Requirements and Availability

Currently, no extraordinary resources are allocated. The proposed policy would require assignment of more foot patrol officers to the mall and/or more squad car patrols. More enforcement would also require more court or administrative actions by appropriate agencies. The additional human service agencies' support programs suggested above would require extensive financial resources. However, given the cost of doing nothing and the ultimate cost to the community incurred by tension in the mall area, some level of outlay would have to be seriously considered. Resources would be needed for additional enforcement and for supports provided by human service agencies. The relative size of the public safety budget, for foot patrols in particular, would have to be examined. Past efforts to develop the foot patrol concept in the community have looked to community development block grants as the funding source. However, other needs are competing for those funds. In the service area, the move to community care and "deinstitutionalization" has led to the transfer of some state dollars heretofore allocated to hospital inpatient care into community mental health budgets. However, recent state funding problems have strained existing programs and led to cutbacks in service areas, particularly in outpatient counseling services for the less severely impaired. Nonetheless, given the frequent incidences of abuse reported on the mall, mental health funds represent a possible source of support for new programming, as do adult protective services funds through the state Department of Social Services. The correctional system has not generally allocated large amounts of financial resources or staff to support prison-based community placement programs. While the local court programs could be of assistance in developing supportive programs for correctional half-way house residents, state prison officials would have to lend their own support to the local effort.

d. Rationality

The proposed policy is rational in the sense that it stems from generally accepted and legitimate means of resolving problems involving citizens' rights. Its practicality would be enhanced by meshing the regulatory and enforcement strategy with a public education and supportive services strategy. Theoretically, the rationality of the policy stands alone without these additional measures.

e. Newly Perceived Self-Interests

The commissioner's proposed policy will succeed if individuals, groups, and businesses are able to expand their range of perceived self- or group-interests served by the policy. A strategy of cooperation and accommodation by business people in the mall area could return more business activity to the mall area. The Merchants' Association and such groups as the Community Economic Development Corporation are likely to see this possibility but may need some assistance in realizing it.

State funding agencies may be helped to see the economies of supporting successful, community-based efforts as alternatives to public disenchantment with community care strategies. This scenario would likely mean more strains on institutional budgets. A key element in subjecting the proposed policy to useful analysis will be Commissioner LaRose's efforts (or the efforts of her policy analysts) to bring these newly perceived self-interests to light.

5. Provide Recommendations

Focus on the strengths and weaknesses or factors peculiar to the issue and suggested by the data generated by the analysis. At this point you are in a position to make any recommendations that are suggested by the data from the analysis.

Summary

In Case 3 we have examined the problem of homelessness in the situation where homeless people are threatened with exclusion from the downtown mall. We considered a proposed policy offered by a city commissioner, Frances LaRose. We have also considered what complementary approaches to problem resolution might be necessary in the commissioner's proposed approach to the problem. The elements to be considered in the analysis of the policy *process* in this case will be considered in chapter 7.

Case 4: Participation of Birthparents

The participation of birthparents in the adoption process of their child is a knotty problem, both for policy and for direct service practice. Let's assume that you are employed as a social worker in a typical private child welfare agency providing adoption and foster care services for children. Conventional practice has been that one or both of the birthparents (i.e., the biological mother and/or father) are assisted in making a decision for a permanent plan for the child at the earliest reasonable opportunity. In general, aside from making the personal decision regarding adoption, the birthparent is limited to the role of a provider of information. The actual adoption plan and placement is seen as the responsibility of the agency and its staff. However, our agency example, Child Services, Inc., has had a policy in place for two years providing that the birthparent is both encouraged and expected to participate in the planning for the care of the child to as great a degree as possible. The Board of Directors has inquired into the functioning of this policy and we have been given the task of providing an analysis of the "birthparents' participation policy."

Child Services, Inc. is a rather small, sectarian, nonprofit agency that places an average of ten or twelve children in adoption monthly. It is a member of the local United Fund. You will recall that the adoption policy was established by the Board a couple of years ago, with limited concern expressed. As a first step, we decide to look at the agency's *Adoption Manual* in order to find documentation of the policy. (For purposes of discussion, please note that the birthparent is referred to in the singular and as the feminine "she"; the infant is referred to as "he." In actual practice, agencies may give more effort or recognition to inclusion of both birthparents. This should certainly be a factor in our analysis, especially when confronting such issues as participation by the natural father and discrimination based upon gender).

1. Identify the Policy Problem or Policy Goal(s)

Focus on the definition or delineation of the *core principles* at stake in the particular problem, policy goal(s), or the specific policy that is to be analyzed. Identification should include:

a. The Policy Problem/Goal and the Policy Statement

The policy reads, in part, as follows:

> Adoption is an experience which is done with the birthparent and not to her. The agency has a great deal of respect for this expectant parent and her commitment to life itself and her child in particular. The agency sees adoption as an opportunity for the birthparent to experience a great deal of personal growth. The opportunity to grow is enhanced by an atmosphere of openness. This openness enables the expectant parent to anticipate some of the grief and loss experience. . . . It is expected that the worker and the birthparent will together develop a particular contract for how the adoption will occur. . . . Finally, the agency recognizes that the experience of giving birth to a child and releasing him for adoption is a lifelong experience. The agency will continue to be available to the birthparent over the subsequent years and will make every effort possible to provide support. . . .
>
> The putative father has long been neglected in adoption planning. . . . Child Services, Inc. recognizes that pregnancy and adoption

are very significant events in the lives of fathers. Therefore, the worker should make every effort to involve the father in the decision-making process.

b. Base(s) of Legitimacy and Source or Location

The *Policy Manual for Child Services, Inc.* contains many procedural provisions and guidelines, such as the means for encouraging involvement of the biological mother and special methods of publishing notice for the putative father. Furthermore, many suggestions of sound professional practice are also interspersed, such as compatibility of the policy with the development of a helping relationship characterized by trust. Thus, having established the source and the wording of the policy, we have taken the first step in our analysis and identified the policy statement. As noted earlier, we are not always blessed with a policy as a given; in this instance, we had an already established policy as a point of departure. Had we not been given this policy to begin our analysis, our first step would probably have been to give more shape or specificity to the issue of birthparents' rights, study the difficulties involved in *a priori* contracting by birthparents in making adoptive plans, or translate certain treatment principles into policy.

c. Targets and Clients of Concern

On the face of it, the target of the policy is the newborn infant, with the agency acting in the capacity of advocate for the child. On a more immediate level, the target is the birthparent, whose full and enlightened participation in the process is solicited from the policy being in place. Our discussion of types of systems in social services suggests that the child is the client system (the system on whose behalf action is undertaken) and the birthparent is the target system (the system in which behavioral change is being sought). The policy also allows for expansion of the target by providing particular emphasis upon reaching out to and including the biological father of the child. We could also speculate at this point in our analysis about the desired and potential outcomes for the target. A birthparent is likely to feel helpless, vulnerable, guilty, and leery of trusting anyone. The policy is aimed at alleviating these feelings. An obvious possibility for accomplishing the desired outcome is to enlist the cooperation of the birthparent-as-client, using interviewing and other casework techniques to obtain the greatest amount of preplacement information that will assist in sound problem resolution. Achieving the desired outcome depends greatly on the theoretical perspectives upon which the policy is founded.

d. Eligibility

We can only speculate from this example that eligibility is not a consideration in application or implementation of this particular policy. Presuming that the client is otherwise eligible for this agency's services, or this service in particular, the policy under analysis does not affect nor is it affected by the question of eligibility. However, there may be a question of this in some states, for example, regarding the rights of a *minor* child birthparent in an adoptive decision process. Minors have more or less a say in their "eligibility" to participate fully in the decision process, depending upon the state in which they reside, and depending upon the normative behavior (i.e., the informal, unwritten policy) of the agency.

e. Effect upon Maintenance, Change, or Control

Clearly, this policy of parental participation is a departure from the norm, at least for this agency. Therefore, it could impact upon system change, as opposed to system maintenance or system control. As a consequence of this policy, the client population and its entitlements are expanded and the system boundaries are opened more broadly.

f. Explicit or Implicit Theories

Some speculation about and/or identification of the theoretical foundations of the policy under analysis can give clues to the incentives for the policy's existence. Increased inclusion of the birthparent may be founded upon the hypothesis that the birthparent's active participation in the adoption process is more likely to result in a successful and functional separation process for the parent. Another (and not necessarily separate) possible explanation is that fuller participation will bring about more successful placements as a result of obtaining the most complete information rather than making decisions under less clear conditions. The theoretical explanation may be founded upon more fundamental values (which we will discuss below), such as fundamental client rights to self-determination. Releasing a child for adoption may be viewed as an act of love by the birthparent, rather than an act of abandonment, and should (according to theory) be supported in a manner that encourages the birthparent's full and active participation in the adoption process.

g. Topography of the Policy System

This policy obviously expands the typical boundaries beyond the office space of the adoption worker. As the biological mother is more fully involved, those in whom she confides are more likely to be involved in the decision process. Furthermore, the explicit reference in the policy to the putative father broadens the service system boundaries by introducing more actors.

By inference, this would seem to place agency birthparents and the agency itself more into contact and interaction with the community in which service is provided. The more service recipients participate, the more open the agency is to inputs—its boundaries become more and more semipermeable to information and values from the community (i.e., broader system) in which it is located.

h. Contemporary Issues or Historical Antecedents

Ancillary issues in our case illustration should be explored. What is the general mood in the community toward unwanted pregnancies and birthparents placing children for adoption? In other words, how reasonable has the agency's expectation been that biological mothers would not only allow, but actually encourage, prolonged or extensive participation in adoption planning? Another possibility is the question of the likelihood of biological fathers being willing to go against what are probably long-standing community norms and voluntarily participate in planning. Can you think of other contemporary issues that might play a part in such a situation in your agency or your community in a similar circumstance?

Let's also consider what some of the historical baggage might be that accompanies this policy. The first thing that comes to mind is the community attitudes that have existed over the years regarding pregnancies out of wedlock, the propensity toward managing such pregnancies in a shroud of secrecy, leaving of details to "professional discretion," and the presumption of few rights, aside from the consent for release being allocable to the birthparents. The process generally was viewed as the birthparent "giving up" the child. Given these community values, there were probably few opportunities for the birthparents or for the agency's adoption workers to have encouraged or even tolerated extensive participation and involvement.

The analyst should also look to historical events within the agency or the community that might have a bearing on the policy. In this case example, let's play out a hypothetical situation. A major factor in the policy's initiation is that a staff member recognized the need in the past and developed a support group for parents who had released their children for adoption. This effort led to communications and visits with a similar agency experiencing similar concerns for this client group, which introduced outside information.

Exploration of this issue would likely turn up such matters as public debate over the number of school-age pregnancies and the number of students dropping out of high school. Another possibility might be that parent training be provided to adolescents and/or young adults. Certainly a recent historical issue could be community debate over sex education in the school system and how the lack of sex education might be related to the increase in unwanted pregnancies. Yet another discussion might center around pregnancies that occur in the later child-bearing years and the issue of whether expectant parents have the right to plan for the future of their unborn child in their own way.

2. Assess Current and Anticipated System Functioning

Focus on the organizational, administrative, and/or environmental functioning of the *policy system* and the interaction of the components in that system. Attention should be given to both current functioning and system functioning anticipated by embracing any proposed policy changes.

For our case illustration we will use the criteria provided in our earlier discussion. The criteria selected are not cast in stone but are, rather, to be selected by the analyst. Here we need to be creative. Some clues to our direction will be found when we look at how or whether the program's design would encourage or deter realization of the policy goal of birthparent participation. We should also study the actual patterns of interaction among or between those who participate in the planning and placement decisions.

a. State of System Boundaries

The first place to look is the boundaries that exist between system elements—between the two birthparents, or between either of the birthparents and the agency worker or, in the case of "open adoptions," between the birthparent and prospective adoptive parents. Are the patterns of interaction any more or less permeable as a result of the policy? For example, there is a tendency to exclude the biological father from planning in adoptions. Many issues in the birthparents' relationship often go unresolved in common practice surrounding adoption planning. The policy analyst would do well to determine the effects of this policy on the boundaries between the birthparents or between the birthparents and others.

b. Authority, Influence, and Leadership

Every policy that is meaningful has some aspect of power that keeps it in place. The board authorized the birthparent policy and is accountable for it. Internally, one might also observe the extent to which the agency's administrative leadership, in the persons of the executive director, program heads, coordinators, or other significant actors, give leadership in pursuing the policy goals. For clues, one might note how often and in what manner the policy arises during orientation of new workers or in staff meeting discussions, and whether its enforcement leaves a paper trail of consent forms signed by birthparents, interoffice memos, and the like. Put another way, one might observe whether the policy, given its legitimacy from the board, is also associated with its necessary sanctions (i.e., rewards and/or punishments). Are new staff assisted in developing effective techniques for involving birthparents or is such involvement valued by staff in discussions? Answers to these questions offer clues.

c. Patterns of Communication

The impact upon communication is fairly obvious in the reference just made to the two birthparents. The policy mandates an increase in bilateral communication between birthparents and agency personnel, perhaps even involving prospective adoptive parents. The policy also reduces, to some extent, the unilateral gatekeeping power of the caseworker. The nature of the participation policy requires both client and worker feedback and, perhaps, some other outside observational assessment mechanisms (e.g., frequency of appointments or more reports of client preferences as opposed to worker assumptions of client preferences).

d. Strains and Constraints

Our earlier discussion suggested that policies or procedures that generate tension in a system are generally seen as "bad," whereas the introduction of variety sometimes generates new and creative interchange among or between system components. Surely, variety in perceptions and preferences is at least more likely to occur in more democratic or participatory decision-making environments. The introduction of a new participant in the adoption process—the birthparent—adds variety. It might be axiomatically stated that, the more new information is introduced into the system, short of overload, the greater the system's ability to do work. The principle of client participation generates more problem-solving resources. In this case, "doing work" is arriving at a problem resolution. Consequently, entropy (the tendency toward disorder and inability to do work) is reduced by the policy since significant actors are involved in doing the essential decision work.

Another perspective is that, because the current policy adds more information to the decision system, each of the parties might be confronted with more criteria with which to plan and make ultimate recommendations and decisions. While more information presumably leads to more enlightened decisions, it also introduces more variables and reduces the *probabilities* of total agreement in perceptions and judgments. Thus, the policy increases the likelihood of the birthparents not being in concert—between themselves or with the staff worker. This would appear to be one of the costs of democratizing the process, which will be discussed further. At this point, we at least can say that the birthparents' participation policy (as with the introduction of many other policies) may generate more confusion or disagreement in the adoption placement process because more people are participating in the decision processes (assuming that the policy is being implemented to the fullest intention of the Board of Directors).

e. Resistance to Change

The task now is to determine if resistance to the change created by the policy of participation exists and, if so, what form the resistance takes. The more obvious methods are tuning in on staff complaints regarding, for example, the inconvenience of including birthparents, and looking at the differences in frequency or duration of appointments with clients. Some less obvious possibilities could be agency changes in the use of collateral contacts (such as the birthparents' family) as opposed to direct client contacts, and changes in the rates of home visits or appointments out of the office where staff reach out to the birthparents.

f. Feedback Devices

On the one hand, the policy would seem to allow for corrective feedback to enter into the client-worker problem-solving relationship because both parties would presumably be active participants in the release and adoption processes. On the other hand, no provision is built into the policy for monitoring the effectiveness of the policy, individually or in the aggregate, across all of the agency's clientele. We might think that birthparents' participation is effective and appropriate, but nothing in the policy is built in to assure us of that. Procedures should be developed to correct this deficiency.

A key question is how the system is handling both positive and negative feedback in birthparents' participation. That is, do we have any measures or estimates of the extent to which the policy affects birthparents' participation, such as dropout and "no-show" rates, the incidence of voluntary call-backs, and the number of referrals by former agency clients? Are there any monitoring systems in place, such as client feedback during or subsequent to receiving services? We need to determine the extent to which clients, individually and collectively, feel they have had adequate opportunity for meaningful participation, or the extent to which they feel they have obtained their contractual goals or treatment plans. This information could be obtained from both the clients and the agency staff.

g. Impact on Agency's Dynamic Adaptation

Evidence of dynamic adaptation might be found in the extent to which staff orientation or training has been altered as a result of the policy of parental participation. Another possibility is the extent to which procedures have been routinized for the inclusion of biological fathers as well as biological mothers.

h. Environmental Impact

This policy is likely to open up a number of related situations in the agency that will foster increased client participation. Given the new-found role of birthparents in the case planning process, it is not unreasonable to expect that this orientation to client participation will influence other program areas in the agency. This could have implications for greater inclusion of minors in case planning, for full family member participation as a condition of receiving services (as some agencies now require), and for more attention to issues involving informed consent of clients and recipient rights.

3. Determine Implications for Selected Values

Focus on the implications for selected values to be used in the analysis of the proposed or desired policy, particularly with regard to the targets and clients/interests affected by the policy. We will continue to explore the policy of Child Services, Inc. that both encourages and expects birthparents in adoption situations to participate in planning for the care of the newborn child to as great a degree as possible. So far, we have considered a number of elements in our analysis of that policy situation that had value implications. We will now give our attention to those elements for a *values* analysis. Remember that application of each values element in our narrative is meant for illustrative purposes; an exhaustive application of each element may not be necessary or appropriate to all policy situations.

a. Adequacy

One could first ask, "To what extent does this policy accomplish the desired effect of achieving fuller participation of birthparents?" Is there really a reaching out by the worker to the mother or father or does the effort by staff, as mandated in the policy and its attendant guidelines, tend to be perfunctory or routine? What evidence is there that there has been any change in the pattern of participation by birthparents? If that information is not available, the policy analyst needs to devise means for obtaining it, and the regular development of such data may even be one of the recommendations of the policy analysis effort.

b. Effectiveness

Another approach is to study whether the policy of participation has, in itself, had some bearing on increased participation of birthparents or whether some other policy or staff behavior has had that cause-and-effect impact. Here we tend to pursue the question of actual effectiveness, since the desired effect needs to be established in terms of the specific means employed.

c. Efficiency

We also need to arrive at some estimation of the efficiencies obtained by the policy. In this policy, we may want to look at the amount of time and effort needed by staff to obtain the desired level of participation. This is not to say that there is some pre-established level of "efficient" versus "not efficient" participation. Rather, it forces the analysis to make visible the extent to which the means employed in pursuit of a policy goal are maximized with a minimum use of the resources available. This perspective helps to establish some of the "costs" of the policy, thereby flushing out the more detailed criteria of cost for subsequent policy decision making. For example, what is the "price" or "cost" in human terms that is extracted from the birthparent for the effort required in carrying out this policy?

d. Impact on Rights, Statuses, and Social Justice

The birthparent participation policy formalizes client rights and statuses. Even if the principles underlying the policy were already embodied in workers' attitudes and practices, the policy formalizes such rights and statuses. The clients' entitlement to expect certain kinds of behaviors is safeguarded by written policy, as are the workers' methods and procedures in bringing the intended policy effects about. That is, both parties in the helping relationship are given explicit expectations in the event that the approach provided by the policy is called into question.

Furthermore, the relative statuses of the two parties in the relationship have become more formalized, without suggesting that the helping relationship has become any more or less sensitive, accepting, nonjudgmental, or growth producing.

Generally speaking, any policy that opens up the boundaries to participation in the decision process could be considered egalitarian, be it in decisions around one's own direct services or the administrative policies of an agency. The client, participant, or recipient of services thus is seen as having some identifiable rights and privileges that place him or her in a relatively egalitarian position in relation to the provider of services. In the birthparents' participation policy we find the biological parents meeting in group interviews with the adoptive parents to share information. The birthparent and the adoption worker each have unique roles to play in this planning process. Policies achieving participation of the receiver of services may not necessarily result in equity (i.e., people in similar circumstances may not be treated in a similar fashion), because there is no way of telling how different applications of the policy are distributed. However, the principle of client individualization is more likely to occur when birthparent participation is implemented uniformly and consistently, in which case equity is at least a reasonable possibility. Furthermore, birthparents are more likely to be treated fairly, and not equivocally, when they are active participants in contracting for adoption planning and in contributing to the adoption process along the way.

e. Self-Determination

The policy directs the agency to move away from the traditional practice of casting the birthparent into the "giving up the child" role and the associated task of providing a formal release in a timely manner. Rather, the policy allows for the birthparent to be a continuous decision-making participant. By fostering birthparent participation during the process, the birthparent's right to self-determination is protected while, at the same time, the birthparent is utilized as a resource in achieving the policy goal.

f. Identity

We have, in effect, already touched upon the criteria of identity. Since self-determination is the very essence of this particular policy, the development or protection of a sense of personal identity is fostered in that the client is encouraged to articulate personal choices, as opposed to leaving them to unilateral professional discretion. Emphasizing self-determination and identity would no doubt lead the birthparents to be confronted by their own values and priorities and enhance their ability to confront their own decision criteria for adoptive release and placement. Presumably, this would produce a more lasting and stable problem resolution for both the child and the birthparents.

Our analysis leads us to conclude that the policy of birthparents' participation in adoption processes provides a formalization of rights and status for the birthparent that legitimizes and supports optimum participation. In terms of a person's identity, this policy appears to foster and support a client's perception of him- or herself as a person of worth who not only has a right to participate but who can make meaningful contributions to the problem-solving process. The birthparent enters the policy process as a team member, a role that contributes to the policy goal of achieving the best possible arrangement for the newborn child and, at the same time, incorporates a professional value for social practice.

g. Individualization

Individualization, a principle providing that the unique nature of the individual will be respected, is very much assured by the commitment to maintain client identity. However, the analyst should be reminded that the policy of both encouraging and expecting birthparents' participation does *not* mean unilateral or irresponsible decision making. Consequently, individualization has its limits in this situation, suggesting that attention be given to individual preferences as meanings within the rather circumscribed context of the birthparents' role in planning, and the rights of the other parties in the adoptive process.

h. Nonjudgmental Attitude

The birthparent participation policy would appear to give tacit and implicit support to holding a nonjudgmental attitude toward the client or client group. After all, the policy provides for a movement away from the very judgmental notion that adoption is a "giving up" rather than a "planning for." Consequently, the meta-message of acceptance of the client is embodied in the policy.

i. Confidentiality

Since the birthparent is not coerced into disclosure of any sensitive information as a precondition of participation, the maintenance of confidentiality is not endangered by the policy. However, the prospective adoptive parents are, in a sense, coerced since they are placed in a "take it or leave it" situation. They can accept the policy or not continue in the adoptive process. The analyst should also be aware that the implementation of the policy is likely to include many more people and relationships than previously during the adoption planning process, thereby making confidentiality more difficult to maintain. This is not to say that the agency or its casework staff would in any way relax their own confidentiality commitments or procedures, but it does mean that staff would have to be all the more vigilant in assuring protection of confidentiality.

j. Indeterminateness

The policy of birthparent participation seems to imply a faith in the systems principle of indeterminateness—that the end states of social problem solving are actually determined in process, that is, they are not predetermined. Expanding the pool of actors and decision makers through the active inclusion of the birthparent gives indeterminateness the opportunity to operate. The policy allows for the end state to be determined in process in that the motives and role of the birthparent are not delimited at the outset, and the plan for the newborn is developed in process with even more information and more actors than is traditionally the case.

k. Multifinality

The policy tends to support the notion that a variety of end states can arise out of similar conditions. Contrary to the presumption that the problem is simply to plan for an "unwanted child that is to be given up," the policy allows for the similar initial state (pregnancy and impending birth) to be seen as an opportunity for a variety of end states.

l. Nonsummativity

The notion that the whole is something different than or more than the sum of its parts is also suggested by this policy approach, because the policy fosters the development of a *holistic* approach to adoption planning. The worker does not see each actor separately and "add up the pieces." Rather, the birthparent and the potential adoptive parents are active group participants in the planning process. Holistic approaches to problem solving may be said to be nonsummative since they view process and outcomes as something greater than the sum of the observable parts.

m. Morphogenesis

Morphogenesis is a human systems principle that holds that human systems have the ability to change forms in process. While individual human systems do not manifest any structural or sociopsychological change as a result of the policy (though such change may come about), the change appears to be organizational. The policy allows for a fundamental change in the nature of the interaction of key components in the social agency system by means of a radically redefinition of the role of birthparent. To that extent, the policy may be said to allow or provide for the morphogenetic nature of human systems—that an organization has within it the resources to fundamentally change its forms.

n. The SCRAPS Test

The processes of adoption planning and placement have long been seen as primarily "woman's work." The biological father has been much less involved in the process, and few agencies have made concerted attempts to include him. Only fairly recently have some states required systematic attempts to locate and include the biological father.

The professions have largely given the task of providing child welfare services to female workers inasmuch as an overwhelming number of child welfare staff working in the area of adoptions are women. This is, no doubt, also a reflection of our societal orientation to the care of children; perhaps the professions merely reflect those values.

The policy also has racial implications. Given the disproportionate rate of adolescent pregnancies and births among a minority population, and the greater likelihood of those birthparents to keep their child, agencies are in even more need of staff who can assist this client group in making decisions. To a great extent, this issue highlights a need for increased numbers of black and other minority staff in adoption agencies in general, and in Child Services, Inc. in particular, to ensure that the minority birthparent group is represented adequately.

The staff of Child Services, Inc. must reach out to that group of birthparents and aggressively inform them of the policy and their entitlements to participation. As with many private child placing agencies, Child Services, Inc. has a disproportionately small clientele from lower income groups. Therefore, special efforts must be made to reach such groups.

4. Establish Feasibility of the Desired Outcomes

Focus on the elements that make for achieving resolution of the policy problem or the attainment of the policy goal.

a. Legality and Foundation

The birthparent participation policy not only has legal foundation (to the extent that identities are not inappropriately disclosed as a result of it) but, in some states, actual attempts to undertake meaningful measures to include the putative fathers (e.g., locating fathers through newspaper advertising) are a legal requirement. Furthermore, most courts would require assurances that the decision for release be obtained with complete knowledge and consent of the appropriate parties involved. Consequently, the policy is in concert with both legislative and judicial expectations. In addition, we find in this and many other policies that an innovation in policy coincides with changing societal norms. Hence, the foundation of support for some policy change is often found in the larger social system as well as within the agency.

b. Power of the Policy

Policy has been said to create a stochastic phenomenon in organizations; that is, that policy creates a certain lawfulness or predictability to the sequencing of future events. In one sense, this is true for the birthparents' participation policy since it mandates the right to such participation. Presumably, as the birthparent becomes involved, more information is added to the decision process and, consequently, the potential outcome is more likely to be known—or at least to be more predictable. However, this analysis could also yield another conclusion: that participation of the birthparent makes future events even more improbable, or less predictable. The inclusion of each additional actor, with more decision prerogatives, may be said to produce a greater number of potential outcomes. In this case, the principle of stochastic processes in human systems helps to generate more light on our analysis and brings to mind even more outcomes that are possible with the inclusion of more key actors in the process.

The birthparents' participation policy has clearly provided for a fundamental shift in power to the birthparent in the adoption-planning process. This is not to say that the birthparent has become a controlling factor, but her influence has increased markedly. We also need to look at whether the board, the agency's administrative structure, and the technology and competence of the staff can assure delivery of the policy goals. Surely the board has the power (legitimate authority) to mandate such a policy. The adequacy of the administrative structure might be manifested in proper procedures for supervision of staff in regard to the policy. Administrative influence might also be observed in the extent to which administrative staff provide leadership in giving visibility in other areas of the agency to the participatory philosophy inherent in the birthparent policy. The staff, of course, exercise the ultimate power in their influence on the working relationship with the birthparent-as-client; the direct service worker enters at the point where the client is confronted. The staff level is where the real power of policy is observed and exercised—or subverted. The staff must have the necessary social treatment skills to ensure maximized client participation as well as the necessary orientation for such participation.

c. Resource Requirements and Availability

Cost is always a consideration in social services, inasmuch as social agencies are chartered to serve the public good with social resources. This is true of both publicly and privately supported programs. There is no question that this policy will require additional staff time, though the demands of the policy could be incorporated into staff approaches to the provision of service. Additional equipment or space would not be required. For the birthparents-as-client, presumably there would be a cost incurred by the demands upon personal time required for increased participation. For the agency, additional visibility would be given to the agency programs in the community, which would have to be weighed as a cost or a benefit. In any event, it helps to be reminded that, besides the criteria of costs, equally important is the question of who sets those criteria. The policy decision examined here impacts upon staff, clientele, the agency as a whole, and perhaps other components in the community. It is important to consider whether the policymaker (in this case the board of Child Services, Inc.) has the interests of each of the affected social components in mind and has the legitimate authority to unilaterally affect each of those components.

By inference, this is a costly policy because, in the short term, it would likely consume more staff time. Presumably, in the long term, it would constitute a wise use of staff resources inasmuch as more appropriate and successful placement decisions would arise and individual clients would experience growth at a time of important decision making. Other cost indices that relate to this particular strategy might include the cost to the agency's public relations—whether the policy would incur more favor or disfavor with the client group it serves and with the community in which the agency is located. In this sense, the policy's approach must be seen as having political costs and, while these considerations may not necessarily be primary determinants, they should be weighed in the analysis.

d. Rationality

Earlier we considered the theoretical foundations of the policy under analysis. However, while a policy may be theoretically sound, it may not necessarily be rational in terms of its practicality, logistics, or workability. The birthparents' participation policy does not appear unreasonably cumbersome; thus, staff can implement it. Here is a point at which practice theory can immediately be translated into workable practice.

e. Newly Perceived Self-Interests

As discussed earlier, an important dynamic for policy change (or policy maintenance for that matter) is the extent to which significant policy actors perceive that their individual or collective self-interests may be served by pursuit of the policy goal. For the birthparent clients, the policy provides for a more open system in which the clients become decision makers rather than providers of information in matters important to their own lives. For the workers, the policy provides support legitimized by board action for pursuit of practice goals that are consistent with professional ethics relating to client self-determination. For the agency, the mandates and expectations of law and the judiciary are integrated with agency practice. Consequently, the policy relates to the self-interest of a number of significant actors and subsystems in the policy field.

5. Provide Recommendations

Focus on the strengths and weaknesses or factors peculiar to the issue and suggested by the data generated by the analysis.

Summary

In Case 4 we have explored the implications of a child placement agency's consideration of a policy that would alter the role and participation of birthparents in the decision-making process involved in making adoption placement plans for their child. Each of the elements for the framework for content analysis has been applied for illustrative purposes. In conducting or producing an actual analysis, you would likely extract your own model and pick and choose only those elements thought to be particularly relevant or for which information was readily available for analysis.

Chapters 4 and 5 focused on the *substantive content* of policy. The focus in chapter 6 will move to developing a framework for the analysis of the *process* of social agency policy. We will examine the elements to consider when analyzing the developmental events that might occur in the formulation of policy in small-scale systems.

Process Elements
for Small-Scale
Policy Analysis

6

The task of this chapter is to construct a framework for analysis of the *process* aspects of policy. Chapter 3 introduced the various origins in the literature that give rise to our framework for this chapter. In chapter 4 attention was given to the content aspects of analysis. Here we focus on the policy process—the *activities* that people engage in to pursue policy interests, rather than the substantive content of policy *per se*. In reality, it is difficult to separate or select out the substantive content, the people process, and the value issues that exist in the play of power. Admittedly, content, values and process cannot be easily separated in real life but, for purposes of developing our analytic skills, we must treat content and process separately here. Dichotomies or trichotomies are not really found in real life. They are false representations of reality. However, we use classificatory schemes in order to break down complex phenomena so that we can study them.

We have incorporated the analysis of values simultaneously in both content and process analysis. As we move through the chapter, we will be developing our own framework, or outline, as was done in the earlier chapters. Once again, it will be up to you to extract from that framework to build your own model for policy process analysis. You can pick and choose for yourself as to what might ''fit'' or be relevant to your particular situation or your particular issue, and on the basis of what information might be reasonably available to you.

As in chapter 4, we will intersperse a case example throughout the narrative of this chapter for illustrative purposes. Chapter 7 will offer other, more detailed, case illustrations.

Case Illustration—Infants with HIV+ Infection

For illustration purposes, we will continue with the policy topic used in chapter 4 in building our framework for content analysis: infants with a positive diagnosis of HIV infection, infants who are abandoned in hospitals. We assumed in that case example that we are employed as social workers in the medical social service department of an urban general hospital, Vistaview Hospital. The hospital is confronted with the growing phenomenon of the increasing number of "boarder babies," infants who were born in the hospital, who are ready for discharge, and who test positive for the human imunodeficiency virus. These infants, often referred to as "boarder babies," are ready for discharge to a community that will not accept them. We presented some detail on this problem in chapter 4.

The hospital is considering a policy of providing a community-based residential care program for these infants outside of the hospital. We have been called in, because of our responsibilities in the Social Service Department and our familiarity with policy analysis, to assist a Task Force on Residential Care for Infants with HIV+ Infection in considering this new policy option. Our task here will be to use the framework for analysis to speculate about how the process of policy formulation might be played out—from the social worker's perspective.

Essential Activities in Process Analysis

In developing our approach to analyzing the content of policy, we established a number of activities essential to policy analysis. We visit this task once again, this time devoting our attention to activities associated with policy process analysis. Those activities are as follows:

1. Identify the policy problem or policy goal (similar to content analysis)
2. Assess the nature or condition of developmental milestones
3. Identify interest group relationships
4. Assess the availability and use of process resources
5. Determine implications for selected values (same as content analysis)
6. Provide recommendations

The tasks of identifying the policy problem or policy goal and of determining implications for selected values are similar to those of content analysis. That is, clear problem/goal identification and anaylsis of values are central to both aspects of policy analysis.

Because the specifics in problem identification are the same for both content and process analysis, there is no point in duplicating that task at the front end. Consequently, the problem/goal definition section of our framework will not be as extensive as it was for the analysis of content. At the same time, however, we need to give the same attention to values analysis in analyzing process as we do to analyzing content.

Major Elements Relevant to Policy Process Analysis

Having surveyed the essential elements of a few process frameworks in chapter 3, we will now attempt to grasp their central differentiating concepts in order to build a framework for policy process analysis. While the activities associated with problem or policy goal definition and identification of values issues are central to process analysis, we will concentrate our discussion on three major aspects especially germane to policy process: (1) milestones, (2) interest group relationships, and (3) process resources. These aspects are extracted and reduced from a number of views of process thinking, most of them noted earlier. Special attention will be given to the explanations of system process that pertain to the policy process at the local or small-scale level.

Milestones embodies such concepts as stages or phases often included in process explanations that emphasize the time dimensions of policy process, such as the completion of certain crucial tasks or the movement through stages or steps thought to be particularly necessary in formulating policy. *Interest group relationships* include concepts that emphasize the competitive or cooperative interaction of policy processes. Included are social actors—individuals or groups—acting in their own self-interests. *Process resources* include tangible and intangible assets and liabilities such as time, money, and access to power, people, talent, and space.

We will now build our framework to do our analysis.

1. Identify the Policy Problem or Policy Goal(s)

a. The Problem/Goal and the Policy Statement

The first task is to develop a clear and concise statement which delineates the policy that is under analysis or the problem that is of concern. As with the analysis of content, the analysis of process must proceed from a clear notion of what is to be the focus. (This is not to say, of course, that the focus cannot change during the analysis.) We might identify an actual statement giving rise to policy action or infer from peoples' behavior what the policy is. That is, peoples' actions can be evidence of the real principles behind their choices and behavior. On the other hand, there may as yet be no "policy" in view and the actors may just be confronting a problem around which policy action is developing.

a. The Problem/Goal and the Policy Statement—Case Example

Vistaview Hospital is a private, non-profit, acute care, general hospital located in the urban center of a city of 500,000. Like other hospitals of its kind, it is experiencing escalating costs, pressure for cost reduction from third-party payors, and continuing demands for the whole range of acute care medical services. Like many other non-profit institutions, Vistaview Hospital is participating in profit ventures under the umbrella of a holding company—in this case Vistaview Healthcare, Inc.. The proposal for developing a residential program for "boarder babies" would be a departure for Vistaview. Neither the hospital nor the parent company has ventured into social service activities outside of the hospital's walls nor have they taken responsibility for long-term care of any kind in the medical community. This is the backdrop for our case illustration. We will restate the policy:

> *Vistaview Hospital shall provide community-based residential care and other appropriate assistance for infants abandoned in hospitals due to a positive diagnosis of HIV infection.*

Let's presume that Vistaview, as a preliminary and tentative step, has indicated that there are at least two options of interest to the Board. One is the hospital's "going it alone" and developing its own residential, outpatient care program for these infants. The second option is to enter into a partnership with Family and Children's Services, Inc. to develop a specialized child care program. Family and Children's Services, Inc. is a private, not-for-profit, multi-service agency that provides counselling services for individuals and families and a range of community-based residential out-of-home care for physically handicapped, developmentally disabled, and other children and adults with special needs. That joint program would provide foster care, respite care, and/or home health care for birthparents or foster parents, and health education and training to various caregivers in the community, not only parents and foster parents but also school personnel and recreational providers, for example.

b. Base(s) of Legitimacy and Source or Location of the Policy

Generally speaking, policies that have a foundation in some bases of legitimacy, or the right to take action or to be brought into effect, have the most power. A corollary is that those who enforce or implement policy, in ideal circumstances, have the legitimacy to do so, or the right to take action. This is not to say, of course, that informal and non-legitimated policy does not at times also have considerable power. However, no policy can move ahead, be applied, or stand alone without some legitimacy, whether that legitimacy is ascribed at its birth, formally achieved by the social action of the policy actors, or informally bolstered by the power of influential actors in the policy system.

There are a number of sources of legitimacy for social welfare policy, ranging from constitutional foundations, judicial and legislated rulings, administrative policy via administrative rules, and executive action (which may or may not have its foundations in these higher levels). The ultimate legal legitimacy is, of course, constitutional mandate. Administrative policy may derive legitimacy from many areas, but its firmest foundation is the double sanction of judicial and/or legislated legitimacy supported by broad popular consent. A good example is the self-regulating behavior of day-care center providers who have meaningful input into state licensing laws regulating child day care and, themselves, take adverse action against peers who violate the administrative rules regarding the statute. Executive policy often has a push-pull sort of legitimacy in the sense that may have the formal legitimacy of a board of directors behind its executive position. But such policy may also have the informal but very real support of the subordinate staff who, technically, have no formal authority to legitimate a particular policy.

In policy analysis it is well to identify the sources, nature, and legitimacy if one is to truly understand the context of the policy under analysis. For example, we can look to the existence of judicial orders, legislated authorizations or appropriations, board or committee resolutions, city or county ordinances, contract agreements or requirements, and other manifestations of the right to take action. These are examples of sources of formal legitimacy.

b. Base(s) of Legitimacy and Source or Location of the Policy—Case Example

The hospital's Social Service Department's right to take action will be found in the sanction afforded by the hospital Board's charge to explore implementation of the policy, either as a solo effort by the hospital or as a cooperative effort with Family and Children's Services, Inc. However, the analyst will first have to determine the level of sanction and commitment presently assigned to this possibility by Family and Children's Services, if the latter option is to be adequately explored. To some extent, then, two process analyses are required. Some clue to the level of support might be found in whether such an eventuality was considered in the present drafts of a strategic plan embraced by each of the two organizations. The official minutes of each board meeting would be obvious sources for documenting the necessary legimation for taking action, as would any executive directives for actions decided upon.

Other issues related to legitimacy will probably need to be explored as well. Some examples are the extent to which the hospital's accreditation by such groups as the Joint Commission on the Accreditation of Health Organizations or the Commission on Accreditation of Rehabilitation Facilities might be threatened or advanced by this policy. One may also have to determine the implications for the accreditation of Family and Children's Services by the Commission on Accreditation of Children's Agencies and its licensing status for the placement of children under the state's Department of Social Services. The ability of Vistaview to obtain necessary licensing might also have to be considered.

2. Assess the Nature or Condition of Developmental Milestones

It is wise to include in our model for analysis some accounting of the temporal and/or developmental aspects of the process of policy. That is, all policy and its analysis should give some consideration to the fact that policy exists within a time dimension. One guide for us here is the emphasis in some frameworks on the notion that policy processes have a life of their own, with certain stages, phases, or tasks being characteristic of particular times in the policy's life. For purposes of analysis it is helpful to think of the *milestones* that are to be achieved over the life of a policy process. Milestones may be thought of as the major developmental tasks that must be performed in the process dimension of policy. These milestones must be included in the analysis to determine whether the policy has satisfied requisite developmental tasks and contains the necessary ingredients for moving through those tasks, and whether certain major events have occurred (or are likely to occur) to achieve the desired policy effects. Some examples are the establishment of an "initiating set" aimed at taking action, the achievement of sponsorship or legitimation, and the recruitment of significant talent in sufficient numbers to carry out the policy action (see Warren, 1963). Other examples might be developing key coalitions and obtaining necessary contractual agreements. Milestones are the touchstones of policy process, the key steps providing bridges between espoused principles and desired end states. They might also be seen as seizing opportunity at appropriate times or points in a policy's history or as fillng a policy space in a vacuum of social action. The first of these milestones is that of obtaining a charter.

a. Identification of the Charter

As we study the policy process in terms of milestones, we will pay special attention to the original impetus for taking action and how that beginning state emerged. We will also observe how key actors obtained the right or support for taking action and what the central substance of their agreements might have been or might be.

Every policy must be founded upon an original agreement or template. The existence of a charter is not only a source of power, but also a fundamental milestone from which policy action can proceed.

The importance of this milestone is best illustrated by administrative rules (i.e., standards or regulations that have the force of law) developed subsequent to some enabling legislation. For example, any regulatory legislation passed by the federal government or virtually any state legislature tends to be quite general, indicating the population or enterprise to be protected or limited and the administrative agency responsible for monitoring regulatory activity. The general purpose of the legislation is also usually stated in the statute. However, federal administrative procedures legislation and the administrative procedures acts of virtually every state require a rather detailed and explicit set of routines for an administrative agency to follow in publishing proposed rules (i.e., administrative policy) in receiving and responding to input offered on the part of those affected and final legislative review prior to promulgation of the rules. Prior to completion of these required steps, many administrative rules are mere policy without authority (as is the case with many guidelines). Once having fulfilled the requirements (publishing proposed rules, conducting public hearings, and passing legislative review), the rule has the firmest legitimacy—the force of law. Likewise the creation of a charter and/or legitimacy constitutes a major milestone that must be considered in the analysis of policy, especially (in this case) when it involves administrative rules arising out of legislated regulatory policy. In this example, the enabling legislation provides the charter for subsequent rule development.

There are other, less complicated examples. A group of social activists agrees to "take on city hall" regarding a community issue or a group of clinicians agrees to put their heads together to "turn the administration around" on an intra-agency policy issue.

a. Identification of the Charter—Case Example

The charter for policy action may be the original agreement or template providing the impetus for the individuals or groups to get the subject of the policy onto the local "agenda." In our case illustration, our analysis might pursue the question of which particular individual(s) within the hospital initiated the idea. In this analysis these individuals would be the "action system," In our case example, we would need to identify what issues were key in redefining the issue in such terms that action was pursued. It could have been that people were moved by an unmanageable critical mass of a patient census, a particularly difficult child's situation or some event that coincided, by circumstances, with other planning activities occurring within the hospital. These and other possible explanations need to be checked out.

b. Functioning of the Action System(s)

The second milestone to consider is the development and functioning of an action system, that is, somebody to do the initial work. In order for social action to take place (i.e., for policy processes to occur) there must be an identifiable set of social actors who assume responsibility for pursuing, implementing, or enforcing the policy. Any analysis of policy must consider who the movers of a particular policy are, what their aims, motives, and/or incentives are, and what next steps toward policy initiation are both necessary and feasible. At the same time, policy analysis must include a study of the necessary next steps for installation, modification, implementation, or enforcement if the process aspects are to be adequately considered. At this point in the discussion, the emphasis is upon the reality of an action system being in place—an essential milestone—more will be said later about the interactive aspects of action.

The presence of an action system—an identifiable set of actors committed to taking action to (or even impede) a particular policy—is, therefore, a necessary element in the process aspects of our policy analysis. A careful analysis of the action system's legitimacy, authority, leadership capacities, membership, individual and collective status, and the overall strategies its members employ are all important dimensions of the action system. A consideration of these aspects of process in policy analysis helps to determine the policy system's capacity to convert issues to public concerns, bring about agenda setting in the organization or community, and determine the parameters within which the policy will take shape. The ability to set the public or private "agenda" is a tremendous asset and a key function performed by a policy action system. In essence, this aspect of policy process analysis is the assessment of the power of the action system—a measurement of the ability of a given set of actors to effect the probable outcomes of future events.

b. Functioning of the Action System(s)—Case Example

The action system's charter (i.e., agreement to pursue policy change) had to have been supported by the members of the action system. Beyond identifying the locus of support from particular Board members, it would also be useful to determine how any particular members of the hospital's middle or upper management were brought into the action system, thereby potentially giving further legitimation to their ongoing efforts at policy change. (Or, in the case of a policy action still in need of support and legitimation, it would be helpful to speculate about what steps should be taken and what actors need to be brought into the action system.) The activities of the action system may illustrate the integral relationship between establishing a charter and obtaining legitimacy. It would also be instructive to identify who played leadership roles, who took on what might be considered the "grunt work" or "dirty work" to get the action moving, who played facilitative roles and what individual or group became the spokespersons for the action system. In the case of a hospital, these roles might be fulfilled by key individuals or entire departments.

c. Key Participants and Their Associated Events

Another milestone in the play of policy and, therefore, in the analysis of policy process, is the recruitment and participation of certain key actors in the policy system. That is, for purposes of analysis, it is important not only to identify whether or not an action system exists but to identify the participants in that action system—who they are and whom or what they represent. The action system is more than the accumulation of individual actors. A determination of the actors' nature and their interpersonal chemistry is essential to an effective analysis.

A definition of the membership of the policy action system would include officials with designated authority, influential media, people with technical expertise, and those who are in touch and have influence with decision makers. Designated authorities are those who hold elected or appointed offices, those named in agreements or contracts, and those who informally emerge as "the leadership." The "media" may consist of radio, television, or newpapers; however, it may also include those who "spread the word" in various ways (e.g., through newsletters or information offices) or influential individuals who move about freely in the neighborhood or the office and become important channels of communication. They may be the gossips, those counted on to "have the word," or those closely connected to significant "grapevines." Clearly then, influential—policy actors need not always be those holding official positions—individuals may be influential because of their own attributes or the group they represent. Influence makers may be individuals, such as key staff; knowledgeable authorities or organizations; prestigious think tanks or research groups; or reference groups of various types. What is clear is that the presence and force of key actors not only play a part in the political processes of policy but also constitute vital milestones in the policy process.

c. Key Participants and Their Associated Events—Case Example

It would be useful to look at the chronology of events that lead to the conversion of somebody's concern into an organizational position to take action. A key here is determining how and by whom the action system was expanded to include more individuals who then lent their efforts in achieving the support of key individuals and, ultimately, the Board. The channels of communication within the hospital need to be examined in terms of what routes were used for the information flow concerning the particular policy proposal involving children with an HIV + diagnosis. This really means identifying the "proximate policy makers" (Lindblom, 1968), those who are closest to or called upon to give advice to those who ultimately make policy decisions.

3. Identify Interest Group Relationships

A number of factors give shape to the analysis of interest group politics in policy process. Some have to do with the sheer power or influence (i.e., the exercise of power) of particular groups; others involve the salience (attraction or valence) of particular policy-related issues for particular groups; and some consist of specific intergroup activities that occur in the context of interest group interrelationships.

a. Power and Influence

It is absolutely essential to estimate the power (i.e., the ability to control the outcomes of others' behavior) and the influence (i.e., the actual exercise of that power) of the various interest groups that are party to a policy under analysis. Making precise measurement, of course, is not likely. Thus, the estimate probably should be based upon historical evidence of the actual exercise of influence behavior in the past or upon speculation about what particular groups might do under hypothetical circumstances. Kenneth Gergen (1968) touches on this matter in his discussion of the concept of "personal efficacy." Efficacy includes both the individual's and the group's capacity to produce desired effects, together with their history of doing so. Some obvious considerations regarding this are: (1) speculation as to the likelihood of a particular group supporting or rejecting a proposed policy and (2) an estimate of whether a particular group is needed to assist in the enforcement or maintenance of a policy position. At this point, an analysis is needed of the *vested interests* various groups already possess, risk losing, or have the potential to obtain via an existing or proposed policy position.

a. Power and Influence—Case Example

As noted above, the action system in our hospital illustration had the authority to take action. Given the range of professional and disciplinary orientations likely to be represented in the original action system and given that this policy exists in a hospital, the particular play of power and influence could be instructive here. Hospitals are generally hierarchically arranged organizations with the medical professionals wielding the most formal power. The actual use of that power (i.e., the use of influence) would greatly depend upon the particular actors and the particular circumstances, however. So, we need to explore whether influence was exercised by pediatricians on the children's unit, the nursing staff who became intimately associated with each of the children in care, or the social workers linked with the community care network. These are just some possibilities. The impetus for power and influence could just as well have come from a powerful and prominent board member or an especially concerned or dedicated member of the hospital's executive staff.

Besides the collective goals of units in a hospital, there could be additional individual or organizational vested interests at work. In considering the possible incentives to Family and Children's Services, Inc., some agencies, for example, are more interested in participating in the interagency communication network for not-so-obvious purposes or in maintaining an "in-the-know" posture. That is, some organizations simply do not want to be left out of the information loop. In summary, potential as well as actual play of power and influence must be examined.

b. Salience of the Issue(s)

Identification of the power and influence of group participants leads us to an estimate of the salience of particular issues for particular groups. The "salience" of an issue is the extent to which any particular issue generates action because of its special meaning or value to the actor. Gergen (1968) speaks of "issue salience" in relation to individual actors in policy processes; here we are speaking to salience giving rise to group action. While individual policy initiatives are not to be ignored (indeed, they were mentioned in the previous section of this chapter), it is group action that greases the skids of *social* welfare policy action.

Consequently, an estimation of the salience of the proposed or existing policy for all groups in the policy system is an essential element for effective policy analysis. In the best of all worlds, these estimates would each have sound empirical bases; that is, each would be based upon "hard" data gathered under established rules of procedure and evidence. A fruitful source of such data could be found in the historical antecedents of contemporary community or organizational issues related to the policy under analysis. However, such empirical data may not be readily available. Nevertheless, one should strive to obtain such data or, at the very least, make a conscious tally of data based only on conjecture.

b. Salience of the Issue(s)—Case Example

The salience of the issue of infants with HIV+ abandoned in any location is obvious. The abandonment of any child in any circumstances has a high valence as a social issue. In this situation we have a highly unusual concommitant variable, however, in the complication of HIV infection. The anguish over AIDS is certainly a salient national issue, too. Given that the hospital was incurring unusually high costs in maintaining these children in what was essentially custodial care for intermittant periods of time, the aggregate cost to the hospital and its financial solvency were surely salient issues for the hospital as a health care organization.

The central issue facing the hospital of having children in need without an organizational response with appropriate services certainly presented a challenge to the hospital, too. After all, were needy children languishing without appropriate medical and social services? Was Vistaview a party to this condition? That would certainly be a salient issue goading the hospital to search for a solution, leading it to go beyond redefining the usual mission of Vistaview—into providing community-based services.

c. Intergroup Activities

Power, influence, and issue salience might be thought of as the static aspects of interest group phenomena. However, the very construct of the interest group suggests social action, or to be more exact, social interaction. And, of course, the literature of political science is full of concepts and their illustrations of the interactive aspects of political processes. Our task at this point in the analysis is to identify particularly relevant intergroup interchanges, cooperative or otherwise, that appear to be essential to explaining the policy process. We need to look at (1) the transfer of favors or resources from agency to agency, (2) bargaining or other forms of negotiating that may explain the process, (3) coalitions that may have been formed (or modified or destroyed), and (4) formal or informal contracts that were established or might be established regarding the policy.

Unilateral transfers versus bilateral exchanges. Our focus now turns to the activities that occur across or between intrasystem boundaries in social welfare policy systems. Regarding the domain of policy substance or the prerogatives of policy actors, social welfare activities tend to be unclear. This lack of clarity is exemplified by the contrasting views of Kenneth Boulding (1967) and Robert Pruger (1973). For Boulding, social policy involves *unilateral transfers* of various commodities, whether money or services, as opposed to exchange transactions. That is, the donor is viewed as giving up something and the receiver as obtaining something. No exchange is presumed—just a transfer—and the commodity is said to move only in one direction. In contrast, Pruger sees social policy as involving *bilateral exchanges* between donors and receivers in which a transaction involves commodities (tangible or intangible), and movement in both directions between provider and receiver. This view is best illustrated by the aphorism "There is no such thing as a free lunch." The most debased and humiliated recipient gives up something—dignity or freedom of choice—in exchange for assistance.

Given that what constitutes right and proper prerogatives in social welfare policy is universally contested, it is no wonder that there are few rules to guide us in the analysis of interest group activities. Nevertheless, a sound analysis must examine the nature of transfers or exchanges as incentives or outcomes for those who engage in policy-making processes.

Bargaining and negotiating. Bargaining and negotiating are especially characteristic of social welfare policy processes, because social welfare resources, being scarce or in demand by a variety of competing interests, are generally obtained through debate. This is not to say that other, more common activities are not present in social welfare policy processes, such as initiating tradeoffs, seriality, or "satisficing" (see Lindblom, 1968). Given the constant contentiousness of social welfare policy, it is particularly important in the policy analysis to assess bargaining and negotiating (and what occurs during these activities).

Bargaining may be thought of as the means by which agreements are reached between two or more parties each pursuing its own interests. Therefore, in policy analysis one should study the commitments made in the agreements themselves as they might enhance or hinder the policy objectives. Negotiating may be seen as a special kind of means by which bargains are obtained and is generally characterized

by particular social rules or norms. Indeed, in collective bargaining between management and labor, such negotiating is regulated by laws.
Consequently, it is valuable in the policy analysis to note what kinds of
agreements (bargains) were made by various interest groups and in
what way (i.e., form of negotiation) bargaining occurred.

Coalition building. Another special activity, related to both negotiating and bargaining, is coalition building. Coalitions are commonly
found in social welfare policy processes, given the competition for
scarce resources and the need for cooperation in the interest of client
service. Coalitions may be thought of as temporary agreements or arrangements made by interest groups in which limited goals of each
group are served while no group's autonomy is surrendered. For purposes of policy analysis, it is helpful to determine the particular goals
selected to bind the coalition(s) together, or to observe which goals are
not binding. It is also important to determine who the coalition's
spokespersons are and to identify the policy principles articulated by
these spokespersons or by the literature the coalition generates.

Contracting. Finally, contracting is a special form of policy activity that has great potential for policy analysis. This includes the processes employed and the forms obtained by such contracting. Contracting may be thought of as a formal agreement upon terms. These terms,
such as the resources to be employed, the conditions under which policies (and programs) will be pursued, and the outcomes to be expected,
guide interactions between two parties and give shape to policies and
programs. Indeed, contracts themselves may be seen as master statements or a collection of principles, each suggesting many policies inviting analysis. Given the increased reliance upon contracting in recent
years—including purchase-of-service contracting supported by such
factors as the Social Security Act, state departments of mental health,
or United Way agreements, and the general inclination to formalize economic relationships—contract elements and contracting are necessary and proper grist for the analysis mill. Some likely provisions are
the usual "boilerplate" policy principles, such as the formal standing
of past practices, the nature of master-slave relationships between parties to the agreements, rights and responsibilities regarding access to
and provision of data and auditing, expectations regarding the form
and frequency of reporting, and prerogatives regarding the movement
or reallocation of funds within a budget. Other contracting elements
might relate to expectations regarding notice of termination of the contract, matching requirements for funding, limitations on subcontract-
ing, output and outcome expectations, and rates of reimbursement.

An important point for the analyst is that contract provisions give explicit suggestions regarding what some of the appropriate criteria for analysis might be. Other criteria for analysis might be suggested by what provisions are *not* in the contract. In other words, what is missing from the contract that would otherwise seem to be a reasonable provision? Furthermore, it should be noted that a formal contract need not be written or in place for the analyst to use contract principles or features for the policy process analysis, because the fundamental questions to be asked pertain to what group interests are being served by existing principles and how there principles were arrived at.

c. Intergroup Activities—Case Example

The plot thickens as we examine the possible intergroup activities involved in developing community-based alternatives for infants with an HIV+ diagnosis abandoned in an acute care general hospital. Given the nature of the policy developed, a number of intergroup interactions are possible: (1) frequent case conferences regarding particular children and their situations, (2) actual case activity by line staff, nurses, physician, social workers, and others; and (3) informal interaction among hospital administrators who share the experiences of their respective staffs' interactions with one another and community service agencies, (4) some interaction with child care service providers in the community who expressed an interest in these children and, in some cases, who were familiar with some of the families involved in these patients' situations. While the reader will recall the decision to explore a cooperative relationship with Family and Children's Services, Inc., the policy also states a concern for children abandoned in hospitals (note the plural). It is possible that, should other hospitals become involved in this policy action other childcare providers besides Family and Children's Services might become agencies of choice for these other hospitals.

Unilateral transfers versus bilateral exchanges. Clearly, the organizations with the greatest incentives to actually engage in coordination of efforts are those who benefit from bilateral exchanges. Others that come along in order to stay "in the know" or work on their own agendas are perhaps more likely recipients of unilateral transfers of information or intelligence. In our case example, the hospital has a great deal to gain in being able to meet its medical mission of appropriately serving these children while at the same time reducing unnecessary use of acute care beds by reaching out to the community. At the same time, the community service agencies, for their own survival and functioning, require sufficient inputs of clientele—the complication of HIV infection notwithstanding. Hence, an excellent opportunity exists for a bilateral exchange of resources, presuming that the Vistaview Board decides to achieve the policy goal by cooperating with existing child care providers as opposed to establishing its own network of community-based services.

Bargaining and negotiating. Agreements by agencies in individual case situations can be achieved through a bargaining and negotiating process. So, too, can interagency general working agreements. In our case illustration, agreements might involve combining routine procedures for referral and screening, joint efforts at an individual child's case planning, or sharing individual agency and/or mutual agency obligations for service delivery, case follow-up, and the like. The context in which bargaining and negotiating occurs is also important in terms of which agencies decide to take the initiatives and which appear to display the least investment in the process.

Coalition building. Given the often unpredictable process of the development of the HIV infection in children and the many roles played in providing service to these children, a high level of cooperative effort is demanded—whether it be within the hospital or the interagency coordination of care efforts. Excellent opportunities for coalition building exist, in that individual units and organizations would be able to enter into agreements to provide community-based care and still be able to pursue their established organizational missions without surrendering any prerogatives to another organization.

Contracting. Contracting likely would demand rather explicit formal written agreements on the particular responsibilities of each unit or organization involved. Should the hospital decide to develop the services on its own, clear lines of responsibility would need to be drawn (possibly through memoranda of agreement) for each hospital unit's responsibility either for community-based care or in-hospital care. Similar responsibilities would have to be codified should cooperative arrangements be sought with existing community child caregivers. Contractual arrangements would be needed with community-based agencies external to the hospital. Agency rights and responsibilities and specifics in case processes would have to be explicated in contractual terms. An example might be the need for clarification of training, orientation and supervision responsibilities concerning the actual caregivers, such as home health aides, caseworkers or case managers, foster parents, respite care workers, and recreational workers.

4. Assess the Availability and Use of Process Resources

Now we come to the fourth step in the analysis of policy process. The achievement of social goals requires resources. Analysis of the social welfare policy process is no different in this regard. Analysis itself requires resources. An important point for the analyst to recognize, however, is that "resources" constitute a rather broad category. In fact, many of the elements that we have already discussed might fall under the rubric of "resources." Surely, the efficacy, power, and influence of individuals or groups should be considered in any analysis of resources; so, too, should the ability to bargain or negotiate, and acquire legitimacy for a desired policy. In our analysis, however, we will include the more tangible, perhaps even quantifiable, aspects of resources for movement of the policy process. In particular, we will focus on resources in the form of (1) the social actors or personnel participating in the policy process, (2) the technology employed, (3) the financial resources needed to bring the policy to fruition, and (4) the considerations related to time as a resource.

People Power

In assessing resources, one should identify the people necessary for the job of bringing the policy to fruition. The analyst must ask how much effort was expended and by whom, which gives some evidence of the salience of the policy for particular groups and the relative value of the principles articulated in the particular policy at issue.

Technology

A corollary to the question of people power is that of technology—the existing skills and/or talents used in the policy process. People's skills are considered technology, as well as mechanical or electronic technology available to the policy actors for the attainment of policy goals. Some examples of the latter are computer facilities, office space, and communication facilities. Communication facilities are especially important because policy principles are of no value unless they are communicated. Furthermore, an analysis of communications capacities suggests who the gatekeepers and filterers of communications are in the policy system (e.g., intergroup liaisons, spokespersons, press officers, or even messengers). Also, an analysis of communications technology leads the analyst to look for particular media. Newsletters, flyers, and even electronic bulletin boards are examples of formal channels; people of like interests who come together and possess the ability to move the word quickly throughout a territory are examples of informal networks.

Finances

Access to or the use of money in its various forms is an obvious criterion for analysis of the resources of policy processes. A clear illustration would be the presence of cash contributions to campaigns or drives. Yet another would be the ability to hire people to staff a social action effort or campaign for a preferred policy outcome. There are, of course, other factors pertinent to financial resources in policy processes, such as the availability of office space or access to locations for public meetings. Another is the ability to have funds available to conduct mailings or other advertising efforts.

Time

Our final criterion for resource analysis is the use of time in policy processes. Time can be seen as an asset or a liability. When adequate amounts of time are available to develop and conduct effective campaigns for system-wide support, time is an asset. When insufficient amounts of time are available, time is a liability. One can also observe how significant policy actors utilize time in achieving policy goals, such as being patient, playing brinkmanship politics, issuing ultimatums on short notice, or building time tables for time-consuming participatory processes.

4. Assess the Availability and Use of Process Resources—Case Example

People Power

Like most acute care general hospitals, Vistaview has had to reduce staff as a cost-cutting measure. There is not likely to be sufficient people available to implement this policy relying solely on existing or internal resources. Staff-patient ratios are the highest they have ever been. On the other hand, community placement would reduce internal workload; on the other, the program development involved and the staffing needed to maintain a placement program would also demand the use of these resources. Possibly even more staff time would be needed for development and maintenance of the program than is being devoted to the existing, albeit undesirable, situation.

Technology

The hospital clearly possesses the technology, as well as can be expected at this point in the state of medical management to provide medical care for those with HIV infection and those with ARC or AIDS. However, while some individual staff have technical expertise and experience with community-based care (e.g., some nurses with home health care backgrounds and some social workers with out-of-home care placement experience with children), the hospital is not organizationally equipped with this technology. Their forte is medical care in an acute care general hospital setting, not community-based residential and other supportive care. Consequently, we would have to see some extensive staff development activities of the hospital staff or, on the other hand, the hospital would have to opt for interagency agreements for the use of existing community agency resources for those who are equipped to provide child care services. This latter option being the case, this project and policy process would likely benefit from an even broader range of disciplines and professional services available in the community. Given the multiproblem nature of the clientele to be served, a variety of staff technology would need to be involved.

Finances

If Vistaview Hospital opts to develop the program itself, there would be extensive out-of-pocket costs requiring considerable amounts of up-front financing. The interagency coalition option would require extensive investment of staff time but less out-of-pocket expense and less extensive organizational investment of capital. The costs for case staffings, placement planning, and case follow-up would be considerable, but their cost/benefit ratio would be beneficial as compared to the costs of these children occupying acute care beds.

Time

Time allocated to interagency meetings is time lost to other direct services within the hospital. However, time is a valuable resource that is now being inefficiently used, in that hospital professional staff are devoting that resource to a function not within the mission of the organization, i.e., long-term custodial care of infants. In terms of the process of developing this policy proposal and its associated program, there would be extensive demands upon staff time for program planning and policy implementation. No doubt considerable time has already been invested in moving the problem from an individual concern to an organizational agenda item, in gaining legitimation to move ahead, and to program planning.

5. Determine Implications for Selected Values

In this section, we will apply the same values elements outlined in chapter 4 for analyzing values in policy content analysis to our case illustration of children with HIV + diagnosis abandoned in a general hospital. The descriptions or explanations of the values elements need not be repeated here since the reader can easily refer to Chapter 4 for review of that material.

Case Illustration—Infants with HIV + Infection

a. Adequacy

This process holds promise of providing more appropriate services to infants in the hospital found to be HIV +. The process of policy development itself would appear to be adequate, at least on the face of it, inasmuch as it has been legitimated by the Board and there is still space to manuever within the policy directive. The policy is now enabling a program planning process to proceed. The process has been adequate from both a vertical and horizontal perspective, too, in that the hierarchy has sanctioned the effort and the various professional disciplines are in support of the policy initiative. That is, support is adequate in the sense that it is both *Board*-based and *broad*-based.

b. Effectiveness

As indicated above, successful policy provides for a stochastic process; policy gives order and predictability to a system. This policy process supports the orderly and predictable development of policy inasmuch as those charged with direct patient care have initiated policy action which, as a result, obtains legitimacy and support at the highest policy level. On the other hand, it remains to be seen just how effective the formulation process can be when more social actors in the form of community agencies become more intimately involved in achieving the final goal.

c. Efficiency

The logic behind the policy process involved in soliciting the participation of other community agencies is that more can be obtained by coordinating existing community-based services for this particular population in need. While a principle driving the need for a community care coalition for abandoned infants may be efficiency, there are certainly real programmatic benefits to be made available to these children. It is likely that there is a mix of motivations held by those who participated in the policy process, some pushing for creating efficiencies and others for achieving a new level of effectiveness. At any rate, there were relatively little process resources needed to obtain sanction for this policy, given that there was little research to be done on the wisdom of the policy. There is much more research to be done in the subsequent decision of whether Vistaview Hospital should be the direct alternative care giver or whether it should enter into a coalition with existing agencies.

d. Impact on Rights, Status, and Social Justice

The policy process entailed in developing any coalition of agencies would enable each agency to maintain its own prerogatives as to how it wishes to deliver services to these children and their substitute care givers. However, while the process itself would help children or their surrogates to maintain their right to appropriate care, the children or their surrogates most likely were not involved in the development of this policy. Only to the extent that patients/consumers are on the hospital Board, can they be said to have participated in the development of the policy. Nevertheless, this policy process has acted on behalf of these infants and, to that extent, it may be said that these childrens' rights and status are thereby being served.

e. Self-Determination

Clearly, no infant placed in care has the ability to refuse or accept these alternatives to care. Because they may have been abandoned, their natural parents would not be involved in determining the desirability of placement (though some may not have surrendered parental rights) nor would they have participated in the policy's development. However, it is possible that the guardians or parent surrogates might be included in the more detailed operationalization of this policy.

f. Identity

This policy process should contribute greatly to the self-image of those who participated in the policy action system inasmuch as these individuals saw a service need that could be meshed with organizational goals and then moved that problem definition to the point of obtaining policy legitimation by the board for further program planning. The collective self-image of the board was also likely enhanced to the extent of their pride in being able to rely on staff skills and input to support and shape their policy choices in policy development, program planning, and resource allocation.

g. Individualization

Individualization is the central objective in the policy observed in this process. The policy process is aimed at developing plans and services that are unique to the needs of each client. Also, to the extent that the input of each professional discipline was or will be appropriately considered in the policy's development and implementation, it may also be said that the policy process allowed for professional individualization.

h. Nonjudgmental Attitude

It is not likely that a judgmental attitude prevailed in this policy development process. Given the fact that there are widely held stereotypical views in the social environment regarding those who are infected with the HIV virus (e.g., presumptions of drug abuse or promiscuous behavior), it would have been quite easy for some elements in the policy action system to foster a victim-blaming frame of mind and condemn these children. The fact that the policy was established is testimony that prejudicial attitudes did not prevail.

i. Confidentiality

The maintenance of confidentiality is essential in the case of an HIV + diagnosis, as was noted in the case illustration in chapter 4. However, in terms of policy *process*, the maintenance of confidentiality is also essential when it comes to negotiating with potential care providers. Such information should only be provided when there is a clearly discernable "need to know" regarding specifics of any particular child's symptomology.

The maintenance of confidentiality will continue to be a difficult responsibility in carrying this policy process forward, given the number and variety of external services that will have to be provided.

j. Indeterminateness

The policy on providing community-based residential care and other appropriate assistance for abandoned infants with HIV infection is consistent with the principle of indeterminateness on at least two counts. This principle—that the end states of social processes are determined during the life of events—is apparent in the open-ended approach of the policy statement itself. First, the policy indicates that the nature of the program is yet to be determined in process. That is, it is yet to be established whether the hospital itself will provide the program and/or other services or whether a community agency will provide them under the auspices of the hospital. Indeed, it is even yet to be determined whether other hospitals will be invited to benefit from this policy. Second, since the actual arrangements may be dependent upon the outcome as yet to be determined by negotiations with community agencies, the details of policy implementation are yet to be decided by more policy process. This process is still open-ended.

k. Multifinality

The principle of multifinality—that similar original states could properly result in varied subsequent conditions—is clearly possible through this policy. Given experience developed by providing community-based care for this particular population (i.e., infants with HIV +), the hospital is more likely to explore similar departures from the traditional service provision model for other patient population groups in the future. This is a precedant-setting policy, a common precondition to organizational change on a broader level.

l. Nonsummativity

The principle of the whole being something different or more than the sum of its parts is evident, to some extent, in the notion of defining the treatment solution in extra-mural, community-based terms. This policy approach is based upon a holistic view of patient needs when it comes to discharge planning and follow-up services. The provision of residential care is not, of course, simply one procedure to be applied like some surgical treatments but, rather, calls in a number of related subsystems—a fact implied in the recognition of community-based care.

m. Morphogenesis

The principle of morphogenesis—that human systems can change their forms and structure in process—is demonstrated in this policy process in that the organization was able to alter its fundamental conception of service delivery. That is, the policy process allowed the organization to embrace the notion that Vistaview can move beyond a traditional acute care general hospital role, which is not responsible for providing residential care subsequent to the patient's readiness for discharge. On the other hand, there may be no expectation of any morphogenetic change to be undertaken by existing community agencies, except that they would need to adjust their program design, staff training, and policies and procedures to accommodate children who may be in and out of home and hospital due to the progression of the virus seen in young children.

n. The SCRAPS Test

We know that this policy and the process engendered to establish the policy has particular implications for those who are poor and socioeconomically disenfranchised. Most infants diagnosed HIV+ are children of intravenous drug users and individuals who maintain their survival through prostitution. Others born to parents with higher economic status are likely to experience some of the same prejudice directed at them as blame for the behavior of their parents. Therefore, not only does the content of the policy speak to the SCRAPS issue, but the policy process having occurred means that significant elements within the hospital system were cognizant of their responsibility to relate to the needs of those in these population groups. This process is evidence of institutional efforts at combatting the isms. We know, too, that HIV infection disproportionately exists within some minority groups and is presently being found at an increasing rate among women who are partners of bisexual males and IV drug users. Consequently, the process is evidence that the organization, in an institutional sense, is willing to combat some outcomes of racism and sexism.

Summary

This has been an analysis of a policy process in which an urban, acute care, general hospital established as policy that the hospital would provide community-based residential care and other appropriate assistance for "boarder babies," infants born in the hospital who are abandoned, with few alternatives for other out-of-home care, due to their being diagnosed HIV +. The Vistaview Hospital Board developed a policy that asserted its intention to serve these children, crafted in such a way that its implementation would be left open to exploration of the hospital mounting its own direct service program, either by supporting purchase-of-service contracting or by developing some cooperative arrangement or coalition with existing child-care services in the community.

Summary

In this chapter we have reviewed some elements for policy analysis that help to explain the process aspects of social welfare policy. We addressed elements of process that should be reviewed as the milestones, the interest group features for analysis, and the resources to be considered in policy process for analysis. As with the analysis of policy content, we also considered the values implications in the policy process. Application of the elements has been illustrated throughout by reference to a case example involving the development of a policy in which an acute care general hospital would provide community-based residential care and other appropriate assistance for infants abandoned in hospitals due to HIV infection.

We will now apply these policy process criteria to three case illustrations in chapter 7, using the following outline.

An Outline for Analyzing Process of Small-Scale Policy

A. *Essential Steps in Policy Process Analysis*
  1. Identify the policy problem or policy goal(s) (same as content analysis)
  2. Assess the nature or condition of development milestones
  3. Identify interest group relationships
  4. Assess the availability and use of process resources
  5. Determine implications for selected values (same as content analysis)
  6. Provide recommendations

B. *Content Analysis*
  1. Identify the policy problem or policy goal(s)—A focus on the definition or delineation of the **core principles** at stake in the

particular problem, policy goal(s) or the specific policy that is to
be analyzed. Identification should include:

    a. The policy problem/goal and the policy statement

    b. Base(s) of legitimacy and source or location of the policy (in
written form if formal policy or as observed in actual behavior if in informal policy).

2. Assess the nature or condition of developmental milestones—A
focus on the major developmental tasks undertaken or to be undertaken in the policy process.

    a. Identification of the charter

        1) Find original agreement or template for action

        2) Obtain the right or support to take action

        3) Determine substance of the agreement(s)

    b. Functioning of the action system(s)

    c. Key participants and their associated events

3. Identify interest group relationships—A focus on the particular
groups represented in the policy process, identification of their
particular interests, and their interaction relevant to the policy.

    a. Power and influence

    b. Salience of the issue

    c. Intergroup activities

        1) Intergroup transfers and/or exchanges

        2) Bargaining and negotiating

        3) Coalitions

        4) Contracting

4. Assess the availability and use of process resources—A focus on
the resources needed and observable in the policy process.

    a. People power

    b. Technology

    c. Finances

    d. Time

5. Determine implications for selected values—A focus on the implications for selected values to be used in the analysis or desired in the proposed or desired policy, particularly with regard
to the targets and clients/interests affected by the policy.

    a. Adequacy

    b. Effectiveness

    c. Efficiency

    d. Impact on rights, statuses, and social justice

    e. Self-determination

    f. Identity

    g. Individualization

    h. Nonjudgmental attitude

   i.   Confidentiality
   j.   Indeterminateness
   k.   Multifinality
   l.   Nonsummativity
   m.   Morphiogenesis
   n.   The SCRAPS Test
6. Provide Recommendations—A focus on the strengths and weaknesses or factors peculiar to the issue and suggested by the data generated by the analysis.

Case Illustrations
of Process Analysis

7

This chapter provides three case illustrations of small-scale policy process analysis using the framework introduced in chapter 6. We will continue with the case example involving the policy topic of "The Homeless and the Mall People" (Case 5) used for illustration of content analysis in chapter 5 and will add the topics of "Uniform Fee Determination" (Case 6) and "The Community Case Coordination TEAM" (Case 7) as new policy topics for consideration. This way, we will be able to follow two policy issues (i.e., Infants with HIV + Infection, treated in chapters 4 and 6, and Homelessness and the Mall People) through both content and process analysis and still add additional policy topics for illustrative purposes.

Case 5: Policy Process—The Homeless and the Mall People

This case illustration extends the discussion of content analysis begun on this policy topic in chapter 5.

1. Identify the Policy Problem or Policy Goal(s)

Focus on the definition or delineation of the core principles at stake in the particular problem, policy goal(s), or the specific policy that is to be analyzed. Identification should include:

a. The Policy Problem/Goal and the Policy Statement

You may recall that this situation involves a community concern about the use of the downtown mall by various groups in the community. There is particular concern about the relationships between the "mall people," merchants, and other visitors to the mall. "Mall people" is really a label, often spoken in a pejorative context, given to a variety of citizens. Some are homeless, some deinstitutionalized from state facilities, and others just happen to use the mall as their central place for socializing. The population consists of residents of a correctional halfway house, youths, developmentally disabled citizens working at a sheltered workshop in the area, some senior citizens, and some persons on aftercare from the state psychiatric hospital. City Commissioner Frances LaRose proposed a policy, as follows:

> It is the policy of the City of Rapid River that all citizens of the community shall have equal access to all public facilities associated with the Downtown Mall; that the civil rights of no citizen of the community will be violated by any policy or procedure related to any activity of any public or private group while associated with the Downtown Mall; and that all ordinances of the city and laws of the State and Federal governments shall be observed insofar as those ordinances and laws pertain to conduct of citizens on the mall.

Our analyses, first of content and now of process, offer the possibility of a complementary two-pronged policy approach that would provide social service supports to some of the "mall people" and a public education program for others associated with the mall. The goal of each approach is to create an environment in which everyone in the community finds the downtown mall an attractive and satisfying place while, at the same time, the rights of all citizens are honored, the responsibilities of all are properly carried out, and the opportunities for community pride and development are maximized.

The mall, a combination of pedestrian walkways on a closed thoroughfare with arcades housing shops and meeting places, was constructed with both public and private funds. Some city agencies and businesses guard their investments jealously. Some see the mall people as a threat to the ongoing viability of the mall; others view them positively, seeing the creation of a mall environment that is functional for all elements of the city as a challenge. Our present analytic task is to gain understanding about the process aspects of policy development in this situation.

b. Bases(s) of Legitimacy and Source or Location of the Policy

This should be in written form if formal policy or as observed in actual behavior if an informal policy. Each of the principles or conceptual goals of the charter just enumerated has its own source of legitimacy. The regulatory and enforcement approach of Commissioner LaRose's proposal is based on the right and responsibility of city government to take legislative and administrative action. The service approach is legitimated by mandates for service agencies—particularly state and local public agencies—to provide more than custodial care for its clientele. In fact, these agencies are mandated to provide services as the least restrictive alternative to institutional care.

The City Commission has the unquestionable right to take the action implied by Commissioner LaRose's proposal and, while some citizens may not approve of the particular strategy, commission prerogatives in this proposal are not at issue. The service agencies may have to educate funding sources and/or various publics regarding the propriety as well as the responsibility to undertake the services strategy; nevertheless, the agencies possess the necessary legitimacy, if not the actual support, to take action.

2. Assess the Nature or Condition of Developmental Milestones

Focus on the major developmental tasks undertaken or to be undertaken in the policy process.

a. Identification of the Charter

The key concepts providing impetus to policy action here are entitlement to free access, protection of property rights, maintenance of the public good, equal opportunity for participation, and provision of adequate supports to all elements in the system. The latter are all potential elements of the charter—the valued ends that motivate policy action. While competing priorities surround these valued ends at any one point in the life of the policy process, they will have to be pursued in an integrated fashion if the policy process is to succeed. Consequently, we see a number of principles in this charter that give the impetus for further social action, all engendered by formalization of intent articulated in Commissioner LaRose's motion.

b. Functioning of the Subsequent Action System(s)

The group initiating change in the policy system is composed of an active member of the Downtown Merchants Association, Commissioner LaRose, and a staff member of the Human Relations Office of the city administration. There have been some encouraging preliminary discussions with the chief of police, the director of the Community Mental Health Board, and the president of the Rapid River Adult Foster Care Home Owners Association. But the impetus for action has come primarily from the original three: one merchant, the city staff member, and Commissioner LaRose have clearly been the generating force for policy change.

c. Key Participants and Their Associated Events

The regulatory and enforcement strategy required by Commissioner LaRose's proposal requires the broader participation and cooperation of many key elements, such as the police and court agencies, as well as the entire downtown business community. Key decision makers and proximate policymakers in all of these areas must be involved to arrive at a workable policy.

The dual strategy of service and enforcement requires participation of correctional, mental health, public welfare, school, transportation, and housing agency officials. The participation of local officials in these areas would be appropriate, at least in the early stages. Due to the authority structure in funding and program approvals, state-level officials may have to be brought in at a later time. The key participants mentioned thus far will need to play either technical roles such as developing plans and procedures or interactive roles such as bringing various essential elements together.

At least two other significant elements are present in this policy process: the various media in the community and the Community Welfare Planning Council, a companion agency of the United Way. Each of these elements will play system spanning or integrative roles. The Community Welfare Planning Council has the opportunity to bring together numerous key decision makers from a variety of organizations and associations in the community, many of whom are intimately involved in decisions regarding the design and finance of public and private health and human service programs. The integrative function of the media will be crucial not only in helping the public to understand the problem but also in determining the approaches to resolution that the public will support.

3. Identify Interest Group Relationships

Focus on the particular groups represented in the policy process, identification of their particular interests, and their interaction relevant to the policy.

a. Power and Influence

In a legal sense, the City Commission unquestionably has the power to control the outcomes of citizens' behavior with respect to establishing viable ordinances. However, the influence of the commission—the actual exercising of that power—depends upon the commission's ability to be an *effective* leader. Within its legal boundaries, the commission controls the policies and procedures of the Public Safety Department, the Human Resources Office, the Transportation Department, and all affairs pertaining to use of the public portions of the mall.

The issue of power—the ability to control the behavior of others—held by the merchants rests more on the personal efficacy of certain individuals, which is based upon local history that includes many issues other than the mall, and the many interdependencies found within the business community. The leadership that the business community brings to bear on problem resolution will probably emphasize a combination of future commercial developments, recognition of the needs of all citizens, and prudence in financial investment.

The power of the health and human services elements of the community is extensive in terms of *their* ability to control the outcome for the homeless and others who congregate on the mall. This power relates directly to the condition of the mall people, in that agency policy, procedures, and resources intimately affect the nature and quality of services provided. However, the service agencies' ability to exercise that power (their influence) is greatly controlled by many other elements in the community. Some merchants, city officials, the Community Welfare Planning Council, and the media *all* have many opportunities to exercise control as well—over the community's agenda and the level of funding for virtually all social services programs.

b. Salience of the Issue

Perhaps the most important dynamic in this policy problem is the salience of the issue. The "problem" of the downtown mall has high valence, that is, value and investment, to a whole range of elements in the community. Whether one is a responsible public official, an entrepreneur, a service agency staff member, one of the individuals under scrutiny, or merely a citizen observer, the "downtown mall problem" is important. The issue cuts across geography, ideology, income, and time. This level and quality of issue salience suggests that *something* will certainly happen in the way of policy change. The investment is too great for too many people for policy action not to occur.

c. Intergroup Activities

The broad salience and potentially integrative nature of this particular issue suggest that extensive intergroup relationships are necessary. Issues of public access and freedom to move about, successful commerce, the special needs of particular population groups, community aesthetics, and pride are all intertwined, as are the groups that represent those interests and/or responsibilities. To date no ongoing task force or coalition exists to deal with these issues. The city manager's office, the Community Welfare Planning Council, or even one of the special interest agencies could assume leadership. However, no institutional arrangements are in place in the community to bring these various elements and interests together on a regular basis. Their interaction, therefore, is likely to be dictated by ad hoc strategies for solving particular problems. Our analysis will now consider some particular aspects of intergroup interaction.

Intergroup transfers and/or exchanges. Were only one of the policy approaches (i.e., regulation and enforcement or supportive services) to be taken, the reward of opportunity and burden of sacrifice would be bilateral or multilateral in the sense that most of the elements would be giving and getting some rewards out of the policy. If only the regulatory and enforcement approach were taken, there would be a unilateral "giving up" of many existing ways of dealing with the problem. For example, a specific "mall person" whose behavior violated the rights of others would be forced (more directly) to give up such behavior. However, this would not solve the problem of the dissatisfaction that some people feel about other, legal behavior on the mall. If only the regulation strategy were taken, the burden would rest only on the mall people—to either change their behavior or cease to frequent the mall.

The tandem or dual policy approach suggests a bilateral (more democratic) sharing of responsibility for change. All elements—the city, merchants, and the mall people—would have to participate in various ways to resolve the problem. The rest of the public, hopefully all participant-observers, would also have to make certain adjustments.

There are incentives for each of these constituencies to make the necessary adjustments. A refusal to participate and make such changes could signal the ascendancy of any one group and impede the community goal of providing an environment that is attractive and satisfying to all parties concerned.

Bargaining and negotiating. The main vehicle for policy change will be extensive negotiating among all elements. Particular issues for negotiations would involve the City Commission, city manager, and the Department of Public Safety addressing the clarity of the policy and the adequacy of resources to be provided for its implementation. Given the probable changes in working conditions for the police force, some collective bargaining efforts may be necessary to alter some of the terms in existing labor-management agreements. Commitments would have to be made by and with individual business people and the Downtown Merchants Association to the negotiating strategies to be employed. Turf issues are also likely to arise: negotiation about service domains and obligations would be necessary for the health and human services agencies.

Coalitions. The nature of the problem, given its diverse auspices, authority, investment, and incentives unquestionably speaks to the necessity of formal coalition building. However, it is extremely important to recognize that each party in a coalition has a right to expect that individual and/or group interests will be respected and not surrendered to the goals of the coalition. Thus, group self-interests will be recognized, but all in the context of achieving the community goal.

Contracting. Inasmuch as some of the local funding agencies (e.g., mental health) provide services by contracting with existing community agencies, it would be necessary to contract for certain services identified in the policy process, e.g., behavioral management training and transportation skills training. Furthermore, many local agencies' contracts with state agencies would need to be renegotiated, and approved spending plans would have to be modified. Such contractual changes may require new funding; others may necessitate authorization to transfer resources from one program line to another.

Another possible contracting issue that could arise is that one agency or a coalition of agencies may have to assume contractual responsibility to oversee and/or coordinate future plans and policy. The probable parties to such a contract are unclear at this time.

4. Assess the Availability and Use of Process Resources

Focus on the resources needed and observable in the policy process.

a. People Power

The salience of the issue for the community has generated a range of interest in seeking a solution. The self- or group-interests of the range of elements in the community assure active participation in problem resolution. Efforts of key partisans will not be lacking! We have no shortage of people as resources in this policy problem and policy process.

b. Technology

The regulatory aspects of Commissioner LaRose's policy approach will require new efforts in monitoring to assure citizens' rights, which may entail developing a monitoring and compliance mechanism of some sort and putting reporting procedures in place. The enforcement aspects of monitoring will undoubtedly require the addition of additional uniformed foot and car patrols in the downtown mall area.

The supportive services strategy will require staff experienced in behavior training, operation of either daytime activity programs or day treatment services, development and packaging of public education programs in the human service area, and operation of a crisis counseling service immediately available for trouble situations. These are some of the activities that will demand new programs and staff with additional skills, plus the requirements of space, virtually all in the downtown area.

c. Finances

Regulatory and enforcement costs could be paid for by community block grants, while other costs could be borne by shifting some city staff from other programs. Such transferring would affect staffing at the city manager's office, the city Department of Transportation, and the Department of Public Safety.

Costs for supportive services could come in part from the city's general revenue funds. Funding from the correctional services area and the mental health system would likely entail a transfer of state hospital funds budgeted for local programs. This would be possible by reducing the local share of the charge back to the county inasmuch as the support programs would presumably allow for reduced institutional utilization costs, thereby channeling some funds from residential/institutional care into community programming. That is, the county's net cost for care would be lessened, because the county would be paying for community rather than institutional care. Some financial support would be available in the form of reduced rental costs for locating services in the downtown area, because some vacated facilities adjacent to the mall would be available at very reasonable rates.

The opportunity costs of doing nothing would be considerable to all elements. Some would argue that the avoidance of regulation and enforcement could mean the loss of the central commercial district, and that the absence of supportive services would surely entail higher institutional care costs for some mall people who are otherwise maintained by the community.

d. Time

Time is a valuable commodity in this problem resolution since much will have to occur by way of citizen participation and in program planning. The costs of time in public review and debate will be an invaluable investment in terms of ultimate support. Interagency cooperation and planning will require considerable time but will have long-range effects in bringing agencies together to serve the community in this heretofore neglected problem area. Moreover, successful service efforts over time could create a ripple effect that would expand community support for health and human services in general.

5. Determine Implications for Selected Values

Focus on the implications for selected values to be used in the analysis in the proposed or desired policy, particularly with regard to the targets and clients/interests affected by the policy. (We have already discussed values implications earlier in the context of the analysis of the *content* of the policy. Those values considerations are still germane to the issue. However, our task at this point is to consider the values issues in the context of the policy *process*. Consequently, our focus on this point will be to speculate on values implications for matters of policy process.)

This policy problem clearly represents a clash of values concerning the uses of community resources and the determination of what should constitute "appropriate" or "acceptable" behavior in public places. We have two policy strategies under consideration in this analysis. The first is Commissioner LaRose's strategy of regulation and enforcement, aimed at protecting the rights of all elements of the system. The second strategy complements the first and includes providing supportive social services for the mall people and public education efforts for merchants and other downtown visitors. Our analysis will proceed with these two approaches in mind.

The two approaches to the problem, regulation and enforcement on the one hand and supportive services on the other, suggest very different values in problem resolution. The regulatory and enforcement strategy gives the highest value to social control, as does the opportunity to rightfully obtain one's entitlements. This is not to say that social control is necessarily a negative or unwarranted strategy. Nevertheless, the approach assumes that the policy goal can best be achieved through legal management and relational restrictions.

The services strategy values the provision of supports through development of individuals' social skills in such matters as taking the bus, engaging in appropriate behaviors in shops and restaurants, and learning how to properly greet others on the mall. The services strategy holds promise of finding service solutions or supports that might be unique to the needs of the homeless as a particular subgroup. This strategy is also aimed at public education. The fundamental assumption is that individuals are in need of remediation and that community resources should be made available to fill those gaps or meet those deficits.

The two approaches have compatible values, thereby suggesting the potential for success. While each is rooted in a different perspective about social behavior, they are complementary policy thrusts.

a. Adequacy

The policy may be said to have broad or horizontal adequacy in that the citizens of the entire community are affected and not just those who are presently disaffected. The vertical adequacy, or the extent to which the policy and the process affect any one individual in particular, largely depends upon the extent to which each group is represented in the formulation process and the extent to which the policy provides remedies for any one individual. Horizontal or broad policy coverage is achieved in that there is "something for everybody" by pursuing the two policy directions.

b. Effectiveness

Both policy strategies suggest a probable alteration in the sequence of subsequent events, to the extent that attempts at behavioral change are successful. Hence, the combined strategy approach is a powerful policy approach. Both the commissioner's regulatory policy approach and the supportive services strategy are intended to narrow the range of probabilities of citizens' behavior with respect to the mall. Each strategy aims at channeling or shaping the types of behavior on the mall, one through control and the other through education and/or training. Each generates more predictability and lawfulness in the sequence of social processes to follow, and each supports the policy goal of making the mall attractive and readily available to all citizens of the community.

c. Efficiency

This policy and its formative process might be said to be unique in that they have efficiencies with two policy strategies being embodied in one resolution and with diverse interest groups being attracted to participate in the policy problem resolution.

d. Impact on Rights, Statuses, and Social Justice

The commissioner's proposed policy appears to treat all community population groups equitably. The regulatory and enforcement strategy is a leveling device. The supportive services strategy is, on the other hand, predicated on the primacy of the majority's way of conducting affairs on the mall; ironically, the services approach creates a greater burden for change on the victims, currently perceived by many as those with the problem, yet the homeless and those labeled as "mall people" have much to gain in the long run from the services strategy.

e. Self-Determination

Virtually all affected individuals or groups have had opportunity to participate in the policy process. This is true even for those individuals who may be seen as not fully competent to lobby for their own interests since the social service agency representatives have lobbied for them. In fact, the two-pronged approach to the policy solution itself supports the value of self-determination for all parties. The right to congregate and the right to free access are evidence of the protected right to self-determination. The right to participate in the process of problem resolution and policy development is also in evidence here.

f. Identity

The promotion or protection of individuals' feelings of self-worth and self-identity is suggested somewhat in this policy process to the extent that opportunities for expression by all parties are not only allowed but encouraged by the policy process. Public policy is being shaped here through *public* processes, though those who hold the most power and exercise that opportunity are no doubt likely to walk away with the greatest feelings of self-satisfaction.

g. Individualization

Inasmuch as all elements are able to articulate their own perspectives on desired policy outcomes, individualization is operationalized in this policy process. For the "mall people," individualization is honored in the concept that they be accorded the least restrictive environment here; for others in the community, such as businesspeople and shoppers, expressed needs are also considered in part of the accommodations made in the policy process and policy formulation.

h. Nonjudgmental Attitude

There is plenty of space or opportunity for making summary judgments of individuals and groups in this policy process, of course. The potential for stereotypes and prejudice is great in this situation. Those with power and influence can be seen as having more opportunity to influence the shape of policy on the bases of their stereotypes of "mall people." On the other hand, it would not be unlikely for social service people to stereotype businesspeople as solely operating in their own self-interest or in pursuit of personal profit. The more that dialogue and compromise is pursued in a public forum, the less likely that the policy outcome will perpetuate judgmental attitudes.

i. Confidentiality

It is difficult to honor the principle of maintenance of confidentiality in this policy process. Certainly, individuals' rights to privacy can be maintained, but it is difficult to assure that the individuals' feelings, perspectives, and behavior are kept secret when policy problem resolution rests on public dialogue and social interaction. The broad participation of the media in the public debate and examination of the issues makes it even more difficult to maintain confidentiality. The use of a public forum for problem resolution presents certain costs for the maintenance of confidentiality.

j. Indeterminateness

The two-pronged approach of providing both regulation and enforcement along with supportive services suggests the likelihood of a highly unpredictable and indeterminate end state of this policy process. Furthermore, the multiplicity of actions and their associated policy views and positions suggest a myriad of potential outcomes. Policy formulation here is far from being linear and simple. It is multifaceted as a result of dialogue and compromise. The end states of these negotiations will be determined in not only the process of policy formulation but resultant policy implementation.

k. Multifinality

A variety of end states are likely to arise out of this policy process inasmuch as new patterns of communication are likely to have evolved out of the new interaction of people in pursuit of problem resolution here. Citizens are now openly expressing their views in an open forum, merchants are negotiating directly with social service personnel, city officials are found in the role of intermediary, and so forth. The variety of potential end states as a result of the policy process is increased with each new participant and each new relationship.

l. Nonsummativity

The principle that the whole is something other than the sum of its parts is put into operation in this type of policy situation. The goals of maintenance of the public good and protection of private rights and interests all lead to the phenomenon of "satisficing," in which the gains of the majority are maximized and the losses to the minority, minimized. Out of such a process comes a new reality that cannot be expressed in the simple arithmetic of adding up gains and losses of individuals or groups.

m. Morphogenesis

Consequently, the situation of "the homeless and the mall people" takes on a new form. The participatory nature of the policy process moves the issue from one of "we" *versus* "they" to one of "we" *and* "us": "How can this issue be resolved to the satisfaction of all of us?" The picture of those who possess the problem has changed from the small charter group of one merchant, a city staff member, and Commissioner LaRose to broad participation by the community-at-large, including the homeless and the mall people themselves. Consequently, the "policy system" itself has been altered as a result of the policy process.

n. The SCRAPS Test

This issue has great risk of being classist in nature in that those who are homeless, poor, mentally ill, or otherwise not seen as normative in their behavior are usually cast aside and excluded from the policy decision process. To be sure, this policy process requires the active participation of community leadership. Consequently, there is a logical risk of perpetuating the classist nature of policy decision making in the community to the extent that the less privileged or their surrogates (i.e., social service personnel) are not included and that the powerful continue to dominate. Realistically speaking, given the usual workings of community power and influence, it would be naive to suggest that the homeless, the mentally ill, and the poor are equal participants in the play of power. Nonetheless, it would appear that the opportunities for the participation of many elements are maximized in this policy process.

6. Provide Recommendations

Focus on the strengths and weaknesses or factors peculiar to the issue and suggested by the data generated by the analysis. Here is where we should be ready to provide our recommendations, each arising out of the information obtained in the analysis.

Summary

This case illustration has reviewed the process elements of policy development regarding the distribution of rights and privileges involving the homeless and the city's downtown mall. A two-pronged approach to the problem, regulation and enforcement of citizen behavior, along with providing supportive services to the homeless and other mall people, has emerged. The content elements of this issue were reviewed in chapter 5.

Case 6: Policy Process—Uniform Fee Determination

This case example provides an illustration of a process involving two interrelated issues. The first is the development of the Cascade County Community Mental Health Board's system-wide "Policy and Procedures for a Uniform Method of Determining Ability to Pay." This is a uniform fee determination policy and fee schedule for all local agencies operating as contractual services under the county's community mental health program. The second issue embedded in the policy program is a system-wide push for the generation of revenues. This is an effort to support continuation of services in a period of significant funding cutbacks by means of increasing program support through the billing of clients and/or their insurance carriers.

Cascade County, a county of approximately one-half million inhabitants in a standard metropolitan statistical area in a north central state, operates its county community mental health program by contracting out all direct services to various private and public agencies in the county. Board administration, planning and evaluation, and recipients' rights activities are all conducted out of the county board's offices; direct services are operated by twenty-five other agencies through purchase-of-service contracting with the Cascade County Community Mental Health Board.

1. Identify the Policy Problem or Policy Goal(s)

Focus on the definition or delineation of the *core principles* at stake in the particular problem, policy goal(s), or the specific policy that is to be analyzed. Identification should include:

a. The Policy Problem/Goal and the Policy Statement

The central problems here are the absence of a policy and procedures or clear guidelines for the installation of a uniform fee policy, in addition to an increasing need to develop new sources of revenue for problem funding. Chapter seven of the State Mental Health Code, Act 129, provides that the State Department of Mental Health or its designees (i.e., the county community mental health boards) have the authority to establish fee schedules and to bill recipients for services. The "Standards for Community Mental Health Services" subsequently published by the State Department of Mental Health provides that each county board has the responsibility for developing and implementing clearly defined mechanisms for the collection of fees from clients and third parties ("Standards," p. 29).

Approximately five years ago, the Cascade County Mental Health Board chairperson appointed a fee policy task force composed of the board chair, the board's executive director, directors of three agencies contracting with the board to provide mental health services, and representatives of two noncontracting agencies in the community. This group formulated a two-page philosophy and fee policy, and a fee schedule. The policy espoused the principle that those utilizing services be asked to pay for them, that the actual cost of services should be disclosed to consumers, and that no one should be denied services based on inability to pay. There was little comment on the proposed policy during its sixty-day public review, but after its implementation, widespread concern was expressed about the effect of the policy on the poor, the difficulty in assessing fees for nontraditional services (e.g., case management and respite care), and the correlation of the policy and guidelines with Blue Cross/Blue Shield insurance procedures. The lack of specific guidelines and procedures for policy implementation, as well as the proposed fee schedule (viewed as excessively high by many agency directors) led to the policy largely being ignored by contract agencies. A few agencies adopted and followed the policy, others maintained policies and fee schedules of their own, and others did not charge fees. Thus, the first attempt at establishment of a system-wide fee policy and schedule was not successful.

Budgetary constraints due to increasing program demands, the general instability of the state's economy, and State Department of Mental Health cuts in matching funds to Cascade County Community Mental Health reawakened interest in fees as a source of revenue. Another key factor in generating concern was an application by the state for federal reimbursement for certain mental health services under Medicaid (Title XIX), which would require uniform billing policies and procedures to be operational throughout the system. During this period, a reimbursement officer was hired by the board and given the responsibility by the executive director for developing a new fee schedule as well as policies and procedures for its implementation. In cooperation with the financial officer of the Board, study of the possible clinical impact of fee assessment and equitable models for collection of fees was undertaken rather hastily by an ad hoc task force composed of administrative staff and clinicians from a number of contract agencies. With the initial activity of the reimbursement officer and the financial officer, upper and middle management of the Mental Health Board generated a fee policy, specific procedures for implementation, provisions for waiver, and a sliding fee schedule based on ability to pay. The earlier, two-page policy and fee schedule was replaced by a forty-three page document consisting of policy, procedures, and examples of recommended forms.

After the review period, the new policy was accepted by contract agencies with little comment and apparent resignation and was quickly approved by the board. Some minor resistance was voiced and, in response, contractees were reminded that such a requirement had been allowed years previously by the Mental Health Code, mandated by the State Mental Health Department, and was embedded in the current purchase-of-service contracts, although it had not been implemented.

b. Base(s) of Legitimacy and Source or Location of the Policy

This should be in written form if formal policy or as observed in actual behavior if an informal policy. In both attempts at initiation and implementation of the uniform fee policy, there was a solid base of legitimacy in the actions taken. In the first attempt, by virtue of the legitimate authority vested in the role of chairperson, the board chair established a task force; in the second attempt, the board's executive director initiated action in the appointment of administrative officers and another task force. Each action was formally legitimated by the appropriate charter associated with community mental health, the State Mental Health Code, Act 129. The standards that arose out of the act required that uniform policy and procedures be established, although processes for those actions were not prescribed. Consequently, legitimacy may be found in both legislative and administrative authority.

2. Assess the Nature or Condition of Developmental Milestones

Focus on the major developmental tasks undertaken or to be undertaken in the policy process.

a. Identification of the Charter

The initial skeleton of ideas giving impetus to the policy process is the Board chair's and executive director's charge to task forces and/or administrative staff to undertake action for change. Those who then moved forward were operating with a portfolio, as it were.

b. Functioning of the Subsequent Action System(s)

The action system was largely composed of the nominal leadership of those initiating action and engendering subsequent social process: earlier in the form of the board chairperson and later in the person of the executive director. To be sure, many of the contracting agencies who were disaffected with the workings of existing policy and procedures were perhaps more than active cheerleaders on the sidelines.

In each instance the action system was made up of a delimited set of individuals, although the nature of each group differed. The first attempt at organizing the action system tended to be somewhat more open and collaborative in that the board chair appointed board administrative staff, directors of some contract agencies, and even agency directors from the community who were not purchase-of-service contractees with the Community Mental Health Board. The second attempt was more of a closed system approach, with board staff developing the policy and a detailed set of procedures. However, in each instance there was opportunity for review and comment when the proposed policy was published, and a requirement for final, formal approval at a regularly scheduled board meeting. In both events, the entire mental health system was presumably involved (or had the opportunity to be involved at some level), although the action system was much more limited in numbers and representation in the second attempt.

c. Key Participants and Their Associated Events

The common policy development practice of publicizing an administrative policy for public review and comment during a specified period of time is frequently used by governmental agencies. In theory, this provides equal opportunity for public participation and could foster active solicitation of system-wide input and active involvement. In practice, it can also mean solicitation of participation with little active recruitment and suggests little attention will be given to assuring any particular representation or mixture of participants in the process. Furthermore, response or reaction to the input provided is not always guaranteed. In these two situations, however, the leverage exercised by certain actors is much more significant. In the first attempt, the key actors were identified leaders among their various constituencies. Unfortunately, their contribution was a vague and general policy. In the second attempt, the key actors were staff members whose leverage was technical information (it did not derive from elected or appointed legislative authority); however, their contribution was clear, detailed, and specific. Our analysis reveals that not only the actors, but the types of contribution they made (indicative of their roles and positions in the system), were key ingredients in the development of the policy.

3. Identify Interest Group Relationships

Focus on the particular groups represented in the policy process, identification of their particular interests, and their interaction relevant to the policy.

a. Power and Influence

Clearly the efficacy and legitimacy of the power of the board's officers and staff are rooted in the requirements of the State Mental Health Code, the standards for review, and the requirements to be met for Title XIX. The ability to exert influence beyond and outside of these areas is unquestionably connected to the board's funding role. While many of the local contractees exert some leverage through their ability to generate seed monies for local matching funds, the Community Mental Health Board is the conduit to state mental health matching funds and is the local mental health authority under the code. Each element has, in general, a vested interest in having that conduit function well; each has a stake in maximizing funding opportunities. Consequently, we see in the second (and successful) attempt at developing policy and procedures an apparent "resignation," evidence of both contract agencies' ambivalence and realism.

b. Salience of the Issue

Uniform procedures establishing community-wide equity for the recipients of services and maintaining adequate funding levels are issues salient to the entire community mental health system. In general, the absence of equity and a reduction in funding levels would affect all contract agencies equally. Consequently, while any one agency might not be enchanted with particular provisions, there is little argument about the necessity of the policy or its procedures.

c. Intergroup Activities

In this particular policy, we find relatively little evidence of intergroup interaction. The first attempt tended to incorporate a democratic presentation model, but there was little response during the period of public review and comment, and implementation was uneven. In the second attempt at development and implementation, the strategy of using internal board staff precluded much intergroup activity. This is an interesting phenomenon, considering the salience of the issue. One possible explanation might be that while service agencies generally find it distasteful to install fee policies that will place more burdens on their clientele, there is actually widespread recognition of the real necessity to do so.

Intergroup transfers and/or exchanges. At the agency-to-agency interaction level, the absence of apparent conflict is explained by the fact that the mutual interests of the board and contractees are served. The board achieves its legislated and administratively directed mandates for a uniform fee policy and procedures while contractee interests in financial support are maintained.

At the client-to-agency level, however, the unilateral nature of the exchange is enlarged. The client group shoulders an increased share of cost. The recipients of service—at least those who have the ability to pay—are asked to bear an increased burden of the incidence of cost. Those who do not have the ability to pay also feel the burden, as will be discussed later.

There is a mixture of incentives for agencies to participate cooperatively. For example, large agencies, or those that have automatic billing procedures in place, will likely benefit most from increased revenues, which could result in continued growth and independence. On the other hand, smaller agencies, especially those serving largely indigent clients and those with innovative, difficult-to-bill services, have to invest additional resources with little hope of recovering even their billing costs. In some agencies, this could result in lack of development, further financial strains, and inability to compete with larger agencies.

Bargaining and negotiating. There is little evidence here of bargaining or negotiating. However, some attempt was made to study issues, such as the clinical impact of a fee schedule; this is the point at which any negotiating might have taken place. In no event did contract agencies find themselves in a bargaining position.

Coalitions. Given the general passivity of contractees in both attempts at fee setting, there is little evidence of a coalition process. However, given that coalitions exist when the goals of individual parties are served by cooperative efforts, the tacit approval of the second attempt, whether out of resignation or agreement, does give evidence of some consensus.

Contracting. The whole process revolves around a network of services that exists by virtue of the ability of individual agencies to establish purchase-of-service contracts with a planning and funding source. (Of course, the contractual goals of each party must mesh in these instances.) The contractual goals of the Community Mental Health Board include development of alternative methods of generating revenue, compliance with the State Mental Health Code and the standards of organizational or agency performance, and, perhaps, movement towards a decrease in the county's dependence on state funding. In this particular instance, an additional goal might be to compensate for the lack of structure and guidelines in the first policy by providing elaborate detail and forms. The contractual goals of the individual contract agencies would include the maintenance of productive relationships with their funding source, advocacy for client rights, and preservation of the integrity of the agency's services. Both parties (i.e., the board and the contractee) have an interest in providing services in an equitable, efficient, and effective manner to those most in need.

4. Assess the Availability and Use of Process Resources

Focus on the resources needed and observable in the policy process.

a. People Power

Our analysis suggests that neither approach was lacking in necessary people power. The first and more democratic approach included a range of participants. The second and more technical approach included the persons necessary to develop an adequate policy. The success of the second approach derived mainly from the ability to develop and promulgate a detailed and technically sound set of policies and procedures that would give explicit direction to the contracting agencies.

b. Technology

As noted, the board apparently had the technical capacity to produce the policy, procedures, and guidelines appropriate to achieving the policy goals. This technical capacity is evidenced by the lack of negative criticism or rejection of what was produced and the fact of "resignation" (for reasons noted above). One could also infer that a technical rather than a more democratic approach was demonstrated. The latter is evidenced by the need to comply or conform with the state's application for a Medicaid certificate for Medicaid funding of selected services. A technical approach to policy and procedures would more likely result in conformity with state and federal regulations, though there is nothing to preclude that a more participatory process would be less effective.

c. Finances

Except for the cost of the actors' participation in each attempt, no out-of-pocket costs were incurred in the process of developing the uniform fees policy. The whole policy and the process surrounding it, of course, have very significant and broad financial implications for the board and the mental health system.

d. Time

Time was used differently in each instance. The first attempt, being more participatory in nature, used time to develop involvement and investment on the part of the ad hoc task force. The time investment during the period of public review and comment brought little return in terms of input. However, such time is not wasted, because it allows input by those who wish to offer it and serves, if nothing else, as a vehicle to inform the constituency. (Thus, time as a resource also has educational value.) The second attempt used time to develop detail and specificity.

5. Determine Implications for Selected Values

Focus on the implications for selected values to be used in the analysis of the proposed or desired policy, particularly with regard to the targets and clients/interests affected by the policy.

a. Adequacy

One mental set implied in the policy is the work ethic—those who receive benefits should properly pay for them. The establishment of a fee schedule is consistent with this attitude. The assumption that individuals utilizing services should pay for them, even though they have already helped fund them through tax dollars, is consistent with the Protestant work ethic prevalent in the community. To the extent that this policy achieves implementation across the board and coverage is actually achieved, the policy may be said to be adequate. At the same time, thinking in terms of the process aspects of the policy, only if all affected elements are appropriately and adequately represented can we say that the process was also adequate.

b. Effectiveness

Effectiveness can be evaluated from two perspectives or criteria. First, the ability of the policy to order the subsequent sequencing of events or to increase the probability of future events is found in the uniform fee determination policy (i.e., its stochastic power). At one level, the policy, with its detailed procedures, guidelines, and even newly developed forms, tremendously increases the predictive power to make things happen—to increase the probabilities of conformity in uniform fee determination. At another level, the process itself most likely has strengthened the position of the Community Mental Health Board in relation to the agencies it funds. The agencies' growing compliance, and the board's clear statement of its authority, will likely impact the manner in which future contract negotiations occur, the environment in which further policy statements are issued, and the always tenuous line between the agencies' self-determination and the goals of the funding source.

On the other hand, there is a second perspective, and the long-run probabilistic events may differ largely from the scenario above. The Board has consistently called upon contract agencies to collaborate with each other and work cooperatively to plan and implement services. That encouragement has largely taken hold as a result of the Board's power as a funding source. However, if the contract agencies become increasingly more independent as a result of increases in client- and third-party fee payments, there will be a lessening of dependency on the Board and perhaps less of a tendency for collaborative efforts. As the Board's leverage lessens in its funding potential, it may need to establish alternative leverage based on its expertise in such areas as planning, programming, or evaluation.

Another view is more pragmatic—that service systems must maximize use of any and all sources of revenue, and the recipients of services merely constitute one of many such sources.

c. Efficiency

The efficiency of the policy process might be examined in terms of the extent relevant groups can participate with the least amount of time or energy commitment. One perspective is that participatory approaches to policy development are likely to be well received and implemented without resentment and, therefore, elicit broad participation. A second perspective is that complex and detailed policies requiring both technical skill and co-operative processes require more time to process. The extensive reliance on the expertise of staff time may have been the least efficient in the short run but the most efficient in the long run.

d. Impact on Rights, Statuses, and Social Justice

One could conclude that the rights of individuals and groups were honored to the extent that each had equal opportunity to participate fully in the policy formulation process and that fee determination did take place uniformly and consistently throughout the system. Hence, the examination of the impact on rights, statuses, and social justice is just as important in analyzing the content as the process of policy. If the participatory strategy was narrow or selective, social justice was not served; if participation was broad and meaningful, the policy process stands a chance of being fair and equitable.

e. Self-Determination

Clients of mental health services in the community have more restricted access to mental health services in the sense that there are even more eligibility rules with which to conform. Presumably, no persons would be taxed beyond their ability to pay, but the current latitude in deciding to use mental health services would likely be curtailed.

From the agency perspective, this is a "take-it-or-leave-it" situation because the agencies are compelled to comply. The policy is not only promulgated from the top down but is a precondition of existence in the absence of alternative funding sources. Agencies have virtually no choice in the policy decision because their self-determination is severely limited.

f. Identity

Maintaining the identity of the contract agency as an integral member of the mental health system was enhanced more by the first approach to the policy process. The argument could also be made that the first approach promoted a greater sense of ownership and greater acceptance. The second approach, whether viewed as expedient or as a strategy to co-opt input, gives much less recognition to the role of the contractee. It could be said, however, that the role and identity of the contractee agencies are respected in each approach by the provision of the review and comment period.

g. Individualization

There appears to be no threat to the ability to deal with any client or contracting agency as a unique person with self-worth, either as a result of the policy or the process occurring in the policy's development.

h. Nonjudgmental Attitude

A nonjudgmental attitude in the administration of the policy is assured, provided that the guidelines for the policy (e.g., guidelines specifying excluded income or allowable expenses) do not reflect arbitrary or capricious judgments on what clientele do with their own resources. The policy process itself does not appear to reflect any judgmental attitude on the part of the policy developers, although the procedure requiring validation of income seems to imply a lack of trust in the individual's ability to be truthful. While this procedure is practical, it runs counter to professional values—the policy objective could be achieved as well by the client's affirmation by affidavit.

i. Confidentiality

Recipients of mental health services will, as a result of the policy, have to disclose more information regarding their personal finances. This will put more information into the system, thereby creating a need for additional safeguards to assure protection of confidentiality. In terms of the *process* of the policy's development, however, there do not appear to be any implications for maintaining client-system confidentiality. The policy process itself neither risks nor enhances the principle of confidentiality.

On the other hand, agencies will now be forced to develop and disclose more internal information (such as cost per units of services), in order to establish appropriate fees. Thus, the confidentiality of an agency's organizational information is at greater risk. The Mental Health Board's procedures for contract monitoring will have to ensure confidentiality for the agencies pertaining to organizational secrets.

j. Indeterminateness

This policy would seem to fly in the face of the values associated with indeterminateness—that the end products of social processes are determined in process. In the second attempt at policy development, the policies, procedures, and guidelines were more or less handed down; there was little process. Furthermore, from the perspective of the client system, the specificity of the policy and its associated trappings leave little room for an indeterminate perspective. The opportunity for public review and comment and the formal establishment of the policy at an open and formal public meeting would introduce some element of indeterminateness. However, the nature of specific fee schedules and forms would preclude much opportunity for a participatory policy-making process.

k. Multifinality

The principle that a variety of end states can arise out of similar beginnings is somewhat honored in a uniform fee schedule because different family or client circumstances can, or should, be considered and allowed in the implementation of the policy. Thinking in terms of the policy development process itself, however, little space was provided for conceptualizing a variety of alternative outcomes. (Fee schedules become fixed, though their application throughout a system might differ.) Consequently, little evidence is found in the substance or process in policy development of anything other than a rather deterministic view of the uniform fee decision.

l. Nonsummativity

The principle of nonsummativity—that the whole is something other than or greater than the sum of its parts—is demonstrated by the fact of a *uniform* policy being established. Acknowledging the need for uniformity in a fee policy gives recognition to the fact that the implications of such a policy are system wide. Any departure from uniformity and consistency in the policy or procedures from contractee to contractee would be injurious to the entire community mental health system. This was evident in the absence of the policy to begin with and in the first ineffective attempt to create it.

m. Morphogenesis

The ability of the community mental health system to alter its structures or processes is demonstrated in at least two ways. Perhaps because of the sequential/incremental nature of fundamental policy change, the system evolved from one of total commitment to a policy of no fees for services to a policy (albeit not largely implemented but at least sporadically embraced by some agencies), to a uniform, system-wide policy with attendant procedures and guidelines. This led to a fundamental restructuring in the funding base of the system as a whole and for most of the individual agencies.

In the second illustration relating to alterations in system processes, policy development by traditional consensual and representative processes became a more technical, unilateral process. This shift marked a fundamental departure from the system's usual way of approaching policy and program development. The resiliency of the system is evident in at least these two illustrations.

n. The SCRAPS Test

The fee policy could result in a significant decrease in utilization of mental health services by the poor. The elderly, many of whom rely on fixed incomes and live on the margin of or in poverty, often hesitate to use mental health services, fearing social stigma. They are also often reluctant to reveal personal financial information to strangers, let alone provide verification that they are telling the truth about income. Similarly, the poor, many of whom also have strong reservations about utilizing mental health services, will be reluctant to comply with the verification requirement. Of the agencies serving the poor in Cascade County, many are small; for these agencies the cost of initiating the complex billing procedures would be a financial hardship offering little opportunity for cost recovery. Thus, we could reasonably predict cutbacks in such agencies, which would result in decreased services to the poor.

The situation described above may explain the high level of resistance by these agencies to the policy development process. The policy may ultimately result in a decrease in services to the poor and the elderly and could eventuate the merger or termination of some smaller agencies.

The policy could work its toll on female clientele of the mental health system inasmuch as women are overrepresented as clients in the system and that, for example, being black or a single head of household geometrically increases one's chances of being poor if one is a woman.

6. Provide Recommendations

Focus on the strengths and weaknesses or factors peculiar to the issue and suggested by the data generated by the analysis. At this point we are free, even obliged, to provide any recommendations that arise out of the information generated by the analysis.

Summary

This case illustration reviewed the development of a uniform fee determination policy by a county community mental health board for an entire county mental health system and its twenty-five contractual provider agencies. By observing two attempts at developing the policy, each with a different strategy, we have obtained additional insights.

Case 7: Policy Process—The Community Case Coordination TEAM

This illustration exemplifies the actual problems in coordinating interagency efforts in delivering social services in many communities. In our case example, twenty-one human service agencies in Valley Falls, a population area of nearly one million, have coalesced to form a Community Case Coordination Team (hereafter referred to as TEAM), which has the stated purpose of "improving the coordination of existing area services to dysfunctional multisystem clients." The coalition is composed of public, private, voluntary, and governmental agencies from a variety of jurisdictions and political boundaries in the immediate geographical area. However, as will be noted in our analysis, the initiative for the policy process arose from the efforts of five agencies primarily serving a transient, low-income clientele in our fictitious Middleside neighborhood.

1. Identify the Policy Problem or Policy Goal(s)

Focus on the definition or delineation of the *core principles* at stake in the particular problem, policy goal(s), or the specific policy that is to be analyzed. Identification should include:

a. The Problem/Goal and the Policy Statement

This first section will give some shape to the problem generating the policy process and some definition of the policy itself.

The Middleside neighborhood, a densely populated area characterized by a mix of small industries and both multiple-unit and large, single-family, older residential units near the center of the central city, provides the geographical focus for our policy. Middleside is heavily populated by single, indigent street people and a large number of destitute individuals who are products of the move toward deinstitutionalization over the past few years. It became apparent to many of the agencies serving the area that poor interagency communication contributed to underutilization of necessary services for some citizens of the area, while other clients were using disproportionate amounts of those services. Yet another group of residents were inappropriately using the service system at the expense of those who were very much in need of available support services. As the broad areas of service gaps and duplication became increasingly problematic for the responsible agencies, poor coordination of agency services became more of a threat to needy citizens and clients and an issue for the agencies involved.

The TEAM was originally established by five agencies as an integral part of each agency's program operations. That is, the new interagency coordination policy required each agency to treat interagency coordination as an integral part of its program operations in an effort to "improve the coordination of existing area services to dysfunctional multisystem clients." Until the establishment of the TEAM, no formal mechanism for coordinating services existed. The factors that contributed to that state of affairs included increased agency specialization and independence, ambiguity in case management responsibilities, differing funding sources, and an atmosphere of growing territoriality and competition. Other problems included a lack of understanding by agency staff of the operating procedures of other agencies, different treatment philosophies among the agencies, and a lack of available resources for interagency coordination activities. Many of the clientele in the Middleside neighborhood experienced conflicting advice and services from those agencies.

A five-member coalition of agencies included the emergency room of St. Louis Hospital, the Valley Falls Police Department, the Salvation Army Mission Center, Transitions Detox Center, and The Bridge, the county mental health program's daytime drop-in center. A staff member from a neighboring county health department, on leave to complete a graduate program in social work and serving a student field-education internship at The Bridge, was assigned to chair the TEAM. She was chosen because she was an older, experienced worker who, having recently been employed by a local family services agency, was known to Valley Falls professionals. She was also seen as occupying a neutral position.

Eventually, the original five-member coalition developed a number of more specific goals for other agencies to consider. The TEAM, which utilized the "case conferencing" method of agency interaction, assured all potential participating agencies that no new system would add any additional steps in service delivery or become a requirement of participation. More specific goals were articulated over time: (1) to formalize and strengthen existing information networks in interagency communication or coordination; (2) to service problematic cases common to two or more member agencies by engaging in case management during regular and scheduled team meetings; (3) to determine more specific case management responsibility and procedures for shared management, with ongoing feedback on progress; (4) to review referrals of multiproblem clients and formulate appropriate service plans; and (5) to influence community policy, planning, and resource development regarding services to dysfunctional multisystem clients by issuing TEAM reports and recommendations to member agency participants.

b. Base(s) of Legitimacy and Source or Location of the Policy

This set of actors derived their legitimacy first as individuals and next as a collective action system from the organizations employing them. In one sense, then, their legitimacy was legislative in that each agency was legally constituted and had as part of its own mission the service activity being pursued by its staff in the Middleside neighborhood. Sponsorship of the five agencies was both public (the Valley Falls Police Department and the Bridge, a county mental health agency) and private (St. Louis Emergency Room, Transitions Detox Center, and the Salvation Army Mission).

2. Assess the Nature or Condition of Developmental Milestones

Focus on the major developmental tasks undertaken or to be undertaken in the policy process.

a. Identification of the Charter

The charter for policy action serving as the original agreement or template may be found in the impetus by the original five agencies to pilot the case coordination idea. Our analysis might pursue the question of which particular individual(s) in which particular agencies actually came forth with the idea.

The action system's charter to bring about change in the service system itself was subsequently supported by the agreed-upon responsibility of each team member. The five proponents of the plan, each a member of middle management as program coordinators in the neighborhood, simply requested permission to proceed with the pilot as an experimental project. Each member, in turn, was expected to report back on pilot project experiences to their own administrative head, thereby further legitimating their ongoing activity with the TEAM project. Here we can see the integral relationship between establishing a charter and obtaining legitimacy.

b. Functioning of the Action System(s)

As noted above, the action system was composed of five individuals and their associated agencies, each of which had a right to take action. After only three meetings, the goals and objectives enumerated above were more formally developed. An early strategy centered around serving the indigent population of the neighborhood and the service activity of case conferencing. If the TEAM experienced some success in adhering to the multiagency case conferencing strategy, it was believed that other agencies would join. In summary, then, the key action system activity was formally developing TEAM goals and objectives and carrying out a group decision to primarily serve the indigent population through case conferencing. They saw in this agreement the ability to attract other agencies to their mode of operation.

c. Key Participants and Their Associated Events

A key participant in the project was the TEAM chairperson, who was known to the professional community but who, as a graduate student from another county, was not seen as motivated as others might have been to serve agency or personal self-interest. The agencies involved were also key players in that each had extended experience with the client population on a daily basis, and their accumulated knowledge of client needs gave the TEAM credibility. The original TEAM of five had a mixture of professionals and "paraprofessionals," which demonstrated to members who later joined the TEAM that professional status did not create barriers that would interfere with the team approach to case coordination. The Police Department did not have any experienced human service personnel on staff, though it had recently embarked on a neighborhood foot-patrol strategy and officers were receiving more human relations and community resource training. The hospital and the community mental health staff were experienced social workers, while the Transitions Detox Center (except for visiting volunteer physicians) was staffed primarily by trained volunteers. The Salvation Army Mission, a multipurpose agency comprising a range of professional and volunteer staff, served as the framework for staff interaction and also contributed a meeting room for the regularly scheduled TEAM meetings.

In summary, these five agencies represented a range of professional and disciplinary orientations. As line staff from each of the agencies became more involved in TEAM interaction, an atmosphere of professional parity developed. That interaction then served as a model and linkage to their counterparts in other agencies in the ongoing TEAM program.

3. Identify Interest Group Relationships

Focus on the particular groups represented in the policy process, identification of their particular interests, and their interaction relevant to the policy.

a. Power and Influence

As noted above, each member of the action system had authority to take action. The range of professional and disciplinary orientations represented in the original TEAM influenced newcomer individuals and agencies to identify with existing TEAM members. Perhaps one of the greatest sources of influence was the actual success of more efficient service attributed to case conferencing.

Besides the collective goals of the agencies, there were additional individual or organizational vested interests at work. Some agencies, for example, were more interested in participating in the interagency communication network for other purposes or in maintaining an "in-the-know" posture. That is, some simply did not want to be left out of the information loop. Another large agency was testing the political waters regarding a single track or point of entry into a country-wide service system. (That fact, at one point, was a serious threat to the continuation of the TEAM experiment.) Yet another agency used the TEAM project as an entree into a new program that it was preparing for the Middleside neighborhood. As in all coalition-type efforts, it is important for the process analyst to recognize that each discrete organization in a coalition has the right to maintain its own goals. Coalitions are maintained when organizations can pursue common interests that derive from the goals that each organization rightfully reserves for itself.

b. Salience of the Issue(s)

The central issues facing the agencies were needy clients without services in the Middleside neighborhood and tremendous duplication of agency efforts in other areas. These salient issues were translated into expected client and agency outcomes. Some client-specific outcomes were: (1) interagency case conferencing for a coordinated treatment plan; (2) a broadened range of service alternatives and resources for each client; (3) involvement of professional services from many disciplines; (4) an integrated community response to client needs; (5) greater specificity regarding primary case management responsibility; and (6) a more appropriate matching of client need to agency service. Some agency-specific outcomes were: (1) integrated community approaches to dealing with service gaps; (2) coordinated agency responses to system manipulators; (3) strengthened interagency relationships; (4) clarification of agency roles in the human service matrix; (5) improved ability to provide clients with the least restrictive alternatives; and (6) pooling of resources in extremely problematic client situations. As one can see, there are a variety of incentives for social action that made this issue a salient one.

c. Intergroup Activities

Given the nature of the policy developed here, essentially three types of intergroup interactions emerged: (1) coming together for the regularly scheduled case conferences convened by the TEAM chairperson; (2) actual case activity by line staff; and (3) informal interaction among and between agency administrators who shared the experiences of their respective staffs' interaction with other agencies as a result of the TEAM project.

Unilateral transfers versus bilateral exchanges. Clearly, the agencies with the greatest incentives to engage in coordination of efforts were those then engaged in bilateral exchanges, while the agencies who came along in order to stay "in the know" or work on their own agendas were more likely recipients of unilateral transfers of information or intelligence. From another perspective, the underserved client population was more likely to benefit from the bilateral exchange, while those residents of the neighborhood who were recipients of intensive neighborhood services were more likely to give something up as a result of the TEAM project.

Bargaining and negotiating. Agreements by agencies in individual case situations came about totally through a bargaining and negotiating process. The context in which bargaining and negotiating occurred not only included what agency preferences might have been but how each agency's responsibilities were perceived by their colleagues in the TEAM meetings. For example, greater specificity in designated responsibility for case management of clients on aftercare from the state hospital came about when the state hospital liaison became regularly involved, along with the staff of The Bridge and staff from the work activity training center. Agreements were negotiated in process. The absence of such agreements had heretofore been a major weakness in the service system.

Coalition building. The entire TEAM project may be called a formal coalition building effort, arising out of the initiative of five agencies and resulting in an informal coalition of twenty-one such agencies.

Contracting. While this particular case illustration does not provide evidence of formal contracting taking place, there were extensive examples of interagency contracting occurring through the development of case plans in TEAM meetings. To some extent, an "anticontracting" approach was taken in that "recommendations for action" were developed as opposed to specific treatment plans. To be sure, client goals were established, the participating member agencies became committed to assigning staff resources to particular client situations, and agreements to pursue particular progress goals were made. In this way, accountability to one another was established at the client or case level while specific interagency contracting was avoided.

4. Assess the Availability and Use of Process Resources

Focus on the resources needed and observable in the policy process.

a. People Power

The process appears to have been adequately staffed in that each of the participating agencies assigned staff liaisons to the TEAM project. The initiating group was made up of middle management staff of the core group of five agencies. Another key people resource was the person assigned to serve as chairperson of the TEAM. No voluntary group effort can succeed without at least some amount of effort at group maintenance. However, given the project's commitment not to develop yet another layer of bureaucracy and another service, the formal logistical support of that effort was minimal in terms of ongoing staffing of the TEAM itself.

b. Technology

Since so many different agencies were involved, the policy process benefitted from the range of disciplinary and professional services available in the community. Given the multiproblem nature of the clientele served, a variety of staff were necessarily involved in the TEAM case coordination efforts. Staff ranged from volunteers with minimal amounts of training in some agencies (e.g., the volunteers from a neighborhood church) to highly trained staff from one of the mental health outpatient clinics. Thus, a range of problem-solving technology was brought to bear.

c. Finances

This policy required minimum out-of-pocket expenditures. The Salvation Army was reimbursed by the United Way for expenses incidental to making the facility available for TEAM meetings. There were some expenses for mailings and phone calls. The cost to each agency of having staff available to meet in TEAM conferencing was, of course, extensive. Some "opportunity cost'' was incurred in that staff time was lost to what otherwise would have been direct client contact. However, the benefit/cost of case coordination in comparison to individual case work, though not computed, appeared to be worth the TEAM effort. Evidence of this conclusion is found in the growth of the TEAM project from five to twenty-one agencies over the nineteen-month project period.

d. Time

As just noted, the time allocated to interagency meetings was time lost to what otherwise might have been direct service. Another time factor is the possibility of lost opportunities from staff efforts going into this project as opposed to alternative efforts. Because it is impossible to determine what opportunities were or were not forgone by each of the twenty-one agencies, this time factor cannot be obtained. Time is a necessary resource, and in this instance, one that appears to have been available, given the apparent success in drawing agencies into the process.

5. Determine Implications for Selected Values

Focus on the implications for selected values to be used in the analysis of the policy, particularly with regard to the targets and clients/interests affected by the policy.

a. Adequacy

The process resulted in the provision of more adequate services to neighborhood residents, in that a more holistic approach was taken toward client assessment, service planning, and service delivery. On the aggregate, more horizontal adequacy was achieved in that the entire neighborhood was "covered" as a result of the process and a large number of service providers were included in coordinated case planning that heretofore were not.

b. Effectiveness

We stated earlier that successful policy provides for a stochastic process—it gives order and predictability to a system. The outcome of the TEAM approach in this policy process gave order and predictability in a number of ways. The first is that agencies increasingly came to know what to expect as a result of engaging in interagency cooperative case planning and case management. The second is that the client group perceived more readily that agencies would be working together to provide services to them. Curiously enough, as a general principle, the inclusion of additional agencies makes the service situation itself more—not less—predictable, because the client and the participating agencies can begin to develop reasonable expectations of what services ought to be provided.

In the TEAM approach, the apparent theory behind the policy process is that more can be obtained by coordinating case planning and case management services to an indigent population in a particular neighborhood. The principle driving the process appears to be one of efficiency rather than effectiveness, in that the emphasis is upon the better utilization of existing resources.

c. Efficiency

The analyst should be aware that the policy does not foster strategies of integration of services or the development of a comprehensive service for Middleside neighborhood residents. These approaches would be entirely different strategies and suggest an emphasis upon service effectiveness, as opposed to efficiency. The strategy employed in the TEAM process brought about coordination of efforts without building a new program or service or without altering the way in which any agency served the neighborhood (other than participation in TEAM conferences). The presumption was that participation in TEAM conferences would bring about case coordination. Consequently, the analysis suggests that the focus of the process was more on creating efficiencies rather than achieving a new level of effectiveness.

Nevertheless, a minimal amount of process resources were needed to bring the policy to fruition. Volunteer resources were used to chair the project, agencies did not have to alter their own internal policies or procedures, and did not surrender any autonomy. In comparison to the major outcomes provided for the residents, the adjustments in agency procedures were minor.

d. Impact on Rights, Status, and Social Justice

The policy process enabled each agency to maintain its own prerogatives for delivering services to the residents of the area being served. At the same time, neighborhood residents were able to claim their rightful access to community services and increase their status on the agenda for their share of community agency resources. The interests of social justice were served in that a more proper balance between community need and community response was obtained as a result of TEAM coordination—incurred at the expense of the community and the agencies and not at the expense of the clients of the Middleside neighborhood.

e. Self-Determination

Each resident of the neighborhood would, like any resident of the city, have the opportunity to receive or refuse services. Clients who were subjects of case conferencing by the TEAM gave express permission to have their situations discussed in the TEAM conferences via the legal and ethical requirement that a written and signed release of information and a statement of informed consent be obtained for each client for whom a conference was held. This requirement was automatic for some agencies and not done at all in other agencies. Consequently, development of this procedure was a major task for the policy process. One element lacking in the attempt at client self-determination—at least in the collective sense—was the absence of any clients or client group in the TEAM policy process itself. That is, client representatives were not utilized in the initiation or planning of the case coordination approach. The policy analyst would need to determine whether that client participation would have been helpful or appropriate in this policy situation.

f. Identity

This policy process should contribute greatly to client self-image because each citizen of the Middleside neighborhood, client or nonclient, could assume that the community as a whole was interested in the neighborhood as a result of so many community-wide service agencies giving their attention to this task. Residents of the neighborhood could rightfully conclude that they were being recognized as citizens who, as members of the community, were entitled to services and that the service system was taking steps to appropriately deliver those services.

g. Individualization

A central objective in the policy observed in this process is, in fact, individualization. The policy process was aimed at developing plans and services unique to the needs of each client.

h. Nonjudgmental Attitude

When clients engage in behaviors that maximize the availability of services for themselves, they are sometimes labeled as manipulative. Such labeling may be judgmental on the part of service providers since the "manipulative" behaviors may, in fact, be indicative of resourceful clients who are able to access what is rightfully theirs in the community. One cannot deny that some citizens consume inordinate amounts of community resources, inappropriately or otherwise. However, the issue of judgmental attitudes implicit in "ganging up" on some clients should at least be considered on a case-by-case basis.

i. Confidentiality

The maintenance of confidentiality was a difficult task in this policy process, given the extensive number and variety of service providers involved. In a formal sense, it would appear that the policy achieved confidentiality, although in this instance, this is very difficult to conclusively determine. The policy analyst could use the process analysis to develop techniques whereby confidentiality would be better assured. Some possibilities are making the issue of confidentiality a topic at TEAM conferences, formalizing staff in-service training in maintenance of client confidentiality, or developing more explicit procedures for obtaining informed and written client permissions.

j. Indeterminateness

The TEAM policy process shows evidence of indeterminateness—that the end states of social processes are determined during the life of events. This is apparent in the open-ended approach of the five-member initiating system who opted for a strategy of using a pilot demonstration to bring along an undetermined group of agencies for subsequent participation. In other words, while initially there were some preferences as to which agencies and even which particular staff might have participated, the membership of the group and the experiment was subsequently open. Furthermore, the resultant reports to the home agencies' administrative supervisors of each TEAM member were not established at the front end but, rather, were left to be determined during the life of the TEAM project.

k. Multifinality

The principle of multifinality—that similar original states could properly result in varied subsequent conditions—is evident in the approach that the TEAM took to case planning. The TEAM concentrated on developing interagency treatment "recommendations" and not hard and fast treatment plans. As you will note from our earlier discussion, the notion of formal case-plan contracting was avoided. Thus, the agencies involved were free to develop plans in process while, at the same time, their commitments to one another were honored to the extent felt reasonable. This approach provided an informal accountability system.

l. Nonsummativity

The principle of the whole being something different or more than the sum of its parts is evident in the concept of case conferencing. Recognition of the need for a holistic view of a person is illustrated by the acknowledgment that no single agency can adequately serve the needs of an individual. Case planning and case management is not simply a collection of individual services but an approach to client problem solving that must be coordinated if one is to provide a holistic perspective for the client.

m. Morphogenesis

The principle of morphogenesis—that human systems can change their forms and structure in process—is demonstrated in the TEAM policy process. No single agency altered its mission, goals, or fundamental procedures during or as a result of the effort. However, the nature and process of interagency interaction was fundamentally altered by the activities serving Middleside neighborhood residents.

n. The SCRAPS Test

The TEAM policy process has particular implications for the poor and socioeconomically disenfranchised in many communities. Many clients are transient and indigent, living in high-density neighborhoods where little outreach has been pursued by a majority of local agencies. To some extent, agencies extended their efforts into the Middleside neighborhood because of their vested interests (minimizing duplication of efforts). Eliminating gaps in services was also a motivating force.

The particular neighborhood has a disproportionate number of black residents, relative to the number of black citizens in the rest of the Valley Falls area. Factors of social class and race, then, appear to impinge on the policy process in the sense that the poor and disenfranchised were apparent beneficiaries of the TEAM's coordinating efforts.

6. Provide Recommendations

Focus on the strengths and weaknesses or factors peculiar to the issue and suggested by the data generated by the analysis. Here is where we should be ready to provide our recommendations, each arising out of the information obtained in the analysis.

Summary

This case has been an analysis of a policy process in which a Community Case Coordination Team in the Middleside neighborhood was developed—initially as a pilot experiment—to bring about coordinated case planning and case management for an indigent and highly transient client population. Essential milestones of the establishment of the initiating set and development of a broadly based legitimated charter were achieved, as well as demonstration of the adequacy of the pilot effort. The vested interests of individual agency participants were honored and participating organizations were not required to alter agency services or expected to commit unusual amounts of new resources to the TEAM efforts as a condition of participation. The appointment of a chairperson permitted minimal staff resources to sustain group leadership. Analysis of value elements leads the analyst to the conclusion that the generic values of social work and appropriate values of human systems were evident, although the maintenance of confidentiality was specifically identified as being at risk.

Having presented the frameworks for the analysis of both content and process and provided case illustrations of each, we will move to considerations in the presentation of these analyses in particular contexts.

Essentials in the Presentation of Policy Analysis

8

Up to this point, we have focused primarily on the elements of policy *analysis*. Our sole concern has been what goes into the analysis of content and process, including the values implicit or explicit in social welfare policy. A range of elements have been identified for the analyst's consideration; first, an analysis of the substantive content of actual or proposed policy content, followed by an analysis of the processes that occur in the development of policy, each in the context of the essential value issues to be considered in social welfare policy. A number of detailed illustrations were provided. The analyses in each of these three areas have been detailed and lengthy. However, one cannot ignore the complexities of the real world and reduce complex problems to simple conceptualizations. Now we have another task—communicating those analyses to others. The focus shifts to the form and style of our presentation of these analyses.

Our presumption is that we analyze policy in order to inform, teach, influence, and persuade. Indeed, as Paolo Freire (1972) has noted, all education is a political act, and policy analysis is certainly aimed at educating others. We are not so naive as to suggest that policy analysts are value-free technicians able and desirous of cranking out enlightenment. As professionals, policy analysts engage in these activities not only for personal edification or professional development but also as a service to others, whether a client group, an agency director or supervisor, a policy-making board, a county commissioner, city council members, or a state legislator. However, the analysis of social welfare policy is but one task of professional social welfare practice; another is the task of effective communication of policy analyses to those we serve. Policy analysis is merely an academic exercise if we are not able to effectively communicate the analysis to people who need to be informed, persuaded, or educated.

In citing a study conducted by the University of North Carolina Department of City and Regional Planning, Ziter noted that policy practitioners from all levels of government felt inadequate in the communication and process skills that their work required of them (Ziter, 1983). Yet, in Ziter's own study with public welfare officials in Utah and with the North Carolina sample, policy analysts reported spending from 18 to 25 percent of their time providing written and oral presentations to professionals and approximately one-third of their time providing written and oral presentations to laypersons (p. 47). In a study of oral, public presentational skills of social workers in the state of Michigan, Flynn and Jaksa (1983) found that both managers/administrators and direct service practitioners felt that they lacked necessary skills in presentation of policy material and were highly motivated to develop these skills through in-service training or staff development. Presentational skills, then, are complementary to the exercise of policy analysis skills.

Much of this presentational activity takes place in political arenas. As Mahaffey (1972) points out, certain barriers exist for social workers, however, in working in these environments. These barriers include limited knowledge of governmental structure and process, a disdain or aversion to "politics," lack of patience with procedures, and an inability to empathize with the many viewpoints presented by decision makers. Yet the proper form and style of policy presentations are interrelated with these environmental realities.

In this chapter, we will focus on general considerations for three particular types of presentations of policy analyses: (1) the organization of written legislative analysis, (2) the presentation of oral testimony, and (3) the development of position statements. These three forms of presentation are most commonly used as the vehicles by which policy analyses are communicated in the social welfare context. The three chapters that follow provide more detail and illustrations of each of these three types.

Legislative Analysis

For our purposes here, legislative analysis is the analysis of policy or policy proposals that are provided to support policy decisions in a legislative arena. The most obvious environment for such presentations is state senates or houses of representatives. We are often called upon to make policy analyses available to state senators or representatives, or to their staff who might be conducting studies or investigations. However, these same analyses might also go to state administrative agencies or various interest groups that are becoming knowledgeable about the issues encompassed by our analyses. Consequently, legislative analyses may have audiences beyond a strictly legislative group.

Furthermore, legislative analysis is not restricted to the arena of state legislatures. Legislation and legislative analysis occurs in city councils, county commissions, and the board rooms of various voluntary and private organizations, such as the United Way and community councils. These settings develop *legislation* within their own contexts in terms of establishing policy or in developing rules and guidelines, and otherwise set forth the boundaries of social welfare policy in their own domains. They are precisely the small-scale, local-level arenas in which policy analysts are called upon to communicate their products. When any of these groups are in the process of decision making, legislation in its own particular context is being developed. Policy analysis is one of the essential techniques for helping those decision makers develop such legislation.

Giving Testimony

Human services professionals are sometimes called upon to provide their analyses during formal studies or investigations.[1] On these occasions, the analyst (or some person representing the organization associated with the analysis) is often called upon to make an oral presentation. These presentations of policy analysis must give particular attention to the style and form of communication. (These demands will be discussed in chapter 10.) Testimony can be provided in a range of environments such as a city council's hearing on allocations for general revenue sharing or block grant funding for human services, a community mental health board's ad hoc task force, or a state commission. These are only a few examples.

Position Statements

Position statements are another way of communicating policy analyses. They may be directed at legislative sessions or provided to interested parties during the conduct of hearings or campaigns centered

---

1. Our treatment of the topic of giving testimony here does not include testimony in an administrative hearing or a court of law. These situations are of a different type and purpose; they are primarily to decide issues at law by employing rules of evidence in making decisions concerning fact. Our treatment here refers solely to testimony in *legislative contexts.*

around a particular issue. Position statements may also be issued to the general public or to news media. They may take the form of lengthy and detailed position papers, brief press releases, letters to the editor of newspapers, or presentations made to specific individuals. In contrast to legislative analysis or testimony, a position statement is intended to influence others by taking a stance on a particular issue. Position statements present certain considerations in addition to those presented by legislative analysis and the giving of testimony. These matters will also be considered in chapter 11.

Organizational and Interorganizational Analyses

The reader is reminded that the outlines for content and process provided in previous chapters may also serve as models for style and form of presentations. However, we must add the caveat that these outlines developed for analysis are likely to be too detailed and, most of all, jargon-bound for organizing a presentation, such as providing analyses to state representatives or city council members, giving testimony to a county budget and finance committee, or issuing a position paper for an action group. The outlines for analysis, while practical for internal use as models for presentation, are primarily intended as guides for surveying the essential elements of content, process, and values. The reader is reminded that, when policy analysis is conducted at the service or request of another, the analysis must be "packaged" in a way that effectively communicates what has to be said. The analytic effort has value only to the analyst and not to those who will depend on the analysis for taking action.

Policy analyses conducted for one's supervisor, agency executive, board of directors, or interagency action group are preferably presented with the detail and in the form of the outlines of analysis in the case illustrations used for Cases 1 through 7. That form, style, and level of detail may be appropriate when it is "kept in the family," so to speak. In these instances, much depends on the time available, conventions or expectations in a particular agency for conveying information, the amount of detail expected, and so forth. What we wish to focus on in this and in subsequent chapters are those situations that require special style and form in the vehicle conveying the analysis.

Essential Characteristics of Policy Presentations

Social welfare policy analyses must be knowledgeable, thorough, and technically sound. However, it would be erroneous to assume that each analysis possessing these characteristics will automatically be positively received. The approach used to convey an analysis, in order to be effective, must first and foremost have credibility if it is to have the desired impact upon its target. Credible analyses can be characterized as those which are (1) perceived by the receiver to include a sufficient number of the essential elements relevant to the issue(s), (2) are comprehensive and inclusive of the appropriate variables and information and yet, (3) are provided in a form and style that are comfortable and usable and, of course, (4) are accurate and informative. Before providing direction on the form and style of legislative analysis, testimony, and position papers, this chapter will explore some of the features of form and style that are generic to all three types of policy presentation instruments.

The Form of Policy Presentations

There are a number of possible formats for policy presentations. Legislative analysis and position papers, for example, differ in shape and/or structure. However, some issues of form should be included in the development of *all* policy presentations. These issues are: (1) identification and sponsorship of the analysis; (2) simplicity and clarity of the policy statement; (3) the presentation's basis in sufficient historical or contemporary background; (4) balanced argument; (5) projections of impact; (6) size or length of the policy document or oral presentation; and (7) conscious use of perceptual and physical layout.

Identification and sponsorship. The presentation should first offer a clear statement identifying the author(s) of the analysis and the agency, organization, or group sponsoring it. The identification of the analyst could include job title (and mailing address or phone number) but not other titles, and should be devoid of credentialism. Often opportunities arise to offer other information on one's preparation or credentials relevant to the issue at hand, but credentialism is not the proper or effective way to establish credibility. On the other hand, credibility is in part established by being clear about the organizational base from which the analysis emanates. Here it is important to identify your unit, office, agency, or group so that the target of the presentation has the proper context for your analysis.

The policy statement. The next item of form to consider is that there be a clear statement "up front," in brief but adequate terms, of the proposed policy or remedial action being proposed. Generally speaking, a policy analysis is aimed at an individual or a group of decision makers who are considering or are about to take some action. That action may be to maintain the status or form of an existing policy. Nevertheless, the reader or listener should know at the outset what the policy under analysis is about and, particularly, what action is proposed or favored. In fact, as a matter of form and strategy, the analyst should quote the policy statement and/or describe the proposed action at the beginning and again at the end of the presentation. Placement at the beginning is not only a practical aid to those asked to consider the analysis but also establishes the analyst's credibility since the reader or listener is clearly informed of what the analyst is proposing. Additional placement at the end of the presentation provides a way of summarizing the issues, the analysis, and the proposed action. In other words, planned redundancy can be functional.

Recognition of background issues. Very few issues in the area of policy analysis stand alone and are not in some way interdependent with previous or contemporary issues in the system. The policy presentation should, again as briefly as possible, give some recognition to those issues when they are relevant. This recognition communicates a number of things to the target of the presentation: first, that the analysis is based upon a knowledgeable and informed understanding of the issue(s) surrounding the policy under consideration; second, that the analyst has the interest of the target in mind by providing orientation or education about related matters or is at least reminding the target of the relevant issues involved; and third, that the analyst is attempting to be helpful in establishing his or her credibility by providing concrete evidence that he or she takes the interest of the target listener or reader at heart and is not simply pursuing some secret self-interest.

Balanced argument. In some instances the analyst is not expected to take a position or to offer recommendations, but in others the opposite is true. It is, of course, extremely important for the analyst to be clear about the charge or the assignment and the role he or she is expected to play. In other words, an analyst should be clear about his or her rights and responsibilities, depending on the authority and assumptions under which the analysis is being provided.

It is generally worthwhile to know what the issues are in a balanced argument and whether "opposite" positions or points of view are actually articulated in the presentation. While all of the alternative positions may not be noted in any analysis or its presentation, it is wise to be inclusive in the analytic activity. At the very least, by "doing one's homework," the analyst is more knowledgeable and better prepared to answer follow-up questions, and, thereby more credible.

When the presentation of analysis is not aimed at urging social action or at persuasion, the analyst should present arguments against as well as for the relative merits of the choices or courses of action under consideration. After all, policy analysis has as its purpose the enlightenment of people in the process of problem solving. While it is true in argumentation and debate that the proponent of an idea or action should offer the "warrant" or convincing claim or proof, veracity and adequacy of information are still key in presentation of policy analyses. Clearly, there is no expectation that an individual taking a position will provide convincing arguments for "the other side." However, when taking a position is not the function of the analysis, a balanced presentation is essential.

Projections of impact. Assuming that most decision makers are honest people trying to meet their responsibilities and do their job, the analyst plays a key supportive role. The decision makers should be well advised about the impact of a particular choice or course of action, and the policy analysis is useful in helping "speculating out loud" about the potential effects of the decision. It is also important to consider the impact, or the possible unintended as well as intended effects of the decision. This does at least two things for the target of the presentation. First, it helps to put the decision back into perspective. People do not make choices just for the sake of making decisions; rather, they make choices because they want a particular outcome to occur. By providing statements of impact, the analyst helps to focus on the fundamental purpose of the decision and the accompanying analysis. A second function of identifying impact is that it is consistent with the complementary functions of the decision maker and the analyst. The decision maker needs information to make the best decision possible in all good faith; the analyst is there to provide that information. By shedding light on both intended and unintended possible consequences of the policy action, the interests of both parties (decision maker and analyst) are served.

Size or length. It is very difficult to give any rules of thumb regarding size or length of the presentation except to say that the presentation should be as short as is reasonably possible and yet include all necessary information. Generally more space and time are available for the more lengthy and detailed analytic presentations provided for internal use. Prior experiences about what the agency, the staff, or the group usually needs helps us to determine what is appropriate to discuss. Furthermore, when a presentation is developed internally, it can always be reduced in time or size with early feedback.

Complex detail cannot be irresponsibly reduced to meaningless minima. Yet, the analyst must acknowledge the reality that he or she may have little time on the stage when the actors are busy people, perhaps themselves playing many roles. When the analyst has been invited to provide an analysis, and if there are not a number of competing issues or interests involved, it may be reasonable to "think big" to some extent and not be parsimonious. In such instances, the role the analyst plays is more like that of a consultant. However, in many policy analysis situations, there is limited time and space and the policy analyst is in competition with others for those resources. Consequently, we might think in general terms of legislative analyses being approximately two single-spaced or four double-spaced typewritten pages. Testimony, which should be available in both oral and written forms, should be no longer than five minutes. (If those receiving testimony or conducting the hearing desire more time, especially for their own questions and interchange, it is their prerogative.) The oral and written presentations should contain the same information. Position papers probably vary the most in length. When directed at the media, they should be no longer than one and one-half pages. If a position paper relates to a very technical matter and is being presented to a study commission or committee, the paper can and should be much longer than the other types of presentation.

Perceptual and physical layout. One final word about form. A good rule of thumb is to use, wherever possible, the perceptual images and/or physical arrangements of the written work in such a way that you will call attention to the main sections or rubrics of a presentation. In written work, this means using capitalized and/or centered headings, marginal or paragraph headings, or any form which is able to catch the eye of the reader. This enables the reader to quickly see what you intend to be seen—the main concepts or arguments. So, too, with verbal presentations. It is helpful to paint mental pictures, such as indicating, for example, that there are "three main points to consider," and then proceeding to say "the first is . . . ," "the second is . . . ," and so forth. Another helpful aid is to summarize, in concise terms at strategic points in a presentation.

The Style of Policy Presentations

Other considerations in presentation of policy analyses are equally important; they cannot be classified as matters of form, layout, or particular categories of content. These considerations might be called the *logical necessities* of policy analysis, and they should be reflected in policy presentations. Patti and Dear (1975) refer to the necessity of being timely, balanced, responsive to the request, and focused on relevant alternatives. We will focus here on the requirements of objectivity, languaging, targeting, inclusiveness of key variables, consistency with relevant values and goals, and appropriateness to the policy under study.

Objectivity. A policy analysis, professionally provided, should aim at being objective and factual. This is not to say that a policy presentation, where appropriate, cannot make recommendations and take positions. However, even when positions are taken, the analysis and its manner of communication should be as objective as possible and based upon best estimates of what is factual. This means that the analysis and its presentation must be descriptive and analytical and that "feeling" arguments (e.g., "I feel" or "we feel") are neither appropriate nor helpful in achieving the desired ends. We do not mean that values do not enter into analysis. Indeed, we have stressed that point in earlier chapters. Mahaffey (1972), in speaking of lobbying, makes the point well in noting that values and philosophy can only be maintained by social action that proceeds with clearly defined objectives by carefully relating means to ends. This suggests that valued ends are pursued in a context of norms requiring objectivity and specificity.

Languaging. The policy analyst has a difficult task, because the subjects of analysis are often complex problems involving very technical issues. However, to the greatest degree possible, the analytic presentation should employ words that the average individual understands. With the omnipresence of photocopiers, visual media, and electronic mail and file transfer via computer networks, the audience for one's analytic presentation indeterminably grows. While the target or primary audience must be kept in mind, it is often impossible to know by whom or how an analysis will be used at some point in the future. Furthermore, explanations contained in the analysis should be complete, simple, and fully understandable.

Targeting. As was just noted, the policy analyst must always have the particular target of the analytic presentation in mind. This factor is primarily emphasized by Dear and Patti (1981) and Kleinkauf (1981). This could mean determining what particular issues might be relevant or what perspectives might be important to the person or group commissioning or receiving the legislative analysis, testimony, or position paper. Recognition of these factors is important in the key words, idioms, special symbols, or images that are used in the presentation. Policy analyses are undertaken not only for resolution of a problem but also for people. The people who are targeted for analyses must be kept in mind when deciding how to communicate the analysis.

Smith (1979) has stressed the importance of knowing, for example, a legislator's role conception (or orientation) as a key variable in the decision process. For instance, Smith notes that a legislator's self-concept may be that of facilitator, neutral person in an issue, or resister of change. From another perspective, the decision maker may be more program- than policy-oriented. Knowledge of these role conceptions is very helpful in developing and presenting the analysis. That is, it is very important to determine what particular role conception is held by those who might use the analysis so that the presentation style can relate to that role conception.

Inclusiveness of key variables. The previous chapters devoted to content, process, and values had the task of being reasonably inclusive of the variables generally thought to be relevant to all social welfare policy analyses. It is the analyst's responsibility to determine which of these elements are essential and to show the target of the presentation that the relevant elements or variables have been adequately considered. At a minimum this would include consideration of (1) who the proposal or policy is designed for, (2) what the existing level of need is, (3) the level or scope of the remedy recommended, (4) its cost, (5) delivery mechanisms, (6) resource requirements, and (7) method of administration. Two other special considerations are often overlooked, (8) the opportunity to offer suggestions, or at least give recognition to what possible measures might be established *a priori* to assure the decision maker that the accountability needs can be honored, and (9) recognition that changes in policy often create a ripple effect regarding need for subsequent administrative rules or guidelines for programs or people ultimately pursuing the policy goal. Making suggestions gives the analyst an opportunity to be creative and offer evaluation approaches that could be considered humane, appropriate, or consistent with the values of the profession. A recognition of the ripple effect could make visible, to the extent possible, the implications of a policy decision in terms of future needs for change.

Consistency with values and goals. We have already said a good deal about values in policy analysis. Here we want to emphasize that the presentation of policy analyses should be made in ways that are consistent with appropriate social and professional values. When the policy choices are in conflict with dominant values or professional ethics, the policy analyst has an obligation to make such realities known to the target of the presentation. In the same vein, the analysis should help the analyst and the target see the extent to which the proposed policy or option might actually be in concert with the original goals set forth by the overriding policy or the program currently in existence. First and foremost, the policy choice must relate to and not be in conflict with the basic needs of individuals or groups.

Appropriateness. Lastly, we will consider the category of appropriateness, because certain matters must be attended to in presenting an analysis that speaks to the question of good common sense. The analyst should remember, for example, that the analysis and its presentation must reflect that social problems rooted in multiple causes cannot generally be remediated by one simple approach. Or, complex problems cannot be solved by simple solutions reflected in naive policy. Another consideration is that massive needs usually require massive amounts of resources. This means that substantial efforts need to acknowledge the need for substantial amounts of support. Yet another consideration is that the policy solution proposed or selected must be internally consistent with companion policies related to the same problem. Given the belief that all things in real life are interrelated, no policy stands totally alone.

Summary

This chapter has drawn attention to the fact that analyses are not only conducted about problems or choices but are also conducted for people. Furthermore, issues involved in the communication of analyses must be addressed to maximize the effectiveness of the analysis. This chapter has set forth a number of essential elements in presentation of policy analyses, particularly those matters related to questions of form or style. These elements are summarized in the general outline that follows. Subsequent chapters will include more specific guides to providing legislative analyses, giving testimony, and presenting position papers.

Form and Style in Policy Presentations
(An Outline)

1. *The form of policy presentations*
    a. Identification and sponsorship
    b. The policy statement
    c. Recognition of background issues
    d. Balanced argument
    e. Projections of impact
        1) Intended
        2) Possible unintended
    f. Size and length
    g. Perceptual and physical layout
2. *The style of policy presentations*
    a. Objectivity
    b. Languaging
    c. Targeting
    d. Inclusiveness of key variables
        1) For whom the policy proposal is designed
        2) Existing level of need
        3) Level or scope of remedy
        4) Cost
        5) Delivery mechanisms
        6) Resource requirements
        7) Method of administration
        8) Evaluation
        9) Need for consequent rules or guidelines
    e. Consistency with values and goals
    f. Appropriateness

Legislative Analysis

This chapter deals with the task of developing legislative analyses—those policy documents aimed at informing and/or influencing those involved in the decision-making process in legislative arenas. These decision processes occur at the local level; thus, "*legislative* analysis" does not refer exclusively to analyses of propositions being considered by state and federal legislatures. In the practice of social welfare policy at the local or small-scale level, there are a number of situations in which policy practitioners require written presentational skills that can effectively convey policy analyses. Some of these possibilities were mentioned briefly in chapter 8. For example, a member of an inter-agency coalition may be asked by the United Way board of directors to develop an analysis of a proposed new policy for governing United Way membership requirements. A social action group may need to develop a formal written analysis for presentation to a county board of commissioners considering a policy decision to reorganize the county's human services system. A staff member of a city human relations department may be called upon to present an analysis of a proposed city ordinance regarding the use of a particular block grant or revenue sharing program or the limitations to be placed upon a tax abatement policy. A neighborhood organization may wish to present its analysis of a proposed zoning ordinance to a planning commission. These are but a few examples wherein human service professionals have an opportunity to become a part of the legislative process through the preparation, development, and presentation of legislative analyses.

Kleinkauf (1989) suggests a number of considerations to be given to legislative analysis, each of which might be considered as analytical steps. These steps, offered in the form of a checklist of more than 40 questions, require analysis of the substantive issue, the process and issues relevant to the committee handling the proposal, a fiscal analysis, an assessment of the political likelihood of the passage of the particular bill, and an assessment of the support and opposition for the proposal. Her perspective is largely on larger-scale policy systems, however, that is, on legislative analysis in the larger, state house or senate arena. Our focus is on the smaller scale, because we are concerned with making the practice of policy relevant to the environment of most social work practitioners.

Legislative processes

Effective legislative analysis does not occur in a vacuum. It happens in the context of local customs and rules about how legislative proposals are introduced, how they are formally (and informally) considered and/or adopted, how lobbying occurs, and so forth. Legislative analysis is not static technical skill and event, it is a dynamic and processual phenomenon. It falls within the domain often referred to as "doing your homework" day after day. Legislative analysis also takes place in the context of lobbying—knowing the process by which a proposition becomes official policy or a bill becomes law. Other related concerns might involve knowing how to tap into a decision-making network, knowing how to draw upon informational resources, and being able to determine the proper timing for intervening into the process with one's analysis. While these concerns are themselves topics of a whole range of literature, it would be well to consider a few of them in the special context of legislative analysis.

Lobbying

Lobbying is a set of events and activities that surround the bringing of organized information and influence to bear upon the decisions suggested by a legislative proposal. As mentioned earlier, there are a number and variety of factors involved in effective lobbying. However, in relation to legislative analysis, we must stress that there is homework to be done by the policy analyst which is really a part of the development of legislative analyses (see Dear and Patti, 1981). The analyst should try to determine when and why the proposal was introduced, by whom, and for what reasons. Formal drafts of the proposal must be obtained. Thus, one must do a considerable amount of work prior to developing the analysis.

A very important step is to determine, perhaps through a committee aide, legislative assistant, the city or county manager's office, the agency's public communications officer, or an agency's program director immediately involved in the issue, the sequencing or timing of a number of key events. For example, the analyst needs to know the routines used by a decision-making group *vis-à-vis* the sequencing of important events, such as whether, when, and how the matter is first considered by a particular committee, subcommittee, or administrative office. Being knowledgeable about these events/factors not only provides early opportunity to gather information but also helps the analyst to begin building his or her own timetable for when the analysis must be completed. These efforts may also offer some suggestion regarding the content as well as style and form of analysis and presentation likely to be most effective. Having attended to these details, the policy analyst might be able to clarify any questions about committee procedures and timetables and, consequently, be in a better position to determine the best time(s) to introduce the legislative analysis.

We have provided a general characterization of the need to tune into the process of lobbying. The key concept here is that each legislative process has its own peculiarities, and legislative analysis demands learning what they are: legislative analysis is thus one part of the lobbying process.

Use of Informational Resources

A good habit to develop is to routinely contact the proposers of a policy or piece of legislation (e.g., legislative aides or administrative assistants, council members, directors, etc.), not only to solicit their opinions but to ask for references regarding their sources of information. When governmental policy is being proposed, the administrative or executive offices are also likely to be preparing analyses. It is helpful at such times to identify, for example, the person or office within the state Department of Health, the city's planning department, or the public liaison person of the agency who serves as a contact person—in the absence of or in addition to using one's own organization's internal information resources. Then, of course, the usual library and computerized information resource systems are helpful. Newsletters of associations or various interest groups are excellent resources in helping the analyst determine the positions held by competing interests surrounding a policy decision. These sources often provide the view ''from the trenches.''

A Habit of Doing One's Homework

There are volumes and courses of study concerning the area of legislative and other political policy processes. Our task here is not to summarize them. Rather, it is to develop helpful outlines for analysis—at this point legislative analysis in particular. The key point is that the associated activities such as lobbying and resource utilization are not one-time events. Their work is ongoing. Effective, thorough, and credible legislative analyses are a reflection upon the individual's or group's sensitivity to the processual aspects of the policy effort and reflect an accumulated knowledge of what is behind an issue. The analysis is also a reflection upon those who routinely familiarize themselves with these issues, processes, and resources so that their analyses have a "goodness of fit" with the milieu. When the proposed legislation, ordinance, or policy appears to be outside of the analyst's realm, he or she is well advised to bring in those who understand or are sensitive to key issues, procedures, or symbols in that particular policy environment. Put simply, get someone to help with the homework. Get consultation.

A General Outline for Legislative Analysis

As with all presentations of policy analysis, the legislative analysis document must address the standard set of who, what, when, where, and why questions—sometimes called the "five W's." Then, too, the analyst should consider the range of elements suggested in previous chapters for using the guides for analyzing content and process. However, for the analysis to be reasonably considered by busy people who are likely to have a number of analyses to review, it must be *packaged* in a way that meets the mutual needs of both the provider and the reader of the analysis—the analyst (or the group that the analyst represents) and the decision maker. To be reasonably well received, the analysis cannot be a simplistic summary of complex events; neither can it be a voluminous dissertation. It must consider a wide range of issues in sufficient depth, yet it must also be compact and to the point. We discussed some of these guidelines in terms of form and style in the previous chapter.

The standards described above may seem impossible to achieve. Nevertheless, the outline on the following pages attempts to be as thorough as the analyst ideally should be. This outline has been applied by many students and the author, over time and in its many forms, to a variety of legislative policy situations. There are other forms to be used, especially if one is completing a policy analysis as a staff member of an administrative agency of government. However, we should first look at a more generalizable format for legislative analysis. After that, a case illustration will be provided.

Statement of the Policy Proposition(s)/Provision(s)

As with all other types of analyses, the legislative analysis should begin with a clear, uncluttered, and brief statement of the law, rule, policy, proposition, or guideline that is being proposed. What is being proposed or is under consideration should be uncomplicated and clear to all who read the analysis. It should be stated in only one or two sentences and should be as free as possible from jargon and reference to concepts that would be unknown to readers (particularly to those readers who are decision makers).

The Proposer(s)

The person(s) or group(s) sponsoring the policy proposal should be identified, particularly in terms of their formal positional titles and/or organizational affiliations. Formal policy is acted upon in public and this is a way to bring the identity of the key actors to light. This is both courteous and good politics.

Authority or Legitimacy

The analysis should identify, early on, the statute, court ruling, ordinance, board directive, executive order, administrative directive, licensing requirement, or other source of authority or legitimacy for the existing and proposed action that has a bearing upon the action to be taken. Identifying the source of authority may suggest the opportunities and/or constraints for action that might exist and help the decision makers to more readily determine their prerogatives and range of latitude. To some extent, this helps those who read or hear the analysis in some instances to determine the extent of discretion that may be allowed in considering the policy proposal.

General Concepts

This portion is the main body of the analysis and should enumerate and clarify the concepts that particularly relate to this particular proposal. This is where the analyst can summarize the shape and nature of the problem that exists or characterize the proposal offered as a remedy. This section should especially make clear: (1) why this particular approach is proposed, and (2) how the methods or means proposed are presumed to be particularly suitable to the matter under study. This is also the point at which factual data can be brought in, along with an explicit discussion of the value considerations. Some possibilities for discussion are the way the problem is stated, the implications of the means to be employed if approval or passage is obtained, and/or to the departure from or congruence with prior conceptualizations of the problem or ways of dealing with the issue.

The analyst should take care that this section of the analysis be aimed at bringing out the facts found in the background data while giving focus to the central issues. More speculative analysis comes in later in the analysis. Specifics concerning implications for financing for the target, client, or service systems, and the possible arguments for or against the proposal, should come later and separately in the analysis.

Intended and Possible Unintended Effects

Next, the analysis should speak fairly and objectively to the intended and possible unintended effects of the proposal upon the target, client, and service systems, indicating the potential impact upon each. It should also shed light on the potential ripple effect upon such matters as existing administrative rules, guidelines, companion policies, or the implications for other requirements or programs associated with the proposal.

Fiscal Implications

Assuming that human cost issues have been addressed, fiscal implications should then be considered. The analysis should shed light not only on the revenue and expenditure aspects of the proposal but also on the fiscal implications of *not* taking action (i.e., the opportunity costs).

Advantages and Disadvantages

This section should list, in very concise fashion, the arguments both for and against the proposal, unless the analyst is trying to persuade the readers or listeners to adopt a recommended course of action. In that case, the burden of raising counterarguments rests with the proposal's critics. The analyst should also identify which groups and organizations, if any, have taken positions for or against the proposal or any of its provisions. Preparation and presentation of this material is helpful for the analyst in development of the background information and serves as a practical support service to the decision maker as well. Whether the analyst happens to be for or against a particular proposal, this is the point at which both or many sides to an argument are made visible, thereby assisting the decision maker and likely enhancing the credibility of the analyst. This is not to say that the analyst may not personally take a position—just that the position is provided separately, at the end of the analysis in terms of recommendations.

Recommendations

Depending upon the charge and task given to the policy analyst, this section should be the only point at which the analysis purposely takes a position. If the analysis is developed at the request of an executive director or a board of directors, the recommendations may suggest what the agency should do, and why. On the other hand, if the analysis is being prepared for a county commissioner or state representative, the recommendations may speak less directly to organizational interest and more to a range of interests. The important point here is that the analyst may be expected to take a position and have every right to make recommendations, but these recommendations must be identifiably separate from the rest of the analysis.

Author's Identity

The final statement should identify the author of the analysis, not only to provide a signatory but also to offer a convenient way of being contacted for further information. Cosignatories may be required in some administrative agencies; this matter will be addressed when we consider analyses provided by administrative agencies of government.

Our outline, then, would be as follows:

A General Outline for Legislative Analysis

1. Statement of the proposition(s)/provision(s)
2. The proposer(s)
3. Authority or legitimacy
4. General concepts
5. Intended and possible unintended effects
6. Fiscal implications
7. Advantages and disadvantages
8. Recommendations
9. Author's identity

We will apply this outline to Cases 8 and 9. Case 8 deals with the same issue illustrated in Case 6 in chapter 7 regarding the uniform fee schedule proposed by a community mental health board. At this point, however, Case 8 analyzes the proposition from the perspective of a contract agency offering field-based services to elderly citizens. Case 9 deals with analysis of a piece of state legislation, written from the perspective of a local substance abuse services agency, involving the decision of whether to make application as a local screening program.

Legislative Analysis by Governmental Administrative Agencies

Before moving on to case illustrations, however, we will discuss one more legislative analysis situation with its own set of distinguishing characteristics. This is the context wherein the policy analyst, a staff member of an administrative agency of government, is asked to provide an analysis of a piece of proposed legislation. Often, when a piece of legislation is proposed by a legislator (e.g., a state senator or representative, city commissioner or council member, or county official), a civil servant employee is called upon to provide an analysis of the policy proposal. This situation differs from the others in that the administrative agency (e.g., the State Department of Public Health, the City Planning Department, or the County Human Services Department) is also a part of government. That agency may currently administer some aspect of the program to which the legislative proposal is addressed and/or may have some responsibilities in the future regarding that proposal.

In some instances, this situation may bring a set of factors into play that are somewhat different from those discussed at the beginning of this chapter. The legislative analysis will become a public document and may be taken by some as being the department's (i.e., the administrative agency's) own position on the policy proposal. The analysis may very well reflect the more narrow organizational position of the particular department or agency. A question may arise about the agency's role or position in the policy proposal (i.e., whether the agency sponsored, supports, or opposes the bill). After all, those who legislate should properly seek the advice of those who implement in order to determine the feasible impact or desirability of a proposal under consideration. This would include the analysis in the context of some estimate of the general effect of the proposal upon the responsibilities already assigned to the administrative agency or office. The analysis may, on the one hand, be developed solely for top-level agency management or, on the other hand, may serve as an informational piece for all agency staff members, other agencies, and/or the general public. Let's face it: policy analyses are political, as well as technical, documents and exist in political environments.

There are also certain protocols regarding notice of authorship that are determined by local circumstances. Consequently, while the analysis may be developed by a particular policy analyst, the document itself may be signed or countersigned by a designated responsible agency official. The actual analyst may or may not be identified.

The elements discussed earlier in regard to other legislative analyses would also be considered in such an analysis, as well as the following questions:

1. What is the bill number or title of this proposal and who is the sponsor? What is the current status of this bill or proposal?
2. What is the intent of this bill or proposal? What does it purport to achieve or what problem does it aim to remedy?
3. What existing legislation, rules, or policies are directly related to this bill/proposal?
4. Was the bill/proposal introduced at the agency's/department's request?
5. For whom is the bill/proposal designed and what is their need?
6. What are some possible effects, intended or unintended?
7. What are the potential programmatic and fiscal implications of this bill/proposal?
8. What are the values implications?
9. What are the arguments for and against (or advantages and disadvantages) of this bill/proposal?
10. What is recommended as the agency's position?
11. Who is the author?
12. Who is the agency's responsible person?

With these questions in mind, the following checklist should be of value in providing an analysis of proposed legislation written from the perspective of a governmental administrative agency. This checklist will be applied in Case 10, a legislative analysis of a rule impact statement.

A Checklist for Legislative Analysis by Governmental Administrative Agencies

1. Bill number, sponsor, and status
2. Intent of the proposal/policy
3. Related legislation and/or rules

4. Agency's role in the request
5. Target of bill and level of need
6. Possible effects
7. Potential programmatic and fiscal implications
8. Values implications
9. Arguments for and against the bill
10. Agency's position
11. Author/signatory
12. Responsible person

Case 8: Legislative Analysis—Uniform Fee Schedule

The following case application will demonstrate that legislative analysis at the local, small-scale level need not be restricted to policy developed by a state or federal legislature. We will use our illustration from Case 6 in chapter 7 on uniform fee determination as the example.

You might recall that, in the Case 6 situation, the Cascade County Community Mental Health Board had established a system-wide policy for all contracting agencies, entitled "Policy and Procedures for a Uniform Method of Determining Ability to Pay." In this illustration of a legislative analysis, we will take the perspective of Seniors, Inc., one of the twenty-five local agencies contracting with the Mental Health Board. Seniors, Inc. provides services in the mental health system's outpatient services category, which in this situation consists of a variety of field-based mental health services to citizens fifty-five years of age or older. Among these services are case and program consultation, educational services, counseling and psychotherapy, case management, volunteer services, and information and referral services. You are one of the program managers of the agency and have been assigned the task of providing an analysis of the Community Mental Health Board's proposed policy, which has been circulated among contract agencies for a sixty-day review and comment period.

1. Statement of the Proposition

The Community Mental Health Board has proposed a policy stating that those receiving services from the mental health system shall be assessed a fee to contribute to the cost of services provided. A sliding scale based on ability to pay is proposed, and a procedure for fee waiver is established so that individuals not able to pay will not be refused service. The recipient of service is required to present verification of income and, if a full or partial fee waiver is requested beyond that provided by the sliding scale, the individual is to present verification of hardship. Refusal to do so will result in the recipient being billed for the full amount of services. Individuals having insurance carriers that provide reimbursement for mental health services are required to sign a standard assignment of benefits/release of information form or incur the cost of services themselves. Proposed procedures outline methods for implementing the policy, the process wherein exceptions may be made, and a description of the fee waiver process.

2. The Proposer

Impetus for the policy has come from the Cascade County Community Mental Health Board, which, in turn, has been required by the State Department of Mental Health to take policy action in this area.

3. Authority or Legitimacy

The authority for such an action is clearly provided in Chapter Seven of Act 129, the State Mental Health Code, which provides that the department (or its designees) have the authority to establish fee schedules and bill recipients for services. Furthermore, the "Standards for Community Mental Health Services" provide that each county board has the responsibility for developing and implementing clearly defined mechanisms for the collection of fees from clients and their parties ("Standards," p. 27). While the proposed policy is within the state department's and Cascade board's authority, there is some question about whether Section 4 of the "Standards" contains certain constraints. Provisions allowing the use of fee collection agencies to secure payment on delinquent accounts may, in fact, be a violation of Section 4 of the "Standards," which protects clients from disclosure of their identity as service recipients to any organization or individual without their written permission. This limitation on agency authority needs further clarification.

While the proposed action is within the legal prerogative of the local board, this policy and set of procedures is a radical departure from the historical posture of the local community mental health board regarding client fees. The relatively unilateral nature of the policy, while within the authority of the Cascade board, is also a radical departure from normally accepted community practice in Cascade County.

4. General Concepts

This policy is directed at two separate but associated issues related to the community's mental health system. The first is the Cascade board's desire to develop uniformity in fee-settling and billing and collection procedures within the service system. The second has to do with generating new sources of revenue in order to maintain the level of client services in the face of reductions in available state dollars. The emphasis is on placing more responsibility for payment upon the recipient and/or third parties (including Title XIX) and more responsibility for implementation upon the contract agencies. Presumably, the policy is also aimed at achieving equity among the recipients of services in the state and the county.

The sliding scale approach is presumably aimed at pegging fees to the individual's ability to pay and is also based upon the assumption that such an approach will not be a deterrent to a person seeking or receiving services. The policy's procedures concerning verification are also presumptive of the fact that individuals cannot be counted upon to provide accurate financial information short of proof through such means, for example, as providing an affidavit attesting to the accuracy of information provided.

5. Intended and Possible Unintended Effects

The intended effects of the proposed policy appear to be fundamentally fiscal in nature—to expand the financial resource base of community programs. While some professional literature suggests that therapeutic and/or motivational value may be attached to fee-charging, this does not appear to be an intended effect here.

However, the policy could result in a significant decrease in utilization of mental health services by various target populations. The elderly are often hesitant to utilize mental health services, fearing social stigma; many rely on a fixed income; others are reluctant to reveal personal financial information to strangers. Additionally, many minority clients and those of lower socioeconomic groups already have reservations about the mental health services' responsiveness to their needs and would be even less likely to seek services. Thus, this policy initiative could further deter many individuals from utilizing programs that are available.

The proposed policy could also deter development of innovative mental health programming. Workers in field-based settings such as nursing homes, apartments, and residential facilities would have to engage clients in fee determination discussions in an atmosphere where such conversations would be neither comfortable nor appropriate and in many cases could be detrimental to the development of a therapeutic relationship. An alternative might be for clients to travel to an office setting (thereby defeating the purpose and style of field-based approaches), or perhaps initiation of such approaches as telephone/mail contacts. The latter would also probably discourage service utilization and would not increase revenues, and the staff time required would still need to be funded.

The policy appears to be conceptually based upon the image of practices traditionally found in outpatient clinics and hospital settings. In services fundamental to Seniors, Inc., such as case management and consultation, the client is sometimes the family, sometimes an organization, or even the mental health system. The goals and services are not easily cost billable to the client or a third party. An unintended effect may be a move backward into traditional approaches to providing clinical services to individuals.

6. Fiscal implications

Assuming the maintenance of the same level of case activity, the policy would generate new revenue or at least replace revenues lost through reductions in state funding. Sources of such revenue would be individuals and third party payees. Funding generated would differ from agency to agency, depending upon variations in cost per unit of service, the economic level of the clientele, and the uniformity of criteria actually applied in assessing full and partial fee waivers.

All contract agencies would incur billing costs and increased reporting costs. Those agencies without such procedures in place would incur substantial front-end costs, generally ranging from $7,000 to $12,000 annually per agency.

7. Advantages and Disadvantages

Possible advantages of the proposed policy would include increased funding for mental health services and greater independence for Cascade County contract agencies. Also, those who utilize services would more routinely pay for at least a portion of the cost directly, an approach which may be more attractive to the taxpayer. Lastly, the policy would assure uniform procedures, thereby increasing the likelihood of systematically obtaining certification for Medicaid billing.

Disadvantages would include the startup costs for the contract agencies, both financial and with respect to staff morale, each of which could result in a deterioration in the quality of services offered. There may be reduction in service utilization by some high-risk or high-need groups, for example, the elderly, the poor, and minorities. Some innovative field-based programming may be discouraged due to the difficulty of implementing the policy in nontraditional settings. Finally, this radical departure from encouraging individual program development and management by community agencies may fundamentally alter the service system's manner of cooperation in program planning and provision.

8. Recommendations

The following recommendations might be considered by Seniors, Inc.:

    a. The Cascade County Community Mental Health Board should be encouraged to delay implementation of the policy until more detailed information is available on the assessment of possible outcomes for all agency clientele.

    b. Analysis should continue in special areas of consideration, espe-
cially service utilization by the elderly, the poor, and minority citizens; also, the financial cost of implementation should be further assessed in light of the current budgetary strains already felt
due to reduced allocations in each of the agencies.

    c. The County Board should obtain a state attorney general's opin-
ion on recipients' rights issues concerning confidentiality and the
use of fee collection agencies.

    d. A task force should be convened, composed of contract agency
personnel, Cascade Board staff, and other appropriate community groups to: (1) consider and examine other sources of revenues, and (2) review other means of adapting current and proposed fee policy procedures.

(Signed)
Position or Title
Date

Case 9: Legislative Analysis—Screening Application

The application of the legislative analysis outline in Case 8 illustrated a
policy that was developed and proposed by a local funding agency and
analyzed from the perspective of a contract agency. In Case 9 we will
look at another situation often requiring legislative analysis, that is,
when an agency needs information on the content of a piece of legislation prior to making a decision or taking a position.

    In Case 9, Crisis Services, Inc., an agency that provides alcohol and
drug abuse rehabilitation services in downtown Arapahoe City, is ex-
ploring the possibility of becoming a designated screening agency for
the State Department of Substance Abuse Services. Before making application to the state, the executive director of Crisis Services, Inc. has
asked for an analysis of the legislation and appropriate recommendations.

1. Statement of the Provisions

Public Act 410 (P.A. 410), particularly Section 222(8), provides that, before imposing sentence upon an individual for particular violations,
the court shall order screening and assessment by a person or agency
designated by the State Department of Substance Abuse Services to determine whether the individual is likely to benefit from rehabilitative
services, including alcohol or drug education, and alcohol or drug treatment programs. The court may order the individual to participate in
and successfully complete one or more appropriate rehabilitative programs and require that the person pay for the costs of the screening, assessment, and rehabilitative services.

2. Proposer(s)

This law, introduced in the last session of the state senate as Senate Bill 803 by Senator Ralph Kline (D., Crystal City), was part of a "package" of three bills supported by the State Department of Substance Abuse Services aimed at stiffening the penalties for drunk driving in the state. The primary organization supporting the legislation, in addition to the State Department, was People Against Drunk Driving (PADD), a national organization with local chapters in the state.

3. Authority or Legitimacy

This program is authorized by state law, particularly P.A. 410, Section 222(8). Should Crisis Services Inc. become a designated screening agency, authority would derive from P.A. 410 and the administrative rules developed under the act and administered by the State Department of Substance Abuse Services.

4. General Concepts

P.A. 410 requires, after someone has been convicted on either a charge of Operating Under the Influence of Liquor (OUIL) or Operating While Intoxicated (OWI) that, prior to sentencing, the court shall order that individual "to undergo screening and assessment by a person or agency designated by the Department of Substance Abuse Services" to determine whether he/she might benefit from an alcohol or drug treatment and/or rehabilitation program. If the screening and assessment agency determines in the affirmative, then the court may order, as a part of the sentence, that such person successfully complete one or more such programs.

The basic purpose of the "package" of three drunk driving laws enacted during that period was to attempt to decrease the high number of deaths and injuries on state streets and highways caused by drunk driving. The basic assumption underlying P.A. 410 is that stiffer punishment of drunk drivers is not enough; they also need treatment and/or rehabilitation so that they will no longer be a public menace when they are driving.

5. Intended and Possible Unintended Effects

a. On Targets (Persons Convicted of Drunk Driving)

Persons convicted of drunk driving who may not otherwise be willing to get treatment or rehabilitation will not be required in many cases to seek such services. P.A. 410 provides a very strong incentive for such persons. The law will hopefully result in a decrease in the number of deaths and injuries and in an increase in the number of persons treated or rehabilitated. Private medical and automobile insurance carriers will need to determine whether they will cover the costs of court-ordered assessment, treatment, and/or rehabilitation, which could result in higher premiums. The courts, particularly probation departments, will need to work more closely with substance abuse treatment centers (such as Crisis Services, Inc.), which, in turn, should bring about increases in staff work loads.

If a person has neither sufficient funds to pay the costs of screening, treatment, or rehabilitation nor a third party to pay such costs, this legislation could impose a very real hardship—particularly on low income groups. It could result in refusals of or negative attitudes toward services.

b. On Intended Service Systems

P.A. 410 will likely increase the number of clients who come for services to agencies prepared to deal with these problems. Given the current economic situation, P.A. 410 may counter the effects of reduced state funding cutbacks by helping such agencies survive current funding difficulties. On the other hand, the legislation could cause even more financial difficulties for these agencies since some may be confronted with clients who refuse services or clients who are unable or unwilling to pay for services already received. Furthermore, whether or not they are able or willing to pay, clients coerced into obtaining services are not likely to cooperate fully in the service process.

6. Fiscal Implications

If the Detoxification Unit of Crisis Services, Inc. were to become qualified by the Department of Substance Abuse Services as a screening agency, a staff person who meets the state's qualifications for screening agents would have to spend time with persons referred from the courts. Therefore, there is need to determine: (1) how many OUIL/OWI (i.e., "drunk drivers") would be referred to the agency for screening and assessment each month; (2) whether the county court would be willing to collect the screening fees from the offender and then reimburse the agency; and (3) what the standard fee for screening and assessment would be. Current estimates obtained in discussions with state agency personnel suggest an average of fourteen cases per month for this agency, that the billing process may be negotiable, and that the fees have yet to be established.

Since these costs must ultimately be paid by the offender, the financial burden on those who do not have adequate insurance coverage, especially the poor, will be substantial. Unless the courts are willing to underwrite the costs in those instances, it will be difficult for substance abuse agencies to admit such persons into their programs and survive financially.

7. Advantages and Disadvantages

There are some merits in making application to become a screening agency under P.A. 410. Although becoming a screening agency may not be cost beneficial *per se* (given the potential difficulty in collecting screening fees), the agency might receive clients for the Detoxification Unit and the Turnaround Program who might not otherwise come to these programs. Also, from a public relations standpoint, it would be useful to become a screening agency, if for no other reason than to develop a closer working relationship with the courts. Finally, it would be consonant with the goals of the agency to become an active part of a statewide effort to reduce deaths and injuries caused by drunk driving.

There are also sound arguments against making such application. First, it probably would not be cost beneficial—at least at the outset—until some of the aforementioned problems were resolved. A major portion of at least one full-time equivalent staff person and perhaps a number of staff persons' time would be required at the outset, and screening fees probably would not cover these costs. Second, the agency could find itself receiving an increase in the amount of "difficult" or unwilling clients due to the coercive aspect of the legislation.

8. Recommendations

The agency would do well to continue negotiations with the local court, because the latitude for working within the provisions of state law seems to reside at the local level. This particularly pertains to the considerations mentioned earlier regarding the expected rate of referrals/intake, the court's willingness to collect fees, and the actual fee schedule related to our agency's cost per unit of service. Keeping in mind our agency's mission, and the potential effects on community relations, the agency should continue to explore the matter.

(Signed)
Title or Position
Date

Case 10: Legislative Analysis—Rule Impact Statement

In Case 10, the state legislature is considering a bill aimed at improving the economic climate affecting opportunities for the development of small businesses. The bill is in the House Commerce Committee and, while it may seemingly be unrelated to social services affairs, it could unquestionably affect two existing statutes involving the licensing and regulation of out-of-home care facilities for children and vulnerable adults. As a staff member in the State Office of Regulatory Services, you have been asked to prepare a legislative analysis of the bill for review and possible approval by the director of the office and the director of the State Department of Social Services. We will use "A Checklist for Legislative Analysis by Governmental Administrative Agencies" in this analysis.

1. Bill Number, Sponsor, and Status

House Bill 6077 is sponsored by Representative King et al. and, at this writing, is being considered by the House Commerce Committee.

2. Intent of the Bill

The bill's intent is to improve the economic climate affecting opportunities for the development of small businesses in the state. This legislation would require administrative agencies to prepare a "small business economic impact statement" when proposing new administrative rules. The purpose of such a statement would be to assess the cost impact of proposed rules on small businesses. The legislation also encourages administrative agencies to reduce unnecessary costs to small businesses by such actions as reducing compliance requirements and exempting these businesses from the proposed rule where appropriate. An example might be exemption of a child day-care center from minimum parking space requirements.

3. Related Legislation and/or Rules

The proposed legislation would amend P.A. 508, the State Administrative Procedures Act, by altering the procedures under which administrative rules are developed and promulgated by the state's administrative agencies as those rules pertain to small businesses. The proposed legislation would also result in alterations in P.A. 118, The Child Care Facilities and Programs Act and P.A. 222, The Adult Foster Care Facilities Act. Consequently, the rules for Operation of Child Day Care Centers, Children's Foster Care, and Child Care Institutions would also be affected.

4. Department's Role in the Request

The bill was not introduced at the department's request.

5. Target of Bill and Level of Need

This bill has been designed for owners of small businesses in the state. It includes small businesses operated as for-profit child care facilities and is designed to benefit the small, independent entrepreneur by reducing regulatory requirements on business operations. The bill is also targeted at state administrative agencies and is aimed at limiting their scope in promulgating rules affecting small businesses.

6. Possible Effects

There is no evidence that the intent of the bill is to include such business activities as the provision of out-of-home care. However, "small business," as defined by House Bill 6077, would include virtually all of the child day care, child residential care, and adult residential care facilities currently licensed by this department. Children and vulnerable adults may inadvertently be subjected to unnecessary risks as a result of this bill.

7. Potential Programmatic and Fiscal Implications

a. This bill would affect all licensees providing day care or residential care for children, and for adults in residential or long-term care. In this state, those licensees serve more than 150,000 children in day care homes and child care centers, over 5,000 children in residential child caring institutions, over 300,000 children in summer camps, over 20,000 adults in residential care facilities, and 35,000 adults in long-term care facilities.

b. The bill could reduce the level of protection to the vulnerable citizens served by these licensees if the definition of "small business" in H. B. 6077 is not altered.

c. This bill would affect the State Departments of Public Health and Mental Health with respect to their regulatory responsibilities and in terms of the citizen populations for which they provide programs.

d. The bill would not result in any savings to the department. Considerable staff resources would be required to research the economic impact of proposed rules on the providers of residential or day care, long-term care, and medical services. Substantially lengthened rules would probably be required in many situations, resulting in considerable cost to state government. Consequently, this legislation would require additional staff.

8. Values Implications

To some extent, this bill is an expression of free enterprise and the maximization of opportunity for the small business entrepreneur. It also represents a creative attempt to generate business activity in the state and, therefore, to increase state revenues, and is an expression of current political attitudes toward government regulation. However, unless the bill is altered to specifically exclude providers of out-of-home care from the definition of "small business," the bill is not consistent with the mission and goals of the department, i.e., providing protection for vulnerable citizens.

9. Arguments For and Against the Bill

Given the present climate of economic activity in the state, a boost to the business community would be very welcome at this time. It would also necessitate examination of existing administrative rules and, perhaps, require a reassessment of the need for some of these rules. On the other hand, lacking a redefinition of "small business" to exclude providers of out-of-home care, the bill is unacceptable to the department in its present form, because it interferes with the protection of children and vulnerable adults in out-of-home care situations.

10. Department's Position

The department supports the proposed legislation, with amendments, for the following reasons:

The bill clearly intends to reduce the regulatory burden faced by small businesses. In the present climate of economic uncertainty and hardship, this may be an important goal: While the department does not oppose such an intent, it cannot support this bill as it presently stands because of the adverse effect it would have on the vulnerable citizens served by the licensees and the services provided by various private and public agencies.

This proposed legislation is not designed with health or human services issues in mind. It is not appropriate to subsume the provision of out-of-home care under the definition of "small business" as provided in the proposed legislation. It is believed that, over a period of time, the health, safety, and welfare of hundreds of thousands of vulnerable children and adults receiving care from some of these facilities would be jeopardized as a result of this legislation.

The department recommends that H.B. 6077 be amended, specifically by addition of the following language in Section B (2):

> "excluding those persons or businesses that provide day care and residential care for children and adults, as provided for in P.A. 118 and P.A. 222"

Director
Office of Regulatory Services
Director
State Department of Social Services

Prepared by:
(Signed)
Title or Position
Date

Giving Legislative Testimony

10

While chapter 9 dealt with the development and organization of written legislative analyses as a technical support function, chapter 10 will deal with oral presentations of policy analyses. A logical context to consider here, of course, is giving testimony in the legislative arena. However, we could just as well consider the policy analyst presenting the analysis of social welfare policy in oral fashion in such forums as a speech to a community group or professional association or a radio interview. Public communications involve special considerations, and the policy analyst would do well to prepare for the unique requirements of each. However, these matters are properly the topic of another time and space; each, in itself, demands specific public communications skills. For our purposes, we will focus on the giving of testimony as a means of communicating policy analyses.

Some essentials of presentation were considered in chapter 8, particularly form and style. However, the political contexts of oral presentations via testimony in a policy-making environment demand special consideration.

Types of Testimony Situations

Giving testimony occurs in three basic situations: judicial, administrative, and legislative. The first refers to testimony in a court of law and may generally be thought of as oral presentations having to do with the search for and affirmation of facts; consequently, giving testimony in the judicial situation is not generally a policy analysis function. Though there may be times when an expert witness is asked to give opinions on policy-related matters, oral presentation of policy analysis is not the main function of testimony in judicial situations.

Legislative testimony is most likely to occur during the development of proposed legislation, ordinances, and municipal policies or in policies to be established by such groups as local United Ways or community action groups. It is what most of us commonly think of as "giving oral testimony." Giving testimony is also likely to occur in administrative situations. It may occur in quasi-legal situations, such as the conduct of fair hearings, appeals from administrative action, and development of administrative rules. The first is similar to the search for facts in judicial hearings and is not the focus of this chapter; the third includes hearings on proposed administrative rules and the presentation of policy positions on budget matters—both situations wherein the policy practitioner may be called upon to give testimony.

The actual oral presentation will likely be brief. Considerations of time and length are important and even limiting. Nevertheless, the need to communicate the basic "Five W's"—who, what, when, where, and why—is no less important or compelling.

Basic Essentials of Giving Testimony

Going beyond the "Five W's," Wilcox (1973) has noted the special characteristics of most technical oral presentations. For the policy analyst, this means being aware that the analysis is likely to be directed at a narrow, special audience, such as a committee or staff group, but not ignoring the presence of unintended audiences. Since testimony-giving is often time-limited, there are very real constraints on what should be included or emphasized. Also, testimony is likely to demand instant understanding, unlike a written report that can be reread or discussed. Consequently, special attention must be given to the use of the voice, the use of language, and the use of transitions and imagery.

A most important distinguishing characteristic of testimony is that its intent is usually to persuade rather than communicate facts. This is not to say that a values orientation and/or social change are not inherent in other forms of policy analysis. However, persuasion is generally both the explicit and implicit purpose in legislative and administrative testimony. This is perhaps why Haskitt (1973) gives particular attention to the need for credibility in giving testimony. According to Haskitt, the provider of oral presentations must obtain a high rating in three essential credibility areas: competence, trust, and enthusiasm. Since testimony-giving is listener-centered, the analyst must help the listener to accept not only the content of the analysis but the personality and/or technique of the person providing it. Consequently, the presentation of policy analyses in these situations demands a special form and style. In speaking of the presentation of testimony at budgetary hearings, Wildavsky (1964) emphasizes its unique interactive nature and the analyst's need to role play or rehearse the hearing and the testimony in advance.

Rules of Thumb for Testimony (A Checklist)

Given these overall considerations, the following rules of thumb are offered as a checklist in preparing testimony that involves policy analysis.

1. Recognize the importance of protocol. It is generally best to assume that protocol is important for everyone until or unless the analyst learns otherwise. This means maintaining a demeanor which, without being officious, stiff, or arrogant, conveys firmness and confidence. Protocol also refers to the anticipated routines or rituals, such as manner of addressing the group or the recognition of the hierarchy of committees, such as first presenting to a standing committee prior to presenting to the committee or board as a whole.
2. Avoid being dogmatic. There will probably be value dilemmas or ethical choices to be made in a particular position.
3. Visualize dealing with both a listener (through judicious use of words, symbols, images, and phrases introducing new concepts) and a reader (by using explanatory headings, obvious outlines, and/or numbered or labeled items).
4. Remember that, in real life, only small gains are possible or probable. Many competing interests shape a compromise, and no analyst, except in very rare instances, is likely to be magically persuasive.
5. Be aware that you may have to return to deal with the same set of actors about the same or other issues.
6. Be critical of ideas or concepts but not of people and rarely of organizations. The key here is to know how to disagree without being disagreeable. This means, among other things, avoiding arguments, the use of straw man approaches, and resorting to the "imperial we." At the same time, be firm and clear about your own position.
7. Educate those receiving the testimony about the essential front-end assumptions of your position and provide the necessary basic information without talking down or being pedantic.
8. Be truthful.

9. Speak slowly, audibly, and distinctly, avoiding jargon, sarcasm, and gratuitous humor.
10. Do your homework; learn about the positions of those who will hear the testimony, have a working knowledge of both the central and peripheral issues involved, and, *especially*, be technically prepared in the subject area.
11. Be specific regarding concerns and the proposed remedy.
12. Anticipate the probable criticisms.
13. Be prepared to share written copies of the testimony with hearing committee members and the media.
14. Follow up the testimony with a note or message of some kind to the hearing officers, expressing appreciation and, once again, briefly reiterating your position.

While the checklist is by no means inclusive of all that might be considered, it can serve as a basic inventory of considerations, as well as a tickler for other matters for the analyst to consider when providing testimony. Regardless of the particular list of dos and don'ts that might be used, the important point is that a variety of interactive considerations, in addition to the substantive content and process elements, are brought to bear in the testimony environment. Giving testimony has both technical and interactive aspects, and each needs proper attention.

Organization of the Testimony

The next consideration is the organization of the analysis. The least ambitious approach could include a statement of the identity of the person or group offering the testimony, a brief position statement, and a summary of background information, followed by an explicit statement of recommendations for action. The testimony should be preceded and followed by an expression of appreciation for the opportunity to be heard and an offer of help by the person providing the testimony.

A more elaborate, though not complex, format has been suggested by George Sharwell (1982) in which a brief introduction is followed by a body of testimony composed of three main parts. The first is a statement of the most important point, including the rationale for the position taken and mention of the flaws in opposing arguments. The second is mention of the least important point, along with its rationale and the flaws in opposing arguments. The third part is the second most important point, along with its rationale and the flaws in opposing arguments. The testimony ends with a brief closing statement. The two strategies, which are not mutually exclusive, aim at "winning" on the merits of one's own argument, or by default in showing that the opposing views are not (as) credible. It should be noted, however, that Sharwell's outline was recommended particularly for legislative testimony presentations to a state legislature and may not be as relevant in more local or smaller scale policy arenas.

Given that our interest here is in the more general question of giving oral testimony in a variety of situations, a particular format is not recommended. However, for "all seasons" purposes, the following checklist might be considered adequate for structuring the giving of most testimony, keeping in mind that the analyst can make appropriate adjustments as indicated by the particular circumstances.

A Checklist for Legislative or Administrative Presentations of Testimony

1. Identification of the person or group offering the testimony
2. Statement of appreciation to the hearing committee
3. Brief statement of position
4. Summary of issues, including lack of merit in alternatives
5. Statement of recommendations for action or preferred position
6. Offer of future assistance by the person or group

Case 11 provides a simple and uncluttered sample statement of testimony given by Mrs. Alice Willer, president of L. R. Vincent Homes for Children, Inc., concerning a state house bill regulating the practice of surrogate parenthood. The testimony is being given before a hearing held by the house judiciary committee in the state legislature.

Case 11: Giving Testimony—Surrogate Parenting (Con)

Testimony by

Mrs. Alice Willer, President
L. R. Vincent Homes For Children, Inc.

before

The House Judiciary Committee
State House of Representatives

on

H. B. 5293—The Surrogate Parenthood Bill
(Date of Presentation)

Mr. Chairman, and members of the Committee, I am Mrs. Alice Willer, President of L. R. Vincent Homes for Children, Inc. The L. R. Vincent Homes is a nonprofit service offering substitute care for children, organized by a statewide federation of local agencies, each of which is guided by a citizens' board of directors. We thank you for giving us this opportunity to present our views on House Bill 5293.

The member agencies of L. R. Vincent Homes across the state strongly oppose in principle the practice of surrogate parenthood and strongly oppose the Surrogate Parenthood Bill.

H. B. 5293 is not in the best interests of the child since:

1. only the wants of the childless couple are considered,
2. the physical, emotional, social, and legal protection needed by the child is denied,
3. the likelihood of subsequent legal entanglement for the child is created, and
4. the status of the child is relegated to that of a commodity.

H. B. 5293 is also not in the best interests of the other parties involved since:

1. all parties are vulnerable to subsequent unpredictable legal actions,
2. the natural emotional attachment of the mother to the newborn infant is denied,
3. a dual class system for adoption will be created due to the economic realities involved, and
4. the identity of each of the parties is not adequately protected.

L. R. Vincent Homes for Children, whose mission is to provide protection and appropriate care for the unprotected child, and whose concerns also extend to the safeguarding of human welfare in general, cannot support H. B. 5293 as an amendment to the continuance of the present adoption code. We urge your complete rejection of this bill.

Thank you, again, for your time and consideration. May we also extend our offer to assist you in any way in your study of this matter. We have provided the Clerk of this Committee with copies of our statement, attached to which is the name, address, and telephone number of our Executive Director and myself, should you wish to contact us further.

Make special note of the content and the form and style of this case illustration. Not only are items in the checklist considered, but the physical structure allows for both mental imaging and quick reading—items are numbered and are specific.

Position Statements

11

Position statements are yet another way of communicating policy analyses. Whereas testimony is offered orally, position statements are offered in writing. Furthermore, position statements, as the name implies, are unequivocally a manifestation of a person's, a group's, or an organization's stand on a particular issue. While a legislative analysis and testimony may provide a clear position on an issue, the analyst need not take a position in either instance, since both may be for the purpose of providing technical information or education. In the case of position statements, however, the expressed purpose is to persuade or to take a stand.

The term "position statement" is used here to mean policy analyses that are committed to writing and aimed at persuading decision makers to choose a specific course of action. Therefore, I include what are generally referred to as *position papers*—which may be relatively brief statements or lengthy documents—and *news releases*, which can also serve as notices of testimony having been given or a position statement having been released. (On the other hand, a press release may stand alone as an announcement of a newsworthy event.) Another example of a position statement is a *letter*, such as a letter to a decision-making group or to the editor of a newspaper. Each of these instruments serves as a unique vehicle for presenting the analysis of social welfare policy.

As with the more detailed or inclusive applications of the content or process outlines provided in previous chapters or with the development of legislative analyses or testimony, position statements must also be concerned with credibility, accuracy, and knowledgeability, and must pay attention to matters of style and form. Again, the context of the situation will determine some unique aspects of style and form. The position statement, however, allows the furthest deviation of all presentation forms from the expectation of a balanced argument or position. This is not to say that the position statement can ignore facts, realities, or the use of common logic; it does mean that a position statement, identified as such and not introduced deviously, is expected to take sides on an issue. Consequently, the person or group offering the analysis needs to determine whether they have the right or authority to take the position and whether the desired (social action) outcome will be positively served. Given the legitimacy for taking action via a position statement, the analyst must be cognizant that analysis then moves to purposive change in a way that is more goal-directed, assertive, and unilateral than other forms of policy analysis. This is important to remember because once the analyst chooses to attach more value or force to a particular position and use the analysis and the associated technical information and process skills to achieve the desired end, the risk of the analysis losing credibility becomes greater. It is easy to become righteous or sanctimonious when one has studied a matter thoroughly and a position has been carefully thought through. If the analyst is mindful of this risk, the opportunity for effective use of the analysis is enhanced.

Discourse Management

Steiner (1977) has suggested that policy development is given direction by what he calls the process of "discourse management." Discourse management is said to comprise three elements: (1) descriptive premises, (2) value premises, and (3) prescriptive conclusions. Discourse management is the process in the development of social policy wherein the descriptive and value premises of analysis are integrated with prescriptive conclusions. Descriptive premises are the statements that the analyst derives from observation, study, and classification of what is analyzed. One might say descriptive premises are the conclusions reached from observing empirical phenomena as a result of one's policy analysis. Value premises, on the other hand, are statements which communicate the preferences of the person making the observations. For Steiner, prescriptive conclusions (i.e., statements of what ought to be done or what course of action should be taken) should be derived from careful development of descriptive and value premises. In other words, one needs to develop a clear understanding of both descriptive and value premises before moving into prescriptive conclusions. Also, overemphasis or exclusion of any of these elements of discourse management impedes policy development.

A position statement properly developed and presented is not only a vehicle available to the analyst but also, given adequate and balanced attention to the elements of discourse management, an effective tool for social action and change. An effective policy analyst will be clear in identifying and separating the descriptive premises from the value premises and will base the conclusions chosen upon a logical connection between the three elements of discourse management. The presentation of position statements forces the analyst to clearly articulate the premises and desired conclusions, and fosters responsible dialogue. This is not to deny the other power and influence aspects of social policy processes; it merely gives focus to the value of these technical and processual aspects of policy. Position statements have a particular function in this regard.

Standards and Pitfalls in Form and Style

Before proceeding, we will consider expectations and dangers inherent in written position statements that go beyond the essentials considered in earlier chapters. Some of these relate to all three approaches; some are unique to the particular type of presentation. Bromage (1973) makes the point that some issues in written communication may be either pitfalls or effective tactics, depending upon their conscious use. These tactics depend on the use of:

1. *Abstract words*. These require the reader (or listener) to visualize the concept and supply the specifics. They may be effective in some circumstances or leave too much to the reader, depending upon the issues, the reader, and other factors.
2. *Passive voice*. This separates the identity of the person taking the position from the issues involved in the position; it also makes the statement less personal, which may or may not be desirable depending upon the particular circumstance. The general rule is that position statements are written in the third person.
3. *Bland language and clichés*. These tactics may also depersonalize or, in the case of clichés, help the reader see what he or she expects or hopes to see; they may also make the position taken or its associated arguments appear sterile or trite.
4. *Jargon*. It is not a good idea to use jargon unnecessarily. Jargon sometimes makes the simple seem complex or vice versa. It may help move the process to a desirable outcome from a political perspective, but it does not enlighten the general audience.
5. *Weasel words*. Words that qualify or hedge tend to deal less with facts and more with opinions and judgments. As a general rule, it

is better to state what is considered fact—as fact—and be clear about value and valued positions.

6. *Silence*. Silence is sometimes used as a means of purposely communicating a position—by ignoring an alternative or another point of view, for example. However, silence is risky when it is interpreted as unfamiliarity with the issues involved.

These tactics can be used to obscure or effectively manage the nature and/or flow of communication. Bromage makes the point that, if the tactics of obfuscation are used for political purposes, the real overall strategy is gamesmanship. In policy analysis, one seldom has the right to make a *personal* decision about using political strategies in position statements. The choice of strategy is often a group or an organizational decision. Decisions about gamesmanship strategies are policy decisions themselves and are to be made by the group or person having the authority to make them, that is, the group using the analysis for its purposes. While the policy analyst may be an integral part of strategic action planning, the analysis itself is the property of the decision-making group, and its manner of communication is the prerogative of that group.

Virtually all authoritative literature in this area stresses the importance of including the ''Five W's'': who, what, when, where, and why. This is especially true in press releases, because the media often cut the release from the bottom up. Therefore, it is important that the ''Five W's'' be minimally but adequately covered in a first paragraph if the essentials of a particular position are to be told.

In all instances it is extremely important to proofread your work and check for accuracy of facts, spelling, titles, and the like. Sometimes professionals destroy their credibility by sloppiness in this area, regardless of the technical soundness of the position statement provided.

Types of Position Statements

Tropman and Alvarez (1977) identify four different types of written instruments used in social welfare policy related work. The first two deal with relatively specific and known audiences: correspondence, such as letters, agreements, and memos; and program records, such as minutes, logs, and reports. The last two tend to have less clear targets or audiences. These are publicity documents, such as flyers, brochures, and newsletters; and substantive documents, such as position papers and study reports. Each of these types has some relationship to the presentation of policy analyses. For our purposes here, the applications with particular implications for the communication and presentation of analyses are position papers, press releases, and letters. We will focus on those three instruments.

Position Papers

Position papers are statements that provide detail and specificity arising out of an analysis and are aimed at both enlightening and/or educating as well as influencing. The position paper tends to be a declaration of a policy stance and may include resolutions or formal recommendations for action. It may also serve as a boilerplate preamble to a charter, a contract, or a formal agreement between organizations. Position papers tend to be issued by associations or organizations, and seldom by individuals. Consequently, the policy analyst's major role in position papers is to assure for the group or organization that the statement is correct and suitable in style and form. Sometimes a position paper serves as an aid to developing group positions and group processes, because its development helps a group or organization to sharpen its own understanding of goals or purposes. Position papers demand specificity and rely upon an organization's own view of its preferences and priorities. This serves both internal and external functions for the organization, since internal elements become better informed about policy positions and priorities as a result of the position paper development, and external elements become educated about the stance of the organization.

The following checklist is suggested for position papers. It should be noted that either these or other headings should be used for the actual paper so that the reader is provided with a visual aid, giving direction to what the writers of the position paper wish to stress.

A Checklist for Position Papers

1. Identification of the sponsor of the position paper
2. Brief summary statement of the position taken
3. Indication of when the position is taken or the circumstances under which the position applies
4. Indication of where the problem occurs and the circumstances under which the remedy offered by the position is likely to be helpful
5. Statement of rationale for the position taken
6. Identification of person or organization for further contact

News Releases

A news release is an instrument aimed at (1) encouraging and helping
the media to utilize the position statement and (2) reaching a mass audience. While a news release may include a large portion of what actually constitutes a position paper, it can achieve useful goals by merely
calling attention to the essentials of a position. Or it may only call attention to the fact that an event has occurred in which a position was taken
or announced by the group presenting its policy analysis.

A news release is one of the technical tools of professional com-
municators. The policy analyst seriously interested in communicating
policy analyses through this medium would do well to consult the professional communications literature, particularly as it relates to public
relations. However, there are some essentials that can be considered
here in the context of presenting policy analyses.

An excellent publication on relationships with the media, *It's
Time to Tell: A Media Handbook for Human Services Personnel* (USDHHS,
1981), is available from the Office of Human Development Services.
This publication is aimed at a number of public relations tasks that go
beyond the presentation of policy analyses. It includes many helpful
hints about the use of news releases. The following discussion is taken
largely from this pamphlet as well as from various experiences in developing news releases.

To be received positively by the media and the audience, a good
news release must not be a disguised advertisement for a position but a
report of an actual event. The lead paragraph must contain the essentials of the "Five W's" because the media, given their time and space
constraints, often cut from the bottom up. If the basics are at least minimally stated in the first sentence or paragraph, the essentials of the position will be communicated. Subsequent information might be labeled
with a heading such as "Additional Facts" or "Supporting Statements" and may or may not be used in the story actually printed or
presented on the air. By including such material, the analysis is not
lost, and the media source may use some of the additional material,
either then or at a later time, particularly when issue resolution is prolonged or the policy issue has a long life.

While the basic essentials of style and form also apply to news
releases, there are some special considerations here. The release
must be headed by a dateline and a byline, indicating when, where,
and by whom the release is provided. Names, addresses, and phone
numbers should be included in case the media seek clarification. The
release must be double-spaced and should use an inverted pyramid
format, with the most inclusive details concisely stated first and fol-

lowed by more facts or background. Standard, white, 8½ by 11 inch paper should be used, with pages numbered (e.g., Page 2 of 2, etc.), and the word *more* at the bottom of a page when more follows. The end of the release should be marked by the single word *end*, or the symbols ### or -30-. Abbreviations are not generally used in the body of the release.

As long as the ''Five W's'' are the lead sentence or paragraph, it is not necessary to use a particular outline for a news release. The outline for legislative analyses or position papers might be used for the remainder of the release.

Letters

Letters tend to be directed at an individual or a narrow audience. They may convey a position to an agency or government official or to the editor of a local newspaper. The broader the readership, the less technical the analysis should be. Aside from the general conventions of sound writing and exposition, there are some special considerations in letters conveying policy analyses.

Because a policy analysis conveyed by letter is often directed to someone holding office or in an administrative position, it is important to properly address the person to whom it is written. Failure to do so may unintentionally communicate naivete, sloppiness, or lack of sophistication, which could inadvertently sabotage the analyst or the group sponsoring the analysis. The communication should be timely; it should be conveyed well enough in advance of the decision point so that the decision maker can benefit from the input and not be embarrassed by learning of the position too late in the decision process. The letter should be clear and specific as to preference or objections and, above all, what you are requesting the addressee to do. Obviously, the same clear and cogent rationale provided in other analyses should be included.

Letters to editors or public officials sometimes have a tendency to berate the officeholder and occasionally are couched in threatening language, implying removal of future support. Such approaches are generally counterproductive and, while they may have some place in the politics of policy processes, they have nothing to do with providing sound policy analyses. Furthermore, it is probably arrogant (and for most of us, naive) to allege or pretend to wield vast amounts of political influence.

The following case examples will illustrate a position paper, two different news releases, and a letter.

Case 12: Position Paper—Surrogate Parenting (Pro)

Case 11 provided an illustration of testimony-giving, using Mrs. Alice Willer's testimony opposing House Bill 5293 regulating the practice of surrogate parenthood. Her organization, the L. R. Vincent Homes for Children, Inc., is opposed in principle to the practice of surrogate parenthood and strongly opposes the bill. In Case 12, that topic is used as a vehicle for illustrating a position statement, this time providing a statement in support of the principle of surrogate parenting and H.B. 5293. The bill, as before, is being considered by the House Judiciary Committee. A statewide action group, the State Alliance for the Prevention for Genetically Transmittable Diseases, has issued the position paper that follows.

Surrogate Parenting

A Position Statement by the
State Alliance for the Prevention of Genetically
Transmittable Diseases

We, the members of the State Alliance for the Prevention of Genetically Transmitted Diseases, declare our support for the legalization and regulation of surrogate parenting in the state.

Central Position

The Alliance is concerned with protecting the rights and interests of those individuals who seek surrogate parenting as an alternative and for those children who are born out of surrogate parenting agreements.

Opportunity

We urge the state legislature to provide for an open forum of public debate on this issue and to adopt legislation which adequately addresses the concerns and issues involved in surrogate parenting. We believe that the widest possible dialogue on the issue could take place if the House Judiciary Committee would hold hearings on H.B. 5293 at various locations throughout the state.

Affected Group

There are many people in our state who, because of a number of health reasons, are unable to conceive healthy children of their own or for whom adoption is not a viable option. Some children are currently victims of questionable surrogate parenting practices; the state should meet its obligation in extending protection to such children.

Rationale

The State Alliance for the Prevention of Genetically Transmittable Diseases recognizes that surrogate parenting is a highly complex, legal, moral, and sociopsychological issue. It is compounded by the fact that there is no current legislation or legal precedent to regulate this uncharted area. We strongly urge the state legislature to enact legislation on surrogate parenting which will recognize the following concerns:

1. To establish the parental rights and responsibilities of a natural father and his spouse for a child conceived through the artificial insemination of a surrogate; i.e., to ensure the assumption of responsibility regardless of the child's psychological or physical condition;
2. To establish the legal status of a child conceived through the artificial insemination of a surrogate; i.e., to ensure that the child will be considered the legitimate child of the natural father and his spouse;
3. To provide for the termination of parental rights of a surrogate; i.e., to ensure that the surrogate shall sign a consent agreement to terminate her parental rights and responsibilities upon the birth of the child;
4. To prohibit any person from engaging in certain unethical conduct, such as arranging a surrogate birth for unreasonable economic gain;
5. To require that certain documents be filed with the state registrar for the purpose of allowing the child access to hereditary information on the surrogate mother, and for making available the identity of the surrogate mother in the event of her consent, such as providing that each surrogate birth acknowledgement, consent, revocation, or contract shall be notarized and filed with the state registrar;
6. To provide for mental screening of the parties involved; i.e., the surrogate mother, the spouse of the surrogate mother, and the adopting parents.

Conclusion

The State Alliance for the Prevention of Genetically Transmittable Diseases is fully aware of the argument against surrogate parenting; namely, that surrogate parenting is a potential "Pandora's box" of problems and conflicts. Nevertheless, we strongly feel that this should be no reason to prohibit surrogate parenting as an alternative for those couples who are either unable to give birth to a child or do not wish to transmit particular diseases to their offspring. Simply because an issue presents problems is no reason to avoid addressing it altogether. Such logic is totally inappropriate and inadequate. We submit that, in fact, many of the existing precedents and much extant legislation on custody in the areas of foster care and adoption provide guidelines and examples, from which appropriate legislation can be drafted to regulate surrogate parenting. As foster care and adoption were new frontiers years ago, so today is the life-giving alternative of surrogate parenting. We urge the state legislature to support and adopt these measures.

Date:

For further information, contact:
    Margaret Michelle, M.D., Chair
    State Alliance for the Prevention
        of Genetically Transmittable Diseases
    1001 Main Street
    This City, This State
    (717) 347-8899

Case 13: News Release—Surrogate Parenting (Pro)

The position paper developed by the State Alliance for the Prevention of Genetically Transmittable Diseases also provides an illustration of a news release. Note that, although Case 13 also covers the basic "Five W's" requirement, the two instruments differ greatly in size and detail.

For Immediate Release
Date:
From: The State Alliance for the Prevention of Genetically Transmittable Diseases, Margaret Michelle, M.D., Chair, 1001 Main Street, This City, This State, (717) 347-8899.

The State Alliance for the Prevention of Genetically Transmittable Diseases will be presenting a position paper in favor of legalization and regulation of surrogate parenthood to the State House Judiciary Committee on Tuesday, March 10, 1984, at 3:00 p.m. at the State Capitol Building, Room 204, Capitol City, This State. The Alliance is "concerned about protecting the rights and interests of those individuals who seek surrogate parenting as an alternative and for those children who are born out of surrogate parenting agreements," said Peter Dale, Alliance spokesperson. The meeting is open to the public and all interested persons are urged to attend or contact the Alliance Chairperson, Dr. Margaret Michelle, at (717) 347-8899.

#   #   #

This news release is an example of a policy analysis presentation aimed at giving notice of an event that is meant to inform and persuade or to urge others to action. In other situations, a policy analysis may have been completed and a news release might serve as an opportunity for more generalized public relations.

Case 14: News Release—Agency Energy Audits

Case 14 is an analysis of energy conservation concerns regarding local United Way agencies. Here the news release as an instrument is used as both a vehicle to inform the public about a particular problem and a means of presenting a public relations image of the agency. In this situation, the vehicle of a news release provides an opportunity of informing the community that the United Way and its member agencies are acting responsibly through efficient and effective use of voluntary contributions. The United Way has studied the recent decision by the State Public Utilities Commission mandating the state's utility companies to provide energy audits to homeowners. The United Way has conducted a review of energy consumption and costs among member agencies and is urging the State Public Utilities Commission to include human services organizations in that mandate. This case also illustrates the point that news releases need not restrict themselves to proposed policy changes under consideration by legislative bodies but are also appropriate in instances involving both public relations and the influence process in making administrative agency policy.

For Immediate Release
Date:
From: The Cummings County United Way, Harold Kelly, President, 129 South West Street, This City, This State, (233) 764-6666.

The United Way of Cummings County hopes to enlist the aid of the State Public Utilities Commission in urging the commission to require that utility companies in the state provide energy audits to human services organizations, effective January 1 of next year. The commission recently mandated that utility companies provide these audits to homeowners.

In issuing the statement this morning at the City Center, Madelyn Brown, Executive Director of the United Way, noted that the United Way and its affiliate agencies have contacted and exhausted all potential sources offering energy assistance to human services agencies. The organization found that there are no available resources, although schools, hospitals, local governments, and public care buildings are eligible for energy assistance grants under Title II of the National Energy Conservation Policy Act.

In the past year in Cummings County, energy costs consumed one-third of United Way's total allocations to its affiliate agencies. Continued rises in the costs of energy will increasingly divert funds from services to maintenance. United Way is, therefore, requesting that the State Public Utilities Commission's mandate of energy audits for households be extended to human services organizations. This effort is one of many steps being taken by the United Way to aid human services agencies during the energy crisis.

–end–

Case 15: Letter—Agency Energy Audits

We will now use the content of the news release on the energy audit, which indicated the United Way's intent to enlist the aid of the State Public Utilities Commission, to communicate by letter to State Representative Bridget Green. While the letter in Case 15 is provided primarily to illustrate the form and content of letters conveying a position, note the courtesy and good politics involved in informing a state legislator from the area about the group's activity. The letter should be on letterhead stationery that displays the agency name, address, and phone number.

Date

The Honorable Bridget Green
State Representative, Third District
     State House of Representatives
City, State ZIP

Dear Representative Green,

     We are pleased to inform you that the Board of Directors of Cummings County United Way has urged the State Public Utilities Commission to require that utility companies in the state provide energy audits to human services organizations, effective January 1 of next year. Our recent press release is enclosed. We have requested that the audits currently mandated for homeowners be extended to human services organizations. In our judgment, this step is necessary because all potential sources of help offering energy assistance to human services agencies have been exhausted. Energy assistance grants under Title II of the National Energy Conservation Policy Act available to schools, hospitals, local governments and public care buildings are not available to the United Way and its affiliate agencies.

     As you are perhaps aware, energy costs have consumed one-third of United Way's total allocation to its affiliate agencies. Continued increases in energy costs will increasingly divert funds from services to maintenance. This is one of many steps being taken by the United Way to aid human services agencies during the energy crisis. We would hope that you could be of assistance in urging the commission to take this action.

Once again, we would like to take this opportunity to thank you for the interest that you have continually shown in the work of the United Way and in the programs of many of our affiliate agencies. Should you have any questions or concerns regarding this or any other matter, please do not hesitate to call me (office—388-2864; home—385-9223) or our Executive Director, Ms. Madelyn Brown.

Sincerely,

Harold Kelley, President

Analysis and the Implementation of Policy

12

Policy is often made by those who seize opportunity. Better policy is made by those who seize opportunity and are adequately informed. If the policy practitioner is to be adequately prepared for the occasion, then policy analysis and attention to its implementation must become a way of professional life. Sound policy practice is not just an occasional academic exercise or a hobby for curious people. Policy practice is a continuous process that must become, at least in some form, part of the conscious routine of the human service practitioner. Whether the level of analysis is only a glimpse at the source of a policy's legitimacy or a detailed examination of alternative policy choices, policy practice must become part of professional routines, hand in hand with providing direct services. While the process of assuring policy implementation may be the responsibility of others, the adequacy and appropriateness of policy functioning is the responsibility of all. Policy drives what we do in meeting social agency responsibilities. This is as true for the direct service practitioner as it is for the planner or the administrator; only the level of focus differs.

Consequently, we have to recognize the fact that policy practice goes beyond analysis—the focus of this book—to the actual implementation of policy. The central focus of this book has been on the analysis of social welfare policy in small-scale systems. The implementation of policy is quite another matter. Yet, as we all know, dichotomies are false in the real world. One cannot really separate analysis from the realities of implementation—putting policy to work or giving effect to the content or the process of policy. After all, we engage in the analysis of policy because we want something in particular to happen, to effect social prac-

tice, and because we have interest in the end-of-the-line outcome—
policy implementation. With this in mind, we will look at some practical
approaches to the implementation of policy. The intent here is not to
heap more work on the task of analysis. While this is not a text on policy
implementation, it is only reasonable to give some parting attention to
issues in the implementation of policy: (1) proactive strategies for implementation; (2) advance preparation of staff; (3) issues in authorization as
opposed to providing appropriations for implementing policy; (4) developing of guidelines or administrative rules that give effect to policy; (5)
monitoring and evaluating the implementation of policy; and (6) appropriate activities for those who manage policy implementation.

Proactive Strategies

Opportunity is often realized by those who are proactive, as opposed
to reactive, in any social process. Initiatives generally increase the
chance of success and goal achievement. There are a number of proactive strategies that are possible in policy implementation. These strategies are either in the external environment of the social agency or in the
agency's internal organizational environment.

A first proactive implementation strategy is to become familiar
with the legislative process relevant to a particular policy issue, whether
it be on the state, regional, or local level. Implementation can sometimes
be "wired in" by what occurs in the earliest stages of policy development in legislative arenas. The parameters of what is possible are often
set or delimited by the earliest actions of policymakers. For example, a
local county commission may require at the outset in its enabling ordinance that a certain percent of the available funding must be allocated to
a particular policy initiative or program strategy, thereby setting some
boundaries on the policy's implementation from the very beginning.
Or, for example, a local United Way may develop a policy statement indicating that certain community needs are the domain of the public sector and others the domain of the private sector, thereby limiting potential for voluntary financial support for social services of a certain type in
the community. These initial parameters control the outer limits of policy. Familiarity with these legislative processes can affect the probabilities of policy implementation, at least in the broadest sense.

Another strategy is to become familiar with the play of power and
influence in the external environment. Policy implementation often
begins at the earliest stages of policy formulation, not at the final point
of passage or promulgation. A technique to achieve early entry might
be regular participation in various legislative networks formed by special interest groups, whether those groups interact through social

action forums, luncheon meetings, newsletters, or electronic conferencing, electronic mail, or old-fashioned "button-holing."

Advance Preparation of Staff

Another proactive possibility for implementation is to provide opportunities for orientation or training for staff in the purpose, goals, and procedures of a particular policy. In fact, some policy implementation is enhanced by the participation of the potential implementers in the formulation of the policy. A next best strategy is to involve staff in the development of guidelines for the actual implementation of legitimated policy. Generally speaking, the rule is the earlier the better in involving those who will implement a policy.

Another possibility is the provision of staff support to committees that are charged with the formulation of policy. Generally speaking, committees (whether comprised of volunteers or paid staff personnel) need persons available to do the detail work, such as generating data that supports decision making, following up on informational inquiries posed by the committee process, keeping records of committee decisions, and bringing in resources needed by the committee to conduct its work. A somewhat less tangible resource needed by committees or task forces is a practical, working knowledge of parliamentary procedure. While the formal Robert's Rules of Order may not be used by a particular committee, some of the central principles of parliamentary procedure may be needed for a productive policy process. Provision of adequate support to policymakers in the earliest stages of policy development is a proactive means for policy implementation. This is not unlike giving proper care to a new lawn.

Authorization vs. Appropriation

Another link between policy and implementation is the fact that there is often a difference between a policy process that provides *authorization* for policy action and the actual *appropriation* of the resources necessary for policy implementation. This reality is commonly recognized in large governmental policy arenas, wherein Congress or a state legislature might invest much time and energy in the political process in passage of enabling legislation while the subsequent appropriation of necessary resources may never see the light of day. The same phenomenon can and does occur at the local, small-scale level. An external funding body or the organization's own board of directors may in fact provide authorization to place a particular policy in effect but not allocate the resources needed to realize the policy goal. We can all likely think of a number of such situations.

Developing Guidelines or Administrative Rules

Formal policy statements are often stated in broad terms encompassing a range and variety of system conditions. Policies are not generally established to govern exceptional situations; they are aimed at giving guidance in general classes of situations. Consequently, policies often demand considerable work in the way of developing guidelines or rules subsequent to obtaining legitimation. Guidelines are suggestions for action that will help people comply with the intent or spirit of a policy. Guidelines often suggest courses of action that may help people make decisions about how they might meet policy requirements. They are often mere suggestions stated in permissive terms (e.g., "may" or "can"). In fact, if "guidelines" are stated in mandatory terms (e.g., as "will," "shall," or "must"), they are formal policies and not guidelines at all.

Another variation on the theme is provided by administrative rules that flow out of regulatory legislation. Administrative rules are standards that have the force of law. Examples of administrative rules in social welfare are those that regulate the provision of child day care or adult foster care. State licensing legislation for providing out-of-home care for children or vulnerable adults is often stated in general terms regarding how to safeguard the health, welfare, and safety of citizens in a myriad of conditions. Consequently, minimum standards become formally sanctioned as administrative rules which spell out the detailed requirements of policy. These rules are often developed by administrative agencies in cooperation with those who are regulated by the legislation. Administrative rules become policy standards which have the force of law.

The policy practitioner has an opportunity to affect policy by participating in or otherwise influencing the development of those parameters that are subsequently given to formalized policy through guidelines or administrative rules. The interpretation of what constitutes sufficient or necessary compliance with guidelines or rules is sometimes arbitrarily decided upon, providing opportunity for the policy practitioner to participate in the "policy space" even after a policy has already been formally established and legitimated. Hence, the process and period of implementation is a potentially fruitful domain for policy practice.

Monitoring and Evaluating the Implementation of Policy

While we may sometimes think that policies have their own source of life and energy, policies are sustained in their effect only by individuals and organizations. Policies are not animate objects, no matter how much we are tempted to reify them. Nevertheless, the implementation of policy can often lead to organizational processes that are sustained by inertia supported by procedures that may or may not be compatible with the initial policy goals. Therein lies the value of monitoring and evaluating policy implementation.

Monitoring refers to those activities aimed at determining whether a particular policy, as agreed upon, is operating effectively. This includes the maintenance of data systems, periodic review of the quality of data, auditing for fiscal or program compliance, and confirming that appropriate procedures are in place for adequate implementation. These are all activities that might be assessed in terms of policy implementation. Sound social practice would regularize monitoring procedures, ensuring that policies that are subject to drift or manipulation were supported by institutionalized monitoring procedures.

Evaluation of policy implementation is somewhat different in focus. Evaluation suggests attaching value to means or methods of implementation. Evaluation, then, requires more creativity in identifying alternative means that might be more desirable for the implementation of a particular policy. Evaluation of policy implementation is an analytical task that goes beyond the analysis of policy content and policy process, the focus of this book.

Management of Policy

Finally, it is obvious that policy has to be managed. Not being animate, policy must be sustained by structures and people. Tropman (1984) refers to the function of the "policy manager" and identifies a number of policy management roles in the areas of knowledge development, interpersonal relationship management, political participation, and organizational and group maintenance and support. The management of policy is, according to Tropman, in and of itself an area of policy practice. Programs need managers; so do policies.

In real life, managers of programs are managers of policy. But policy pervades all organizational forms. Policy is managed by all members of social agencies, even those who are direct practitioners—at least to some extent.

The Ethical Imperative

The purpose of policy analysis goes beyond functional utility. There are also certain ethical imperatives. For example, the Code of Ethics of the National Association of Social Workers (1979) provides a clear mandate for the social worker to develop professional competence: "The social worker should accept responsibility or employment only on the basis of existing competence or the intention to acquire the necessary competence." At first glance, the direct service worker, planner, community organizer, or administrator may assume that competence refers only to the acquisition of technical knowledge and skill directly related to method of practice. While this is where the emphasis for professional development should perhaps be placed, social welfare policy provides the legitimacy, the limits, or the opportunities for the application of that practice knowledge and skill. Policy analysis, at least at some level of detail, must become a part of that practice competence if practitioners are to meet ethical obligations for sound professional practice.

Levy (1976) has said:

> The social worker should know what he is capable of and what he is not capable of and accordingly make the appropriate choice or provision—withdrawal, referral, counsel, guidance, consultation, and so forth—in the best interests of clients and anybody else toward whom he has attributable responsibility. (1976, p.119)

It might be added that the practitioner must make not only the appropriate choice but also the appropriate adjustments. The ability to think analytically about policy issues is one of the tools available to practitioners in making practice decisions. The Code of Ethics mandates the acceptance of professional responsibility to engage in practice that is either based upon existing competence or the intention to acquire such competence. Inasmuch as policy embodies the principles upon which such practice is made possible, then policy analysis must become a regular and important aspect of the practitioner's intervention decisions.

A Task for the Policy Practitioner

The task of the policy practitioner is to be informed and to help others to be informed—clients, colleagues, other decision makers, and the general public. Through adequate policy analysis we become better advocates for client groups; we provide valuable information for program planning; we guide the development of positions for social action; and we become active participants in organizational maintenance or change.

The policy practitioner can participate in and influence the shaping of social welfare policy, but to do so, he or she must be an active participant in the process. The making of policy at the local or small-scale level is highly idiosyncratic and demands the participation of those who are in a position to know or uncover the details. This is a major part of providing social services, whether efforts are instigated by a formal assignment or charge for analysis, or moved by meeting the professional obligation of being "in the know."

What Next?

The first action step for professional development is to make policy analysis part of the practitioner's conscious routine. This means that policy analysis must become a regular part of case assessment and planning, needs assessment, organizational analysis and development, or social action. Since most social workers meet their professional responsibilities at the local and/or small-scale levels, the second step requires that they familiarize themselves with their environments in new ways, since they are not used to seeing their worlds from a policy perspective. This suggests a number of "trial runs" by actually engaging in such analysis. The third step is to acquire skill through experience and dialogue with others over policy analysis products at the small-scale level. But if this dialogue is to take place, individual practitioners must take the initiative.

The Need for Staff Development

Few supports are available for the acquisition of policy analysis skills at the present time, particularly with respect to small-scale policy analysis. This book is one attempt to solve this problem. While small-scale policy analysis has become the responsibility of many who are working in human services, the subject is not likely to be found in their job descriptions and is generally not part of staff development or in-service training programs. The tasks of policy analysis have just "crept in." Yet policy analysis is an integral part of development and survival in local-level human services, and most of us play a part in such analyses whether we know it or not.

To make policy analysis a part of the professional practitioner's routine, we need to make it more visible. This would legitimize related efforts in the area of staff development. If staff are actually engaged in policy analysis activities and accountable for those tasks, and if agency development and survival are dependent on the adequacy of those analyses, then there should be effective staff development efforts in that area. We could start with those policy activities already engaged in by local social and human service practitioners. Some of these activities are cited by Ziter and the North Carolina study (Ziter, 1983) and in a study by Flynn and Jaksa (1983). These or other policy activities could be the focus of efforts for staff training. If the social policy analysis activities engaged in by practitioners need to be codified so that systematic development of practitioners' skills can be obtained.

Summary

We have reviewed models of content and process that have been applied to large-scale policy systems, while giving particular attention to values. We identified what may be considered essential elements of outlines for analysis for small-scale human service situations or issues. We constructed two outlines for small-scale analysis for application of content and process factors in selected substantive areas, and we offered a number of case examples as illustrations. The case illustrations ranged from issues immediately related to direct practice for the individual practitioner to organizational and interorganizational policy matters. We also considered particular issues of form and style in specific situations in which policy analyses are presented externally— "outside of the agency"—including the development and application of checklists for legislative analysis, giving testimony in legislative settings, and developing position statements such as position papers and news releases.

This chapter reviewed the functional utility in considering some aspects of the link between policy analysis and policy implementation and considered the ethical imperatives of policy analysis at the small-scale level. Clearly, much remains to be done, but the challenge promises great reward.

Appendix A

An Outline for Analyzing Content of Small-Scale Policy

A. *Essential Steps in Policy Content Analysis*
1. Identify the Policy Problem or Policy Goal (Similar to Process Analysis)
2. Assess Current and Anticipated System Functioning
3. Determine Implications for Selected Values (Same as Process Analysis)
4. Establish Feasibility of the Desired Outcome
5. Provide Recommendations

B. *Content Elements*
1. *Identify the Policy Problem or Policy Goal(s).* A focus on the definition or delineation of the *core principles* at stake in the particular problem, policy goal(s), or the specific policy that is to be analyzed. Identification should include:
   a. *The Policy Problem/Goal and the Policy Statement.* What, in fact, is the policy problem, the policy issue, policy goal or objective under study? Does it exist in written form or only observable in the behavior of those in the environment?
   b. *Base(s) of Legitimacy and Source or Location of the Policy.* Who or what provides the right to take action and where is that documented (i.e., in written form if formal policy or as observed in actual behavior if an informal policy)?

c. *Targets and Clients of Concern.* Who or what is the object of change and whose interests will be served?

d. *Eligibility.* Who or what will be included and under what conditions?

e. *Effect upon Maintenance, Change, or Control.* What is the intended or unintended effect upon system maintenance, system change, or the control of system elements?

f. *Explicit or Implicit Theories.* What are some likely theoretical foundations or assumptions in this policy approach?

g. *Topography of the Policy System.* What elements might be logically included in the conceptual "map" of the system involved?

h. *Contemporary Issues or Historical Antecedents.* What are some of the other relevant issues that might be associated with this policy?

2. *Assess Current and Anticipated System Functioning.* A focus on the organizational, administrative and/or environmental functioning of the *policy system* and the interaction of the components in that system. Attention should be given to both current functioning and system functioning anticipated by embracing any proposed policy changes.

a. *State of System Boundaries.* What is the nature of communication and interaction between elements in the system as a result of this policy?

b. *Authority, Influence, and Leadership.* What authority, exercise of power, or leadership is given to or needed to effect this policy?

c. *Patterns of Communication.* Who or what are the key system points for communication and in which direction does that communication flow?

d. *Strains and Constraints.* What effect does the policy have upon tension, variety, and entropy within the system? Is that outcome functional or dysfunctional?

e. *Resistance to Change.* What are the issues, forces, or factors that might give resistance to or mitigate against change as a result of the policy?

f. *Feedback Devices.* What devices or channels exist which provide for information that guide the system toward corrective action based upon its output activities?

g. *Impact on Agency's Dynamic Adaptation.* To what extent does policy enhance the system's ability to be more adaptive and self-corrective?

h. *Environmental Impact.* What impact will there be on the general social welfare climate as a result of the policy in terms of any messages, meta-messages, overall implications, or setting of precedents for the overall system?

3. *Determine Implications for Selected Values.* A focus on the implications for selected values to be used in the analysis or desired in the proposed or desired policy, particularly with regard to the targets and clients/interests affected by the policy.

   a. *Adequacy.* To what extent is the goal achieved when the policy is carried out, both in terms of "coverage" for individual system units and overall system coverage?

   b. *Effectiveness.* To what extent is there a logical connection between the means or techniques required by the policy and the policy goal achieved?

   c. *Efficiency.* To what degree are the means employed in goal achievement maximized with the use of the minimum amount of resources?

   d. *Impact on Rights, Statuses, and Social Justice.* What is the policy's impact upon individual, group, or organizational rights and statuses, particularly in terms of equity and fairness?

   e. *Self-Determination.* Does the policy honor the right of citizens to a voice in the determination of those policies that vitally affect themselves?

   f. *Identity.* What effect does this policy have upon the self-image of the beneficiary (client) or the target of the policy and upon the need and right to human dignity?

   g. *Individualization.* To what extent is the need for individuals (or groups or organizations) to be treated in terms of their unique nature, needs, and qualities recognized by the policy?

   h. *Nonjudgmental Attitude.* Does the policy, in its net effect, make unfair or improper judgments about the clients or targets of the policy or make any unwarranted assumptions about the competence of individuals or groups?

   i. *Confidentiality.* Are issues of privacy and security of information given proper attention in this policy or its implementation?

   j. *Indeterminateness.* To what extent does the policy recognize that the end states of social processes are determined and altered *in process*?

   k. *Multifinality.* Is the policy consistent with the concept that original conditions can result in multiple end state conditions?

   l. *Nonsummativity.* Is the policy built on the premise that human aggregations are nonsummative, or that the whole is *different than* or perhaps *greater than* or *something other than* the sum of its parts?

m. *Morphogenesis*. Does the policy recognize that human systems have the capacity to alter forms and processes?

n. *The SCRAPS Test*. Has explicit attention been given to the implications for those who constitute a minority because of their gender, class, race, or age or because of their poverty?

4. *Establish Feasibility of the Desired Outcomes*. A focus on the elements that make for achieving resolution of the policy problem or the attainment of the policy goal.

a. *Legality and Foundation*. Is the policy consistent with legislated and judicial mandates and with administrative and executive directives?

b. *Power of the Policy*. To what extent is the policy likely to influence or order the sequencing of *probabilities* of events in the policy system?

c. *Resource Requirements and Availability*. What demands will the policy make upon such factors as finances, space, personnel, time, power, status, prestige, and credibility?

d. *Rationality*. Is the policy based upon some logical link between the original problem statement and the strategy employed by the policy?

e. *Newly Perceived Self-Interests*. Will individuals, groups, or organizations likely find new incentives in compliance with or support for this policy?

5. *Provide Recommendations*. A focus on the strengths and weaknesses or factors peculiar to the issue and suggested by the data generated by the analysis.

What specific actions would you now recommend to decision makers?

Appendix B

An Outline for Analyzing Process of Small-Scale Policy

A. *Essential Steps in Policy Process Analysis*
   1. Identify the Policy Problem or Policy Goal (Similar to Content Analysis)
   2. Assess the Nature or Condition of Developmental Milestones
   3. Identify Interest Group Relationships
   4. Assess the Availability and Use of Process Resources
   5. Determine Implications for Selected Values (Same as Content Analysis)
   6. Provide Recommendations

B. *Process Elements*
   1. *Identify the Policy Problem or Policy Goal(s).* A focus on the definition or delineation of the core principles at stake in the particular problem, policy goal(s) or the specific policy that is to be analyzed. Identification should include:
      a. *The Policy Problem/Goal and the Policy Statement.* What, in fact, is the policy problem, the policy issue, policy goal, or objective under study? Does it exist in written form or is it only observable in the behavior of those in the environment?
      b. *Base(s) of Legitimacy and Source or Location of the Policy.* Who or what provides the right to take action and where is that documented (i.e., in written form if formal policy or as observed in actual behavior if an informal policy)?

2. *Assess the Nature or Condition of Developmental Milestones.* A focus on the major developmental tasks undertaken or to be undertaken in the policy process.
   a. *Identification of the Charter.* What is the issue that led people to take action and how did that beginning state emerge?
      1) *Original Agreement or Template for Action.* What was the original impetus that brought people together?
      2) *Obtaining the Right or Support to Take Action.* How did key actors obtain the right or support for taking action?
      3) *Substance of the Agreement(s).* What was the central substance of their agreements?
   b. *Functioning of the Action System(s).* What transpired that facilitated (or impeded) those who initiated action?
   c. *Key Participants and Their Associated Events.* Who were the identifiable set of social actors who assumed responsibility for pursuing, implementing, or enforcing the policy change (or policy maintenance)? How did that occur?
3. *Identify Interest Group Relationships.* A focus on the particular groups represented in the policy process, identification of their particular interests, and their interaction relevant to the policy.
   a. *Power and Influence.* Who held the power in this situation and who actually exercised the necessary influence to bring about social action?
   b. *Salience of the Issue.* To what extent was this particular policy issue important enough to explain the participation necessary to achieve policy activity?
   c. *Intergroup Activities.* What particularly relevant intergroup interchanges occurred, cooperative or otherwise, that were essential for explaining how the policy process proceeded?
      1) *Intergroup Transfers and/or Exchanges.* What activities occurred across or between intrasystem boundaries, such as bilateral or multilateral exchanges?
      2) *Bargaining and Negotiating.* To what extent did bargaining or negotiating occur, by whom, and in what manner?
      3) *Coalitions.* What, if any, coalitions were formed and what were the conditions sustaining such coalitions?
      4) *Contracting.* What agreements arose between groups or organizations during or as a result of the policy process?
4. *Assess the Availability and Use of Process Resources.* A focus on the resources needed and observable in the policy process.
   a. *People Power.* What key actors were involved that explain the extent to which the social action goal was achieved?

b. *Technology*. What particular technology, skills, and/or talents were used in the policy process by various social actors?

c. *Finances*. What resources requiring financial support were needed, and how were those financial resources obtained?

d. *Time*. To what extent was time an asset or a liability in this policy process?

5. *Determine Implications for Selected Values*. A focus on the implications for selected values to be used in the analysis or desired in the proposed or desired policy, particularly with regard to the targets and clients/interests affected by the policy.

a. *Adequacy*. To what extent were social action resources adequate to achieve the policy action goal?

b. *Effectiveness*. To what extent was the process able to assure that the desired end state was achieved?

c. *Efficiency*. To what extent were the minimum of process resources used to obtain the desired policy goal?

d. *Impact on Rights, Statuses, and Social Justice*. Were the rights and statuses of individuals enhanced or diminished as a result of the policy process?

e. *Self-Determination*. Was the self-determination of individuals, groups, or organizations enhanced as a result of the policy process?

f. *Identity*. Were the reputations or self-images of any element of the policy system enhanced or hindered as a result of the policy process?

g. *Individualization*. To what extent was the input of each social grouping or each professional discipline appropriately considered in the policy's development?

h. *Nonjudgmental Attitude*. To what extent were stereotypical or prejudicial attitudes in evidence during the policy process?

i. *Confidentiality*. Were appropriate standards of confidentiality maintained throughout the process?

j. *Indeterminateness*. Was the approach to this problem resolution an open one, indicating that policy development would be determined in process?

k. *Multifinality*. Was it evident throughout this process that similar ideas and actions introduced during the process could properly result in various outcomes?

l. *Nonsummativity*. Was it evident that, as a result of the policy process, the final product reflected something beyond the additive properties of the participants' individual contributions?

   m. *Morphogenesis*. Was it evident that the process of participation generated new ideas or new ways of problem solving or policy formulation?
   n. *The SCRAPS Test*. Were the interests served or violated for those who were in the minority because of their gender, class, race, age, or income status?
6. *Provide Recommendations*. A focus on the strengths and weaknesses or factors peculiar to the issue and suggested by the data generated by the analysis.
   What recommendations would you make as to how the process might better occur in the future?

References

Anderson, Ralph E., and Irl E. Carter. *Human Behavior and the Social Environment: A Social Systems Approach,* 2d ed. Chicago, IL: Aldine, 1974.

Biestek, Felix. *The Casework Relationship.* Chicago, IL: Loyola University Press, 1957.

Boulding, Kenneth E. "The Boundaries of Social Policy." *Social Work,* 12 (Jan. 1967): 3–11.

Boulding, Kenneth E. "General Systems Theory—The Skeleton of Science." In Walter Buckley, ed., *Modern Systems Research for the Behavioral Scientist.* Chicago, IL: Aldine, 1968. Pp. 3–10.

Boyd, Lawrence, Jr.; Robert Pruger; Martin D. Chase; Marleen Clark; and Leonard Miller. "A Decision Support System to Increase Equity." *Administration in Social Work,* 5(3/4) (Fall/Winter 1981): 83–96.

Bromage, Mary C. "Gamesmanship in Written Communication." In Richard C. Huseman et al., eds., *Readings in Interpersonal and Organizational Communications,* 2d ed. Boston, MA: Holbrook Press, 1973. Pp. 526–30.

Buckley, Walter. *Sociology and Modern Systems Theory.* Englewood Cliffs, NJ: Prentice-Hall, 1967.

Carrier, John, and Ian Kendall. "Social Policy and Social Change—Explanation of the Development of Social Policy." *Journal of Social Policy,* 23 (July 1973): 209–24.

Cates, Jerry R. *Insuring Inequality: Administrative Leadership in Social Security, 1935–54.* Ann Arbor, MI: University of Michigan Press, 1983.

Cates, Jerry R., and Nancy Lohman. "Education for Social Policy Analysis." *Journal of Education for Social Work,* 16(1) (Winter 1980): 5–12.

Cloward, Richard A., and Frances F. Piven. *Regulating the Poor: The Functions of Public Welfare.* New York: Vintage Books, 1971.

Cox, Gary B.; David Erickson; Hubert Armstrong; and Philip Harrison. "The AGENCY Computer Simulation Model." *Computers in Human Services*, 5(3/4), 1989: 13-27.

Cox, Harvey. *The Secular City: Secularization and Urbanization in Theological Perspective*, rev. ed. New York: Macmillan, 1966.

Cunningham, Patrick M. "Social Welfare Policy and Issues: An Innovative Course Design for BSW Students." Paper presented at the Annual Program Meeting of the Council on Social Work Education, Reno, NV, March 1990.

Dear, Ronald B.; Katherine Briar; and A. Van Ry. "Policy Practice: A 'New' Method Coming of Age?" Paper presented at the Annual Program Meeting of the Council on Social Work Education, Miami, FL, March 1986.

Dear, Ronald B., and Rino J. Patti. "Legislative Advocacy: Seven Effective Tactics." *Social Work*, 26(4) (July 1981): 289-96.

DiNitto, Diana M., and Thomas R. Dye. *Social Welfare: Politics and Public Policy*. Englewood Cliffs, NJ: Prentice-Hall, 1983.

Doblestein, Andrew W. *Social Welfare: Policy and Analysis*. Chicago, IL: Nelson-Hall, 1990.

Dolgoff, Ralph, and Donald Feldstein. *Understanding Social Welfare*. New York: Harper and Row, 1980.

Dolgoff, Ralph, and Malvina Gordon. "Direct Practice and Policy Decisions." *Journal of Social Welfare*, 5 (Spring 1976): 5-13.

Dye, Thomas R. *Understanding Public Policy*, 4th ed. Englewood Cliffs, NJ: Prentice-Hall, 1981.

Easton, David. *A Systems Analysis of Political Life*. New York: Wiley, 1965.

Federal Register, 52(174), Wednesday, September 9, 1987: 34188-34189.

Federal Register, 52(250), Wednesday, December 30, 1987: 49252-49253.

Flynn, John P. "A Guide for Mapping and Analysis of Small-Scale Social Welfare Policy." *Administration in Social Work*, 31 (Spring 1979): 57-63.

Flynn, John P. "Local Participation in Planning for Comprehensive Community Mental Health Centers." *Community Mental Health Journal*, 9(1) (Feb. 1973): 3-10.

Flynn, John P. "MERGE: Computer Simulation of Social Policy Process." *Computers in Human Services*, 1(2) 1985a: 33-52.

Flynn, John P. *Social Agency Policy*. Chicago: Nelson-Hall, 1985b.

Flynn, John P., and James Jaksa. "Social Workers' Public Communications Skills: A Research Report." *Journal of Continuing Social Work Education*, 2(3) (1983): 9-15.

Frederico, Ronald C. *The Social Welfare Institution: An Introduction*, 3d ed. Lexington, MA: D. C. Heath, 1980.

Freire, Paolo. *Pedagogy of the Oppressed*. New York: Herder and Herder, 1972.

Gallagher, James, and Ron Haskins. *Policy Analysis*. New York: Ablex Press, 1984.

Galper, Jeffrey H. *The Politics of Social Services*. Englewood Cliffs, NJ: Prentice-Hall, 1975.

Galper, Jeffrey H. *Social Work Practice: A Radical Perspective.* Englewood Cliffs, NJ: Prentice-Hall, 1980.

Gergen, Kenneth J. "Assessing the Leverage Points in the Process of Policy Formation." In Raymond Bauer and Kenneth Gergen, eds., *The Study of Policy Formation.* New York: Free Press, 1968. Pp. 181–203.

Gil, David G. "A Systematic Approach to Social Policy Analysis." *Social Service Review,* 44(4) (Dec. 1970): 411–26.

Gil, David G. *Unravelling Social Policy,* rev. ed. Cambridge, MA: Schenkman, 1976.

Gilbert, Neil, and Harry Specht. *Dimensions of Social Welfare Policy.* Englewood Cliffs, NJ: Prentice-Hall, 1974.

Hart, Aileen F. "Teaching Policy to the Clinical Master's Student: A Historical Approach." *Journal of Teaching in Social Work,* 3(2) 1989: 35–45.

Haskins, Ron. "Social Policy Analysis: A Partial Agenda." In Ron Haskins and James J. Gallagher, eds., *Models for Analysis of Social Policy: An Introduction.* Norwood, NJ: Ablex Press, 1981. Pp. 203–26.

Haskitt, Harold O., Jr. "When Speaking from Manuscript, *Say* It and *Mean* It." In Richard C. Huseman et al., eds., *Readings in Interpersonal and Organizational Communication,* 2d ed. Boston, MA: Holbrook Press, 1973. Pp. 518–25.

Heffernan, Joseph W. *Introduction to Social Welfare Policy.* Itasca, IL: Peacock, 1979.

Hoos, Ida R. *Systems Analysis in Public Policy: A Critique.* Berkeley, CA: University of California Press, 1972.

Jaffe, Eleizer D. "Computers in Child Placement Planning." *Social Work,* 24(5) (Sept. 1979): 380–85.

Jansson, Bruce S. *Social Welfare Policy: From Theory to Practice.* Belmont, CA: Wadsworth, 1990.

Jansson, Bruce S. *Theory and Practice of Social Welfare Policy: Analysis, Processes, and Current Issues.* Belmont, CA: Wadsworth, 1984.

Kahn, Alfred J., ed. *Shaping the New Social Work.* New York: Columbia University Press, 1973.

Kahn, Alfred J. *Theory and Practice of Social Planning.* New York: Russell Sage Foundation, 1969.

Kammerman, Shiela B., and Alfred J. Kahn. *Social Services in the United States: Policies and Programs.* Philadelphia, PA: Temple University Press, 1976.

Karger, Howard J., and David Stoesz. *American Social Welfare Policy: A Structural Approach.* New York: Longman, 1990.

Keefe, Thomas. "Beyond Radicalism: An Historical-Materialist Framework for Social Policy Curriculum." *Journal of Education for Social Work,* 14(2) (Spring 1978): 60–65.

Kelley, Joseph B. "Educating Social Workers for a Changing Society: Social Policy." *Journal of Education for Social Work,* 11(1) (Winter 1975): 89–93.

Kleinkauf, Cecilia. "Analyzing Social Welfare Legislation." *Social Work,* 34(2) (Mar. 1989): 179–181.

Lastrucci, Carlo L. *The Scientific Approach*. Cambridge, MA: Schenkman, 1967.

Levy, Charles S. *Social Work Ethics*. New York: Human Sciences Press, 1976.

Levy, Charles S. "The Ethics of Management." *Administration in Social Work,* 3(3) (Fall 1979): 277–88.(a)

Levy, Charles S. *Values and Ethics for Social Work Practice*. New York: National Association of Social Workers, 1979.(b)

Lewis, Harold. *The Intellectual Base of Social Work Practice*. New York: Haworth Press, 1982.

Lindblom, Charles E. *The Policy Making Process*. Englewood Cliffs, NJ: Prentice-Hall, 1968.

Lindblom, Charles E. "The Science of Muddling Through." *Public Administration Review, 19* (Spring 1959): 79–88.

Luse, F. Dean. *OUTPST: Education/Simulation for the Human Services*. Park Forest, IL: F. Dean Luse, 1982.

Luse, F. Dean. "Use of Computer Simulation in Social Welfare Management." *Administration in Social Work,* 4(3) (Fall 1980): 13–22.

Lyon, Paul. "Ideology in Social Welfare Policy Instruction: An Examination of Required Readings." *Journal of Sociology and Social Welfare, 10*(3) (Sept. 1983): 376–90.

Mahaffey, Maryann. "Lobbying and Social Work." *Social Work, 17*(1) (Jan. 1972): 3–11.

Mayer, Robert, and Ernest Greenwood. *The Design of Social Policy Research*. Englewood Cliffs, NJ: Prentice-Hall, 1980.

MacRae, Duncan, Jr., and Ron Haskins. "Models for Policy Analysis." In Ron Haskins and James J. Gallagher, eds., *Models for Analysis of Social Policy: An Introduction*. Norwood, NJ: Ablex Press, 1981. Pp. 1–36.

McGill, Robert S., and Terry N. Clark. "Community Power and Decision Making: Recent Research and Its Policy Implications." *Social Service Review, 49*(1) (Mar. 1975): 33–45.

Meenaghan, Thomas M., and Murray Gruber. "Social Policy and Clinical Social Work Education: Clinicians as Social Policy Practitioners." *Journal of Social Work Education,* 22(2) 1986: 38–45.

Meenaghan, Thomas M., and Robert O. Washington. *Social Policy and Social Welfare: Structure and Applications*. New York: Free Press, 1980.

Meltsner, Arnold J., and Christopher Bellavita. *The Policy Organization*. Beverly Hills, CA: Sage, 1983.

Miller, James Grier. *Living Systems*. New York: McGraw-Hill, 1978.

Moroney, Robert M. "Policy Analysis Within a Value Theoretical Framework." In Ron Haskins and James J. Gallagher, eds., *Models for Analysis of Social Policy: An Introduction*. Norwood, NJ: Ablex Press, 1981. Pp. 78–102.

National Association of Social Workers. *Code of Ethics*. Silver Spring, Md., 1979.

Patti, Rino, and Ronald B. Dear. "Legislative Advocacy: A Path to Social Change." *Social Work, 20*(2) (Mar. 1975): 108–14.

Pierce, Dean. *Policy for the Social Work Practitioner*. New York: Longman, 1984.

Pincus, Allen, and Anne Minahan. *Social Work Practice: Model and Methods.* Itasca, IL: Peacock, 1973.

Polsby, Nelson. *Community Power and Political Theory.* New Haven, CT: Yale University Press, 1963.

Prigmore, Charles S., and Charles R. Atherton. *Social Welfare Policy: Analysis and Formulation.* Lexington, MA: D. C. Heath, 1979.

Pruger, Robert. "Social Policy: Unilateral Transfer or Reciprocal Exchange." *Journal of Social Policy,* 24 (Oct. 1973): 289–302.

Quade, E. S. *Analysis for Public Decisions.* New York: American Elsevier, 1975.

Reamer, Frederic G. *Ethical Dilemmas in Social Service.* New York: Columbia University Press, 1982.

Reamer, Frederic G. "Ethical Dilemmas in Social Work Practice." *Social Work,* 28(1) (Jan.-Feb. 1983): 31–35.

Romanyshyn, John M. *Social Welfare: Charity to Justice.* New York: Random House, 1971.

Ross, Robert, and Graham L. Staines. "The Politics of Analyzing Social Problems." *Social Problems,* 20 (Summer 1972): 18–40.

Sharwell, George R. "How to Testify Before a Legislative Committee." In Maryann Mahaffey and John Hanks, eds., *Practical Politics: Social Work and Political Responsibility.* Silver Springs, MD: National Association of Social Workers, 1982. Pp. 85–98.

Simon, Herbert. "A Behavioral Model of Rational Choice." In R. Gore and H. Dyson, eds., *The Making of Decisions.* Glencoe, IL: Free Press, 1964, Pp. 124–26.

Smith, Virginia. "How Interest Groups Influence Legislators." *Social Work,* 24(3) (May 1979): 234–39.

Sower, Christopher; John Holland; Kenneth Tiedke; and Walter Freeman. *Community Involvement: The Webs of Formal and Informal Ties That Make for Action.* Glencoe, IL: Free Press, 1957.

Spakes, Virginia. "Family Impact Analysis as a Framework for Teaching Social Policy." *Journal of Education for Social Work,* 20(1), (Winter, 1984): 59–73.

Spakes, Virginia. *Family Policy and Family Impact Analysis.* Cambridge, MA: Schenkman, 1983.

Steiner, Joseph R. "Discourse Management: Key to Policy Development." *Journal of Sociology and Social Welfare,* 4(7) (Sept. 1977): 1025–32.

Stokey, Edith, and Richard Zeckhauser. *A Primer for Policy Analysis.* New York: Norton, 1978.

Tierney, Kathleen J. "The Battered Women Movement and the Creation of the Wife Beating Problem." *Social Problems,* 29(3) (Feb. 1982): 207–20.

Tripodi, Tony; Phillip Fellin; and Henry J. Meyer. *The Assessment of Social Research,* 2d ed. Itasca, IL: Peacock, 1983.

Tropman, John E. *Policy Management in the Human Services.* New York: Columbia University Press, 1984.

Tropman, John E., and Ann R. Alvarez. "Writing for Effect: Correspondence, Records and Documents." In Fred Cox et al., eds., *Tactics and Techniques of Community Practice.* Itasca, IL: Peacock, 1977. Pp. 377–91.

U.S. Department of Health and Human Services, Office of Human Development Services and the Office of Family Assistance. *It's Time to Tell: A Media Handbook for Human Services Personnel.* No. 0-324-000. Washington, DC: U.S. Government Printing Office, 1981.

von Bertalanffy, Ludwig. *General Systems Theory.* New York: George Braziller, 1968.

Warren, Roland L. *The Community in America.* Chicago, IL: Rand McNally, 1963.

Warren, Roland L. *Social Change and Human Purpose: Toward Understanding and Action.* Chicago, IL: Rand McNally, 1977.

Warren, Roland L. "Truth, Love and Social Change." In Roland L. Warren, *Truth, Love and Social Change.* Chicago, IL: Rand McNally, 1972.

Whitaker, William H., and Jan Flory-Baker. "Ragtag Social Workers Take on the Good Old Boys and Elect a State Senator." In Maryann Mahaffey and John W. Hanks, eds., *Practical Politics: Social Work and Political Responsibility.* Silver Spring, MD: National Association of Social Workers, 1982. Pp. 161–80.

Wilcox, Roger P. "Characteristics and Organization of the Oral Technical Report." In Richard C. Huseman et al., eds., *Readings in Interpersonal and Organizational Communication,* 2d ed. Boston, MA: Holbrook Press, 1973. Pp. 509–17.

Wildavsky, Aaron. *The Politics of the Budgetary Process.* Boston, MA: Little, Brown, 1964.

Wintersteen, Richard T. "Linking Social Policy Study to an Interest in Direct Practice." Paper presented at the Annual Program Meeting of the Council on Social Work Education, Reno, NV, March 1990.

Witherspoon, R., and N. K. Phillips. "Heightening Political Awareness in Social Work Students in the 1990s." *Journal of Social Work Education,* 23(3) 1987: 44–49.

Wyers, Norman L. "Policy Practice in Social Work: Models and Issues." Paper presented at the Annual Program Meeting of the Council on Social Work Education, Reno, NV, March 1990.

York, Reginald O. *Human Service Planning: Concepts, Tools, and Methods.* Chapel Hill: University of North Carolina Press, 1982.

Zigler, Edward F.; Sharon L. Kagan; and Edgar Klugman. *Children, Families, and Government: Perspectives of American Social Policy.* New York: Cambridge University Press, 1983.

Ziter, Mary Lou P. "Social Policy Practice: Tasks and Skills." *Administration in Social Work,* 7(2) (Summer 1983): 37–50.

Index

Values. *See also* Human system
    values
  centrality of, 35–36
  and ethics, 12, 35, 77, 305
  implications of, 76–78
Van Ry, A., 5
Variety, 71. *See also* Strains
Vested interests, 191
von Bertalanffy, Ludwig, 85

Warrant, 255
Warren, Roland L., 30, 40, 186
Washington, Robert O., 29, 37
Weasel words, 289
Whitaker, William H., 42
White House Working Group on
    the Family, 49

Wilcox, Roger P., 282
Wildavsky, Aaron, 285
Wintersteen, Richard T., 5
WISC-WARE, 52
Witherspoon, R., 5
Witte, Edwin, 4
World view, 26
Wyers, Norman L., 5, 22

YAVIS syndrome, 90
York, Reginald O., 45

Zeckhauser, Richard, 50, 53
Zigler, Edward F., 48
Ziter, Mary Lou Politer, 12, 14,
    250